AF752564

Palgrave Studies in Classical Liberalism

**Series Editors**

David F. Hardwick, Department of Pathology and Laboratory Medicine, The University of British Columbia, Vancouver, BC, Canada
Leslie Marsh, Department of Pathology and Laboratory Medicine, The University of British Columbia, Vancouver, BC, Canada

This series offers a forum to writers concerned that the central presuppositions of the liberal tradition have been severely corroded, neglected, or misappropriated by overly rationalistic and constructivist approaches.

The hardest-won achievement of the liberal tradition has been the wrestling of epistemic independence from overwhelming concentrations of power, monopolies and capricious zealotries. The very precondition of knowledge is the exploitation of the epistemic virtues accorded by society's situated and distributed manifold of spontaneous orders, the DNA of the modern civil condition.

With the confluence of interest in situated and distributed liberalism emanating from the Scottish tradition, Austrian and behavioral economics, non-Cartesian philosophy and moral psychology, the editors are soliciting proposals that speak to this multidisciplinary constituency. Sole or joint authorship submissions are welcome as are edited collections, broadly theoretical or topical in nature.

Grahame Booker

# Coercion, Authority and Democracy

## Towards an Apolitical Order

palgrave
macmillan

Grahame Booker
Stratford, ON, Canada

ISSN 2662-6470 ISSN 2662-6489 (electronic)
Palgrave Studies in Classical Liberalism
ISBN 978-3-031-16882-6 ISBN 978-3-031-16883-3 (eBook)
https://doi.org/10.1007/978-3-031-16883-3

© The Editor(s) (if applicable) and The Author(s), under exclusive license to Springer Nature Switzerland AG 2022
This work is subject to copyright. All rights are solely and exclusively licensed by the Publisher, whether the whole or part of the material is concerned, specifically the rights of translation, reprinting, reuse of illustrations, recitation, broadcasting, reproduction on microfilms or in any other physical way, and transmission or information storage and retrieval, electronic adaptation, computer software, or by similar or dissimilar methodology now known or hereafter developed.
The use of general descriptive names, registered names, trademarks, service marks, etc. in this publication does not imply, even in the absence of a specific statement, that such names are exempt from the relevant protective laws and regulations and therefore free for general use.
The publisher, the authors, and the editors are safe to assume that the advice and information in this book are believed to be true and accurate at the date of publication. Neither the publisher nor the authors or the editors give a warranty, expressed or implied, with respect to the material contained herein or for any errors or omissions that may have been made. The publisher remains neutral with regard to jurisdictional claims in published maps and institutional affiliations.

Cover credit: Pattadis Walarput/Alamy Stock Photo

This Palgrave Macmillan imprint is published by the registered company Springer Nature Switzerland AG
The registered company address is: Gewerbestrasse 11, 6330 Cham, Switzerland

# Preface

As a classical liberal, or libertarian, I am concerned to advance liberty and minimize coercion. Indeed, in this view liberty just is the absence of coercion or costs imposed on others. In order better to understand the notion of coercion I discuss Robert Nozick's classic essay on the subject as well as more recent contributions. I then address the question of whether the law is coercive and respond to Edmundson and others who think that it isn't. Assuming that the law is in fact coercive, there is still a question, as with all coercive acts, of whether that coercion is justified. Edmundson thinks that this places a special burden on the state of justifying its existence, whereas it simply places the same burden on the state as anyone else. What I reject is the longstanding doctrine of reasons of state, namely that the state is not subject to the same moral rules as its subjects. With respect to the relation of morality to law, Edmundson thought that another of the fallacies of which philosophical anarchists were guilty was that of assuming that there was a sphere of morality where the law had no business. On the contrary, our concern is with spheres of law which appear to have little to do with morality, which is to say laws against wrongs of the *malum prohibitum* variety, as opposed to wrongs which are *malum in se*.

I then turn to a matter with which Edmundson begins his study, namely how it is that states acquire the authority to do what they do, namely coerce their subjects. While the fact that the philosopher's stone of political obligation has proved rather elusive may mean that a legitimate state lacks the authority to demand obedience pure and simple, Edmundson contends that it can at the very least demand that we do not interfere in the administration of justice. I argue that this attempt to sidestep the justification of the authority of the state fails and that we seem in the end to be having to take the state's word for it that we must do X on pain of penalty P. Nor, as I go on to argue, is it any help to appeal to democracy to remedy a failed justification of the authority of the state. There either is a moral justification for state coercion to prevent harm to innocent subjects, or there isn't, and this holds, if it does, not only at the level of individuals, but also at the level of the state, regardless of its constitutional form.

After concluding that the attempts of Edmundson and others to refute the anarchic turn in recent political philosophy have failed, the withering away of the state foreseen in Marx's eschatology is not as improbable as maybe it once appeared. Though as the recent ham-fisted approach of state authorities everywhere to managing a disease which apparently derived from a Sars bioweapon has shown, they are in no hurry to surrender their coercive powers. To the extent that I have reiterated the Anathemata handed down from the mount in Switzerland, they may be just as unlikely to provoke any response from the powers that be as Schumpeter thought [1954, 418], but rather be drowned out by the fascist chorus from Davos.

Stratford, Canada Grahame Booker

# Contents


1 **Introduction** 1
Works Cited 6

2 **Coercion** 9
2.1 Nozick on Coercion 11
2.1.1 Threats v. Offers 11
2.1.2 The Drug Addict 12
2.1.3 The Drowning Man 13
2.1.4 A Fair Price? 14
2.1.5 Nozick's Slave Case 17
2.1.6 Blackmail 19
2.1.7 Threats/Warnings 20
2.1.8 Rhodes on Coercion 21
2.2 Edmundson and the Supposed Non-coerciveness of the State 24
2.2.1 Plea Bargains and Coercion 25
2.2.2 Sea Rescue and Coercion 27

2.2.3 The Coerciveness of Law and the Presumption of Liberty 35
2.2.4 Malum Prohibitum v. Malum in Se 38
2.2.5 The Coerciveness of the state's Monopoly on Enforcement 40
2.3 Summary 44
Works Cited 45

**3 Authority** 49
3.1 Consent 52
3.1.1 The Appeal to Estoppel 56
3.1.2 Possible Salvation in Associative Obligations 58
3.2 Fairness as a Possible Foundation of Political Obligation 64
3.2.1 From Fairness to Prima Facie Obedience 70
3.3 Edmundson's Response to Philosophical Anarchism 73
3.3.1 Authority Indistinguishable from Arbitrary Rule 82
3.3.2 Moral Discovery as a Possible Source of Authority 85
3.3.3 Law and Morals Do Not Necessarily Overlap 89
3.3.4 The Morality of Taxes in Particular 90
3.4 The Public Goods' Defence 98
3.4.1 Public Goods Via Decentralized Coordination 110
3.4.2 The Authoritative Solution to Prisoners' Dilemmas 135
3.4.3 The Principal-Agent Problem 141
3.5 Summary 142
Works Cited 143

**4 Democracy** 153
4.1 Singer on Democracy 153
4.1.1 Voting as Quasi Consent 161
4.1.2 Fair Play as a Solution to Consent 164

4.2 Democratic Rules 166
4.2.1 Wollheim and the Paradox of Democracy 171
4.2.2 The Relevance of Singer's Models to Large-Scale Democracies 174
4.2.3 Representation and Authority 178
4.2.4 Political Parties 186
4.2.5 The Supposed Virtues of Polyarchy 190
4.2.6 *Rex Nunquam Moritur* 194
4.3 Liberalism v. Democracy; Recent Trends 201
4.3.1 The Democratic Peace 204
4.3.2 Democracy and Property 210
4.3.3 Hayek and the State 213
4.3.4 Democracy and Redistribution 217
4.4 Dworkin on Democracy 219
4.5 Summary 231
Works Cited 232

**5 The Non-fallacy of Anarchism** 239
5.1 Abortion and Liberalism 244
5.2 Private Enforcement 248
5.3 Locke on Punishment 250
5.4 Nozick on Punishment 251
5.5 Blackmail Revisited 253
5.6 Anscombe on Authority 254
5.7 The Appeal of Anarchy 256
5.7.1 The Private Production of Defence 259
5.7.2 Responses to Holcombe 261
5.8 Summary 263
Works Cited 265

**Works Cited** 269

**Index** 289

# 1
# Introduction

In this work I argue that the state is a coercive order and that much of its use of coercion is unjustified. Many assume that the first claim that the state is coercive is quite uncontroversial. However, William Edmundson, whom I discuss at some length, denies this claim, holding that it is one of the fallacies to which those like me, who favour some version of anarchism, are prone. Nor is Edmundson alone in rejecting the coerciveness of the state. Following Raz who thought it important not to assimilate the question of the authority of the state to that of the justification of coercion, Green also denied that the state was essentially coercive, asserting rather that what was distinctive about the state was the nature of its claim to authority (1988, 151), which he in turn rejected.

As John Lucas once pointed out, coercion itself is a rather difficult notion (1985, 56), so I devote much of Chapter 1 to an exploration of it. As a basis for this discussion, I use Nozick's classic article (1997), which as it turned out served as the prolegomenon to his celebrated later work. In the latter part of the chapter I take up Edmundson's rejection of the thesis that the law is coercive. While I have little quarrel with his rather brief account of coercion, I fail to see why it cannot apply to law, and in fact argue that it does.

© The Author(s), under exclusive license to Springer Nature Switzerland AG 2022

G. Booker, *Coercion, Authority and Democracy*, Palgrave Studies in Classical Liberalism,
https://doi.org/10.1007/978-3-031-16883-3_1

Edmundson distinguishes two sorts of law, *malum in se* or those things which morally we would likely prohibit, and *malum prohibitum* or those which are illegal merely by dint of the fact that a legislature has seen fit to prohibit them. Indeed, it is the latter group which clearly illustrates the coerciveness of law, since but for the law they would not be proscribed, and as Edmundson notes, it is widely thought that their legitimacy is dependent upon the state's ability to justify them (1998, 110). We of course think that the burden of proof rests with the state to show that coercion is justified in this second class of cases, which we will argue it fails to do.

In Chapter 2, having argued that the state is coercive, we then address the question of the state's authority to wield the coercive power it does. Such authority has often been thought to derive from consent of one sort or another. Although Green thinks this the most promising of the reasons typically offered for acknowledging the authority of the state it stops short of being a convincing account (1988, 158, 185). Others such as Hart and Rawls have tried to derive an obligation to the state from a principle of fairness, such that if others have submitted to authority in some sort of collective enterprise then one is obliged to do likewise. Again, it is far from clear how the decision of some to accept a particular authority as legitimate in any way commits me to do likewise.

Given that a doctrine of political obligation does not appear to be immediately forthcoming—indeed the main question about it still appears to be much as Simmons thought it was a generation ago, namely whether there is any such thing (1979, 3)—Edmundson decides to lower the bar from an obligation to obey to an obligation not to interfere in the lawful administration of the state. Even if our political overlords would be satisfied with a duty of non-interference, it is still not obvious why they are justified in demanding even that much. Edmundson thinks that there are good reasons for acceding to authority, or at least not interfering in its proper exercise, though in general it seems we just have to take the legislators' word for it that they struck the right compromise (1998, 66). Edmundson considers traffic laws a good example of the coordination achieved by people obeying stop lights and traffic cops, though even he has difficulty in believing that we have a duty to come to a definite stop at a stop sign in the desert with no other traffic in sight. Another issue raised by coordination is the fact that most of those that matter appear to have arisen spontaneously where needed and thus antedated their being legalized.

One of the issues that goes to the heart of the supposed authority of the state is the power to raise taxes to enable the state to do the good that it claims to be doing for us. Whereas Athenian citizens were exempt from taxes, and while the Romans reserved them for conquered peoples, modern states consider them to be a privilege of citizenship. We argue with Nozick that they are on a par with forced labour (1974, 169) or in Rothbard's case, with theft (1978, 51–52), and reject the claim that the supposed need for public goods in any way justifies such takings. Indeed, the ever-expanding public domain is evidence first and foremost of official empire building, and rather than providing much needed benefits to the populace, brings all the shortages and inertia we have tended to associate with centrally planned economies. In the case of state-provided medicine, for example, it should come as no surprise that even in major urban centres 20% or more of the Canadian population do not have a family physician, there are lengthy waiting times for surgery, or that Canada has only 60% of the advanced diagnostic imaging capacity of the average OECD country. Considerations of efficiency aside, there is simply no justification for monopoly provision of health, education, welfare, or any of the other industries which the modern state has taken under its wing.

After addressing the main arguments latterly adduced in support of the state, including the need for law and order and to prevent our succumbing to prisoner's dilemmas, we turn in Chapter 3 to the question as to whether democracy might be pressed into service to provide the missing explanatory link. We argue again that it also fails to underwrite the authority of the state, for reasons in addition to the inability of consent theories to provide any such warrant. In our view democracy is a rather superfluous sideshow which mostly serves to divert attention from the fact that the emperor is standing on the tribune wearing nothing but a laurel wreath. If democracy has been thought at times to be more than just a circus for the entertainment of the masses, it is because it has often been conflated in the popular imagination with freedom, notably the so-called freedom to elect our rulers. According to Rose Wilder Lane, lurking behind the notion of free elections is an old superstition to the effect that control over oneself is achieved by one's control over the government which in turn controls us. Of course, as Lane goes on to point out, it really isn't possible for me to control my controllers, so instead I get a vote, a majority of which will control the state which controls everybody. If I happen to be in the minority, as most of us are on some issue most of the time, this is a sacrifice I should be prepared to make to the great god Demos. The notion of a majority often proves to be a delusion because what amounts to a casting vote breaks the tie. It wasn't just in recent years where a small number of votes decided the Presidential election; Lane reminds us that also happened in 1916 where the outcome changed when a few more votes trickled in from California. The myth that we can control the government which in turn controls us encourages the false belief that government has the authority to control us in order to provide for our welfare (1993, 208–212). If there were any way to guarantee freedom it would be by narrowly limiting what governments are authorized to do, since Jasay reminds us that it is sovereign power, which poses a threat to our welfare, regardless of whether it is a sovereign monarch or a sovereign people (1998, 208–209).

Not that we are attributing any great love of liberty to Joe the plumber—Mencken warned against that years ago (1926, 44–45, 147). What interests the average Joe, as Jasay puts it, is which policy will give him the most money and take away the least (ibid., 218). Of course it is always possible that once having voted, the state will actually take from Joe to give to Mary,[1] or that he will find himself falling victim to one of the myriad ways in which the sovereign state manages to coerce its subjects, such as being fined for plumbing without a licence, which is to say that licenced plumber John has been granted monopoly privileges at Joe's expense.

In conclusion I discuss the third of what Edmundson considers a fallacy typical of the reigning anarchist orthodoxy in political philosophy, namely the view that there is a sphere of morality where the law has no business. No doubt this has an anarchic ring about it, and while the

[1] As Jasay again reminds us, the state possesses nothing except what it has managed to confiscate from its subjects. Having nothing, that is the sum of its contribution to society, despite its apparent generosity with other people's money (ibid., 219).

Wolfenden Report may have made noises like this, it is not a view that I wish to spend a lot of time on. More interesting than Edmundson's worry about *delegalized morality* is what I might call *demoralized legality*, or the *malum prohibitum*, law for law's sake, type of legislation, which serves other ends than what is independently morally wrong. While even under a more libertarian dispensation an individual may continue to enlist others to enforce his justice claims, we see no reason to rule out self-help, any more than present laws rule out self-defence. The Criminal Code allows us in the case of an unprovoked attack to repel force by force provided that the force used is no more than is necessary to enable us to defend ourselves.

However, when it comes to its own actions, as typified by the *malum prohibitum* laws, which, Edmundson admits, constitute the bulk of modern legislation, the state has no compunction about exceeding the limits set by self-help and instead of merely coercing the coercers of the innocent, helps itself to coercing the innocent on a grand scale, which of course it is entirely unjustified in doing. Indeed, its ability to do so gives new meaning to Anscombe's claim that the sort of coercion characteristic of civil society is unique to those ruled by government (1981, 147). For this reason, writers like Anscombe and Nozick will have difficulty in showing how state coercion differs from that of the Mafia, even though they remain convinced that there is a difference. Anscombe thinks we need governments, and our need is what confers authority on them to employ norms not available to ordinary mortals. The only problem with what amounts to the doctrine of *reasons of state* is that it makes it hard to distinguish the Nazi state from supposedly just states, something Edmundson and Dworkin thought was important to do.

Anscombe also seems to have overlooked the fact that the agreement to grant authority to our would-be overlords has to be worked out in the state of nature. The question then arises whether the contract with the agent authority is self-enforcing. If it isn't, then we will need a meta-agent to enforce the initial contract, and a meta-meta-agent to see the agent below him performs as per the contract, which is no doubt what Juvenal was asking in his famous question. On the other hand if contracts are self-enforcing, it isn't clear why we need an authority in the first place, since as Green pointed out, it may be harder to produce than many of the goods which supposedly cannot be produced without it (1988,149).

In fact, as Cusan argued, government does not get into an infinite regress of meta-agents but acts as an anarchic agent acknowledging no power but its own (1979, 153). To the extent that government operates under rules, they are mostly written by its operatives with little or no third-party oversight, and, more often than not, deals are worked out anarchically behind closed doors. Such anarchic relations also extend to many at the fringes of government, such as gangsters hired by the CIA and police departments (ibid., 158). Of course, relations between sovereign states have traditionally been anarchic, as Oye points out, free to pursue their interests as they see fit (1986, 1). Indeed, if we are wondering what the face of ordered anarchy looks like, and as Hasnas reminds us, most of us are justifiably not interested in the disordered variety (2008, 112), we need to look no further than the acts of the sovereign state. And if the sovereign, by definition, does not require an enforcer, it is far from obvious why the sovereign individual does either.

## Works Cited

Anscombe, G.E.M. *Collected Philosophical Papers*, Vol. 3. Oxford: Blackwell, 1981.

Cusan, Alfred G. "Do We Ever Really Get Out of Anarchy." *Journal of Libertarian Studies* 3, no. 2 [1979]: 151–158.

Edmundson, William A. *Three Anarchical Fallacies.* Cambridge: Cambridge U. Press, 1998.

Green, Leslie. *The Authority of the State.* Oxford U. Press, 1988.

Hasnas, John. "The Obviousness of Anarchy." In *Anarchism/Minarchism*, ed. Roderick T. Long and Tibor R. Machan, 111–131. Aldershot: Ashgate, 2008.

Jasay, Anthony De. *The State.* Indianapolis: Liberty Fund, 1998.

Lane, Rose Wilder. *The Discovery of Freedom.* San Franscisco: Fox & Wilkes, 1993.

Lucas, John. *The Principles of Politics.* Oxford: Oxford U. Press, 1985.

Mencken, H.L. *Notes on Democracy.* New York: Knopf, 1926.

Nozick, Robert. *Anarchy, State and Utopia.* New York: Basic Books, 1974.
———. *Socratic Puzzles.* Cambridge: Harvard U. Press, 1997.
Oye, Kenneth A., ed. *Cooperation under Anarchy.* Princeton: Princeton U Press, 1986.
Rothbard, Murray. *For a New Liberty.* New York: Collier, 1978.
Simmons, A. John. *Moral Principles and Political Obligations.* Princeton: Princeton U. Press, 1979.

# 2
# Coercion

In this chapter I would first like to explore the notion of coercion, since one of the steps towards maximizing liberty is to ensure that transactions between individuals are free and not coerced, or at the very least, one should attempt to reduce its harmful effects (cf. Hayek 1978, 12). Some writers such as Viminitz think that coercion is a vacuous notion along with others such as liberty, equality, socialism and capitalism. In particular, he claims that any attempt to produce a non-normative definition of coercion is likely to be vacuous (Viminitz 2001). Narveson, on the other hand, rightly denies Viminitz's claim about the vacuity of coercion, arguing that we can indeed reach some agreement about the sorts of activities which are properly described as coercive, and how it is, for example, that coercion differs from force. According to Narveson there are three ways in which I may acquire goods in someone else's possession: (a) I may persuade him to exchange the item for something I have, such as the requisite amount of coin of the realm; (b) I may kill him and take what I want; (c) I may threaten to make him much worse off if he doesn't hand over the goods. It is only (c) which is properly described as coercion, while (a) is what we'd rather have people resort to, as opposed to either (b) or (c) (Narveson 2001).

© The Author(s), under exclusive license to Springer Nature Switzerland AG 2022

G. Booker, *Coercion, Authority and Democracy*, Palgrave Studies in Classical Liberalism,
https://doi.org/10.1007/978-3-031-16883-3_2

Commentators such as Hayek, again, would concede that coercion, like liberty, is a difficult concept, but that *pace* Viminitz, it is possible to decide what we are or are not talking about, before we tackle the question as to what if anything is wrong with it. Hayek notes further that we may be compelled by circumstances to do X, but it takes another human being to coerce us into doing X; indeed we are coerced where we reluctantly serve the will of another, rather than do as we would have preferred. However, Hayek cautions us against thinking that the victim does not actually choose a course of action, as would be the case if he were forced to point the gun and squeeze the trigger. To be coerced is to choose what one would rather not have chosen (Hayek 1978, 133–134).

As undesirable as coercion may often be, particularly when it gets in the way of an individual's most effectively contributing to society (op.cit. 134), Hayek argues that, contrary to what passes as received wisdom, market transactions are generally not coercive. Even in the case of a supposedly essential service, withholding such a service is not to be considered coercive, particularly if a competitive market can supply an alternative source. In the case of a monopoly provider, the service would need to be essential for the necessities of life, for the conditions under which the supplier agrees to provide it to be possibly considered coercive. Hayek notes, of course, that the monopoly supplier par excellence is the state, a fact which led Trotsky to remark that the old dictum about having to work in order to eat had been superseded by the need to obey in order to eat (ibid., 137).

For Hayek the paradigm cases of coercion are likely to be found at the hands of conquerors, or resulting from various protection rackets, including those presided over by a state. Nor is coercion confined to arm's length transactions, since various intimate relationships are known to also provide fertile grounds. But other than perhaps ensuring that such relationships are voluntary, any more vigorous attempt at regulation might lead to even greater coercion (ibid., 137–8). Although in Hayek's view coercion admits of degrees, from an extreme such as a master slave relationship to the one-off instance of threatening harm, it does not include all cases where our actions may cause others to diverge from a preferred course of action. For Hayek coercion involves a threat of harm designed to produce a change in behaviour (ibid., 134).

## 2.1 Nozick on Coercion

Almost a decade later in his article "Coercion", Nozick picks up from where Hayek left off in exploring what would or would not properly count as a case of coercion. Nozick's article was to form the prolegomenon to a fuller discussion of the conditions under which we are justified in coercing someone.[1] In the spirit of Nozick's discussion, let us consider the following list of the necessary and sufficient conditions for P to be said to have coerced Q:

1. P threatens and is aware that he is threatening Q.
2. P's threat deters Q from doing A.
3. Both P and Q, understand that P intends by threatening Q to deter Q from doing A.
4. As a result of P's threat to do C, Q does not do A.
5. Q offers P's threat as part of the reason for his not doing A.
6. Both P and Q believe that Q would be worse off if he did not back down in the face of P's threat to do C.

As well as covering most of the standard cases of coercion, such conditions will help clarify some of the non-central cases, such as those where, for example, P is mistakenly thought by Q to have uttered a threat, or where the supposed threat is better construed as a warning, as in the case of the mother who says she would have a heart attack, if her son were to do A.

### 2.1.1 Threats v. Offers

Although many have seen employment relationships as typically coercive, like Hayek, Nozick considers it the exception rather than the rule that employment or salary proposals amount to threats, which is to say

[1] "Coercion" 1969; reprinted in *Socratic Puzzles* (1997, 15). The longer study mentioned would turn out to be *Anarchy State and Utopia* (1974). Whereas Hayek tended to equate liberty with the absence of coercion, Nozick thought that while the two notions were connected, it was important to note cases where P could be said to have restricted Q's freedom to do A without it being equally correct to say that P had coerced Q into not doing A (1997, 15).

that a prospective employee is not normally coerced (1997, 24). Thus Nozick suggests a rule of thumb for distinguishing threats from offers: if what P proposes worsens the outcome of Q's doing A, then it is a threat, whereas if P's action improves Q's outcome then it is an offer. The background against which we supposedly measure changes in Q's outcome is what Nozick calls the normal course of events, which is the way Q's universe would have unfolded absent P's intervention. Nozick also understands the normal course of events to include the fact that others will continue to act morally as they have done in the past. Nozick presents the following harder cases as a way of testing his rule of thumb:

### 2.1.2 The Drug Addict

a. P supplies Q with drugs, but instead of offering them at the regular price on this occasion, P will charge Q nothing if he assaults R.
b. P is aware that Q's normal drug supplier is out of action and offers to replace his supply if Q assaults R.

Nozick considers (a) to be a threat to withhold drugs if Q does not perform the required beating. It is a threat because Q would prefer the status quo, or normal course of events, where he received drugs in exchange for money, rather than now having to act as P's enforcer. On the other hand, Nozick regards (b) as an offer, rather than a case of coercion by threat, even though Q might again feel he had little choice but to comply. Here P is not withholding drugs he would have supplied in the normal course of events, since he has hitherto had no dealings with Q, though is making overtures in that direction.

If it remains unclear as to whether a proposal is a threat or an offer, this may have to do with the fact that the notion of *the normal course of events* is itself unclear, since it is supposed to address the case where P does not intervene as well as that where morality requires that he does. Nozick admits that there may indeed be disagreement about the normal course of events, or baseline from which to distinguish threats from offers (ibid., 26).[2]

### 2.1.3 The Drowning Man

Nozick's other celebrated test case concerns a drowning man Q and the conditions under which P is prepared to help rescue him. Q is in the water far from shore, nearing the end of his energy, and P approaches in his boat. Both know that there is no other hope of rescue around, and P apparently knows that Q is honest and will keep his promises. P offers to use his boat to bring Q back to shore if and only if Q promises to pay P $10,000 within three days of reaching shore(ibid., 26–27).

The question then is whether the conditions under which P will rescue Q constitute an *offer* to rescue Q or a *threat* to let him drown if he refuses to meet P's terms. If the normal course of events is that Q would drown without P's intervention, then P is offering to save Q, even though Q may consider P's "salvage" fee exorbitant, and/or well beyond his means to pay. However, if the normal course of events is thought to imply that anyone who is able without assuming undue risk to effect a rescue of a fellow human being in peril on the sea would "normally" do so, then to demand compensation could be seen as a threat, if the victim is unwilling or unable to pay the cost.

Nozick thinks that most observers would probably agree that under such circumstances P was morally obliged to render whatever assistance he could, which is to say that to demand payment is to threaten to let Q drown. This also puts a different spin on the normal course of events understood as the baseline or status quo where Q is prior to P's proposed intervention. Nozick now speaks of the morally expected course of events, as opposed to the normal course of events, to reflect the fact that Q expects that P will now do the right or charitable thing, namely rescue Q.

As to why Q would consider it reasonable to expect that P would do his duty, we could reply that P might do so in the hope that others would

[2] For a clearer characterization of a baseline, see Narveson (2001, 3).

do likewise for him in similar circumstances.[3] If indeed we all benefit by living in a society where the virtue of charity is practised, it does seem a little mean spirited of P to demand payment for helping Q in his hour of need. However, perhaps P is a paid-up subscriber to TANSTAAFL, and would fully expect to put cash on the barrelhead should he ever need rescuing.[4] In fact he might even find such an alternative preferable to Good Samaritan laws which attempt to legislate charity. On the other hand, while Nozick thinks it clear that Q can here expect P to exercise the virtue of charity, he can imagine cases where Q's moral credit is sufficiently diminished for him to be left to the mercy of the waves (ibid., 27).

### 2.1.4 A Fair Price?

In a footnote to the drowning man case Nozick pursues the question of the extent to which price might be a factor in determining whether P's proposal constitutes a threat or an offer. Here we are asked to consider the case where P's practising his violin disturbs his neighbour Q. The cost of getting P to take his practising elsewhere for a year is somewhere between $500, the minimum P would require to do so, and $2000, the maximum Q would be prepared to pay to have P do so. Nozick is inclined to say that payments at the low end constitute offers, while those at the high end are more likely threats, though he admits such intuitions may be hard to justify in the absence of a theory of fair pricing, if indeed any such a theory is possible (ibid., 1997, 339n.28). Undeterred by the lack of a theory, Hayek held that a price increase by a monopoly supplier of water in the desert was obviously coercive (1978, 136), a view rejected by Rothbard, who argued that the owner of a scarce resource was free to dispose of it as he pleased. Indeed, Rothbard thought it impossible to tell at what point a contract ceased to be fair or reasonable, and could be considered coercive (2002, 221).

---

[3] cf. Narveson (1988, 264).

[4] "there ain't no such thing as a free lunch":cf. Gwartney and Stroup (1993, 6) [5]cf.Sowell (2000, 133).

On the other hand, Coase thought that bargaining offered the best route to a mutually satisfactory solution (1988, 99), and was certainly preferable to that of the courts, who typically found in favour of one of the parties at the expense of the other. In his discussion of Sturges v. Bridgman, where a doctor's practice is affected by noise from an adjoining confectionery business, Coase favours an agreement where the confectioner would compensate the doctor for the nuisance, at a level which would not render his operation unprofitable, but greater than the cost of solutions the doctor might consider, such as renovation or moving. According to Coase their ability to strike a bargain is contingent upon whether the machinery's benefit to the confectioner is greater than the nuisance caused to the doctor (ibid., 106). If, as Coase suggests, parties intent on bargaining in good faith can agree on a price, we are dealing with a mutually beneficial offer rather than a threat.

Rothbard also raises the matter of Sturges v. Bridgman, but rejects Coase's view that property rights are less important than determining which solution produces the greater social product. According to Rothbard, Coase's approach ignores the subjective nature of costs, and under the guise of supposedly *wertfrei* social science, imports an ethical norm of *efficiency*, in order to determine mythical *social transaction costs* (1997, 123–125, 141–142). No doubt much of so-called public policy is founded on the belief that Coasean determinations of social efficiency are possible, such as are takings under eminent domain, where governments claim the right to seize property so as to put it to more efficient uses than the individual owners. Not only do such interventions raise questions about the coherence of social efficiency, but also about the state's competence to make such determinations.

The difficulties which Rothbard rightly sees in summing individual costs to arrive at a total social product are not meant to preclude other notions of a social good, by which societies, or institutions within societies, might be compared with one another. In a more Pareto-efficient society, for example, as Narveson has noted, people are able to get on with their lives, relatively free from costs imposed by others (2002a, 82). Indeed, Sturges v. Bridgman or Nozick's musical nuisance presented contexts where people could be said to be impeded in their pursuits by the impositions of others. In Pareto terms some people have improved their lots at the expense of others, in which case some offset, or compensation might be called for. Unlike Coase's no-fault scheme of social efficiency, a libertarian regime attempts to settle such questions by reference to its basic doctrines of freedom of the individual and that individual's right to own property or to homestead. Rothbard reminds us that homesteading did not come to an end in the nineteenth century, but that such a notion may still be of service in deciding who is imposing on whom, or who is trespassing on whose property. For example, if we buy a house in a new development near a long-established airport, although excessive noise is a form of aggression, the airport may be considered to have homesteaded an easement or prescriptive property right to X amount of noise (ibid., 145–146). While the ancient doctrine of prescription may have much to recommend it, the courts did not allow the fact that the doctor in Sturges v. Bridgman had come to a pre-existing nuisance to stand in the way of his being granted the relief sought.[5]

Let us return to Nozick's concern as to whether a proposal to take one's nuisance elsewhere for consideration was an offer or a threat. He was inclined to think that if consideration or the price for which A buys B's promise to perform were at the high end of the scale it might be more of a threat, as might a hefty rescue fee for those in peril on the sea. If two individuals cannot reach a mutually satisfactory agreement, perhaps because one or the other considers it coercive, or because A thinks it unjust he should have to pay for B to take his nuisance elsewhere, or because B believes he is entitled to Rothbard's prescriptive easement, either or both may seek third-party intervention, ranging from simple mediation to more complex forms of arbitration. Such interventions proceed under widely different rules and range from the less costly and coercive to the much more costly and coercive at the litigation end. The decision handed down in Sturges v. Bridgman doubtless not only imposed the usual legal costs, but also substantial economic costs of mitigating the nuisance from which the doctor sought relief, to say nothing of further threats pursuant to non-compliance. Some have denied that the state is a coercive order as

[5] Cf. Coase (1988, 105). However there are other cases where the courts have acknowledged the doctrine of prescription, such as Bass v. Gregory, also discussed by Coase and Rothbard. Brubaker (1995, 246) mentions a Canadian case where the court again found for the plaintiff despite his having come to a nuisance.

the practice of such tribunals would suggest. We shall have more to say about that later in the chapter. As to what it is, if anything, that confers authority on the state to coerce its residents we shall take up in the next chapter.

### 2.1.5 Nozick's Slave Case

Having examined the extent to which threats can bring about changes in the normal or expected course of events, Nozick takes up the question as to whether the normal course of events might itself under some circumstances be threatening or coercive. He asks us to consider the case of the master who beats his slave for good measure every morning but offers to refrain from doing so the next day, provided the slave accedes to a particular request. Nozick suggests that such a proposal amounts to a threat rather than an offer, a verdict he claims we arrive at by attending to the *morally expected* rather than the *normal* course of events (1997, 27). Moreover, with respect to both the slave and addict cases, Nozick holds that the normal course of events diverges from the morally expected one. The slave would supposedly prefer the morally expected course of events where he is not beaten, and as most would argue as well, a situation where he is not a slave in the first place, though this particular deliverance of morality does not appear to be currently on offer. However, since we are not told what the master wants his slave to do for him in lieu of a beating, the proposed change may or may not be preferable to the customary one.

However, the addict would prefer to continue the relatively uncomplicated purchase of his drugs, rather than beat up someone else instead, which is to say, according to Nozick, that the addict prefers the normal to the morally expected course of events. By *morally expected* I take it that he means that peddling drugs is immoral, in which case if morality gained the upper hand, the addict might be out of luck, but, being an addict, he prefers to continue to get his drugs and under the conditions to which he has become accustomed. To the extent that the pusher is proposing to disrupt that practice, his proposal at least from the addict's perspective, can be considered a threat.

By way of response to Nozick, there does seem to be something rather arbitrary about deciding whether the supposed dictates of morality or of customary practice, assuming reasonable inferences can be drawn in either case, should act as the backdrop against which a given proposal can be seen as a threat or an offer. Nozick argues that when the two diverge, we should run with the preferences of the recipient (ibid., 28), assuming, it would appear, that there is some way of knowing what the recipient prefers in a particular instance. On the other hand, Wertheimer, for example, is inclined to place less faith in the sorts of intuitions on which Nozick relies and disagrees that when the morally expected course of events differs from the normal or statistical course, the proper baseline is the one that the recipient B prefers (1987, 211–212).

Wertheimer proposes 3 different ways of setting B's baseline: (1) the statistical test, where what is *normal* in society determines whether A is making an offer or a threat; (2) the moral test, where there is a clear moral expectation that A will perform or refrain from performing a certain act; and (3) the phenomenological test, which is what B rightly or wrongly believes A is likely or morally expected to do (ibid., 207).[6] Wertheimer believes that any one of the three methods of determining B's baseline can help us find a right answer to the question as to whether A's proposal is a threat or an offer, but that, Nozick notwithstanding, there is no need to think that only one of these methods is correct, or that there must be a way of deciding which of the three wins the day (ibid., 212).

In his drug addict case, Nozick claimed that P was threatening to deprive Q of his drugs if Q did not beat up Y. According to what Wertheimer calls the statistical test or Nozick's normal or expected course of events, P's proposal was a threat; a threat, that is, to disrupt Q's normal supply, though when we apply Nozick's moral test, it counts as an offer, since morally one ought to discourage the use of drugs (1997, 28). But as Wertheimer reminds us, what morality requires may not be all that clear, since Q might claim, for example, that he has a moral right to P's continued assistance. If that is the case, there is also the question as to whether the terms of the assistance can be varied without the proposal becoming a threat rather than an offer (ibid., 210).

[6] See also Feinberg (1984, 225).

Indeed, Wertheimer does claim that it is reasonable for Q to expect that P will not hike his prices, or if he does, will not exceed the going rate, which is to say that P's offer amounts to a threat (ibid., 210). But while Q may reasonably hope that drug prices will remain stable, it isn't clear what sort of duty Q's expectation imposes on P to keep them that way, such that not doing so constitutes gouging or a threat. Wertheimer seems to acknowledge that drug selling is a rather skewed case, since, by definition, the buyer is precluded from a free exchange because of his habit. Thus, such a proposal may be an inferior offer, rather than a threat (ibid. ).[7]

### 2.1.6 Blackmail

Nozick considers blackmail to be a classic example of offers that have a coercive ring about them. He believes it should be prohibited because it is not beneficial, with the victim being just as well off if the blackmailer had never made an offer in the first place (1974, 85). While Nozick did not want to rule out all transactions for the purpose of non-disclosure, he thought the need to avoid a protection racket imposed strict limits on compensation. Rothbard, on the other hand, found any such strictures incompatible with the functioning of a free market; taking money in exchange for silence does not involve threats to person or property (2001, 443. n.49). As to Nozick's claim that such exchanges do not make the buyer better off, Rothbard replies that the purpose of the exchange is rather to prevent his being made worse off, a service the buyer seems ready to pay for (1977, 53).[8]

Nozick nevertheless allows as productive an agreement reached with a neighbour to forego erecting an unsightly structure, provided that the neighbour's intention of doing so is genuine and not feigned, for otherwise it would be a case of offering consideration for nothing (1974, 85).

---

[7] Rothbard reminds us that the illegal nature of black markets predisposes them to lower efficiency, poorer service and higher prices, where any attempt at price control is only likely to benefit the monopoly supplier (2001, 786–787).

[8] Similarly, Rothbard holds that there is no justification for the tort prohibition on defamation since an attack on one's reputation is not an invasion of person or property (2001, 157, 443).

But perhaps it is somewhat arbitrary to make the seller's *mens rea* a test of productivity, to head off a possible market in abstentions, analogous to those in indulgences in earlier centuries. Interestingly, Epstein also thinks the law is right to prohibit blackmail because of bargaining problems it shares with cases of private necessity, such as that of Nozick's drug addict. Epstein reports that courts have found that a ship's need to escape peril on the sea may override a dock owner's right to exclude and have limited the compensation owed under private necessity or salvage, if only to narrow the range of bargaining (1993, 56). While we agree with Epstein that the customary prohibitions against force and fraud do not extend to those in imminent danger (2003, 100, 101), one might expect legal scrutiny of Nozick's drowning man case to set similar limits to any fees demanded by the rescuer.

### 2.1.7 Threats/Warnings

Before taking up what he considered to be examples of less central cases of coercion under the rubric of threats/offers, Nozick briefly explored the distinction between threats and warnings, suggesting that a mother who reminded her son that his proposed action might give her a heart attack, was best construed as a non-threatening warning, if only because the mother lacked the ability to produce such symptoms on demand (1997, 21). Nozick returns to this distinction towards the end of his discussion to clarify the point at which an employer's response to a union membership drive ceases being a warning and becomes a threat. Here again Nozick appeals to his notion of the normal course of events, which in this case is largely a function of the employer's expected behaviour in the face of a successful union vote. As noted above, Nozick also sets store by the employer's *mens rea* as a test of whether his proposal amounts to a threat or not. While he does not appear to think that the employer is obliged to stay in business if the union wins (1997, 341, n.38), Nozick does think that the employer has a moral duty to be forthright about his real intentions, and not make a strategic announcement about a possible plant closing which does not reflect his considered preferences.

While there is some jurisprudence which supports Nozick's finding that in some cases the employer's behaviour threatens rather than warns the union (1997, 342, n.42), *pace* Nozick and the courts, it is far from obvious who is threatening whom, when a union declares its intention to sign up members in a hitherto non-union environment. From the employer's point of view, in the normal course of events he would continue doing business in the way he had done prior to the arrival of the union, an option which will no longer be available if the union vote carries.[9] However, Nozick seems all too ready to concede the higher moral ground to the unions, while other writers have noted that unions are no strangers to coercion, both of their own members as well as employers.[10] The prime underwriter of such coercion is of course the state, without whose laws unions could not have wielded the power that they do, and, according to one estimate, cost the U.S. economy $50 trillion over the past half century.[11]

Nozick concludes that while not all ways of influencing people's decisions are coercive, it is characteristic of a threat that one feels that one is doing the bidding of someone else rather than what one might have chosen to do, absent the threat. Indeed, the rational individual typically welcomes offers and rejects threats, or in terms of the status quo, is willing to move from the pre-offer to the offer, but not from the pre-threat to the threat (1997, 41). Q can be considered to have been coerced into not doing A, where Q does A only to avoid what P threatens to do; but if Q's reason for not doing A has nothing to do with P's threat, Q has not been coerced (ibid., 44).

### 2.1.8 Rhodes on Coercion

Rhodes's more recent account (2000) in a sense picks up from where Nozick's leaves off, seeing coercion largely as a matter of separating

[9] Other analyses of the normal course of events in terms of the *status quo ante bellum* cannot be counted on to help us decide whose *status quo* is paramount, that of the union or that of the employer; cf. Narveson (2001).

[10] see Olson (1965, 71).

[11] Woods (2004, 150); see also Hospers (1971, 174, 178–80); Rothbard (1995, 136–138); Henderson (2002a, 109).

threats from offers. Rather than Nozick's approach of generating a list of symptoms for diagnosing the presence of coercion, Rhodes suggests rephrasing proposals involving either threats or offers into conjoined conditional form: if Q does A, then result R will follow & if Q does not do A, then result R will not follow. The algorithm rules then tell us to construe a proposal where the first conditional is an *offer* and the second is *neutral* (i.e. result R will simply not occur) as an *offer*, while if the first is a *threat*, followed by a *neutral* proposal, the total proposal is a *threat*. If the first conjoined conditional is an *offer*, while the second is a *threat*, according to Rhodes we have a *mixed* proposal, where neither offer nor threat predominates (2000, 372).

By way of illustration *Rhodes* asks us to consider a case where Quincy offers Paul $15 for trimming a tree limb, the consequence of Paul not taking up the offer being that he doesn't get the $15. Applying the algorithm reveals this proposal to indeed be an offer, contrary to a supposed tendency, on the part of some at least, to construe such a proposal as a threat not to pay Paul unless he does the work. On the other hand, the case where Quincy holds a gun to Paul's head and demands his wallet permits of the following conditional: If Paul surrenders the wallet, then Quincy will not kill Paul, and if Paul does not surrender the wallet, then Quincy will kill Paul. Since the first conditional is neutral while the second is a threat, the proposal constitutes a threat. However, in the face of what has long been seen as the paradigm case of coercion,[12] Rhodes's procedure borders on the redundant. Further, construing the first conditional as *neutral* seems a bit of a stretch, since it is contingent upon Paul's giving up his wallet, something he would probably rather not do.

In the last variation on this theme, Quincy offers Paul a 10% cut to launder some of his mob money, though it's not really an offer because Quincy will kill Paul if he doesn't do so. This time Rhodes's decision machine cranks out the verdict that the proposal is mixed, i.e., both offer and threat, though it would appear to me, given the company that Quincy keeps, that it is mostly a threat. Indeed, as Nozick pointed out, in contexts where people are known to resort to violence, one doesn't have to utter a direct threat for it to be one (ibid., 20).

---

[12] cf. Hart (1961, 19).

In connection with the earlier tree-trimming case, Rhodes noted that the reason it was an offer and not a threat is that Paul would supposedly not perceive any threat or harm associated with Quincy's offer. It is of course anybody's guess what someone like Nozick's partially described rational man, which, as he sardonically remarked, stopped short of including most of us (ibid., 39), would or would not perceive under any given circumstances. He may well perceive what he has insufficient grounds to or fail to perceive what most others would agree there were abundant grounds to. Such difficulties notwithstanding, Rhodes contends that an agent is motivated to choose a course of action based upon what he believes to be the case rather than what is in fact the case (2000, 372).

As for the two cases which Nozick used to illustrate the less straightforward instances of coercion, Rhodes agrees with Nozick in the case of the slave and disagrees in the case of the drug addict. Whereas in the slave case Nozick used what he called the morally expected course of events to decide that the master's proposal not to beat the slave was in fact a threat, Rhodes resolves it into its underlying conditionals: (a) If the slave does the specified action, then the master will not beat the slave and does nothing; (b) if the slave does not perform the action, then the master beats the slave. Given that the first condition is neutral, while the second is a threat, it is the second which carries the day, which is to say that the proposal is a threat. With respect to the drug dealer, P, who wishes to vary the conditions under which Q gets his supply, such that in lieu of paying cash, Q assaults R on P's behalf, P is also considered by Nozick to be threatening Q, while Rhodes's conditional decision procedure yields the result that the drug case is an offer (2000, 374).[13]

Again, if Nozick is right that such cases are less central to a theory of coercion,[14] the fact that he and Rhodes differ as to the coerciveness of a proposal need not be particularly worrisome. Their failure to agree

---

[13] Nozick might have also been prepared to consider a similar verdict if the terms were made more favourable to Q, such as by providing him with better quality drugs in return for beating up R (1997, 25).

[14] Nozick provides a further list of principles which might show how such non-central cases relate to the central ones, leading to a recursive definition for "P coerces Q into doing A" (1997, 22); both the slave and addict cases are outliers to the extent that they feature incompetent market participants: cf. Epstein (1997, 82).

in the drug case, for example, will no doubt be due in part to their rather different approaches. Nozick allows for moral considerations to form part of the baseline for determining whether a proposal is coercive, while Rhodes eschews baselines, holding that threat avoidance behaviour may be sufficient to establish coercion quite independently of intention[15]; questions of morality only enter into the subsequent justification of coercion.[16] So even if different analyses of supposed instances of coercion don't always produce the same result, particularly in hard cases, there is substantial agreement among those of a generally liberal temperament that coercion is to be avoided wherever possible, and at the very least requires justification.[17] William Edmundson, to whose views we shall be turning in the next section, is no exception, though we shall take issue with his view that the state is not coercive.

## 2.2 Edmundson and the Supposed Non-coerciveness of the State

Having surveyed some of the questions relating to coercion in general, let us now address Edmundson's treatment of coercion, where his aim is to deny the view that the state and its laws are coercive. He admits to having somewhat of a task ahead of him, since the assumption that the law is coercive is now largely taken as uncontroversial (1998, 73). My view that this is as it should be is not confined to old liberals like myself but shared with the latter-day variety, such as Rawls, who holds that political power by definition implies coercive sanctions (1993, 136).

Of the various contexts which may give rise to questions of coercion, and their possible justification, Edmundson mentions that of the celebrated highwayman (1993, 76), which goes back at least to

[15] Nozick insists in his original conditions that both P and Q must be aware that P intends to threaten Q, allowing that Q may be mistaken about being threatened, and is therefore not coerced (1997, 17–19).

[16] Narveson agrees that the case for coercion is to be made out independently of its justification but employs the pre-proposal situation as a baseline for deciding whether the proposal constitutes a worsening of the status quo (2001, 3).

[17] Cf. Skoble (2008, 28–29).

Hobbes (1909, 107).[18] Edmundson contrasts the coerciveness of the highwayman with that of the state, which in enacting a statute against highway robbery, coerces the citizenry from making a career of highway robbery by threat of incarceration. He notes that, according to some, the state's coercion in the latter instance demands justification, in somewhat the same way that the highwayman's coercion did.

### 2.2.1 Plea Bargains and Coercion

Edmundson reviews Wertheimer's two-pronged analysis of coercion claims, at least as the courts have tended to see them, into joint choice and proposal conditions, somewhat reminiscent of Rhodes's analysis. For it to be a case of coercion on Wertheimer's view, the proposal must be wrongful, and the person coerced must have had little or no choice about going along with it (1987, 172). To test this analysis of the legal view of coercion, Edmundson selects a case where a defendant agrees to a plea of homicide in order to avoid the death penalty, but later seeks to overturn his conviction on the grounds that he was coerced. The defendant facing the death penalty may well have had as little choice as the traveller under threat from the highwayman, but the second prong of Wertheimer's analysis requires us to settle the moral status of the proposal. According to law the district attorney is entitled to trade the death penalty for a guilty plea, which is to say the defendant has not been coerced, but if you consider capital punishment morally wrong, as Edmundson does, then the proposal is coercive.

By way of brief comment on Edmundson's assessment of this homicide case, one might have expected someone who did not favour the thesis that the law was coercive, not to find that it was coercive in this case either, thus supporting Supreme Court jurisprudence to the effect that plea bargains are not inherently coercive but voluntary agreements liable to enforcement. We might also ask how such a case would fare at the hands of other accounts of coercion discussed earlier, namely those of Nozick and Rhodes. Nozick's slave and drug addict cases show

---

[18] cf, Jasay (1991, 19).

that it can be more difficult to settle questions of coercion which take place within morally problematic contexts such as slavery or drug addiction. As already noted, Nozick seems to have thought that in both cases the proposal was more of a threat than an offer and therefore coercive. As for the plea bargain case, I suspect that Nozick might have been inclined to agree with Edmundson that it was also coercive, given that the defendant, at least in retrospect, saw it to be so, and given Nozick's presumption in favour of the recipient's preferences in such cases (1997, 28).

Rhodes on the other hand thought it possible to determine the coerciveness of a proposal independently of any moral judgement about it. We saw above that Rhodes's biconditional decision procedure suggested that the proposal to have the drug addict perform an additional service for his drugs was not coercive, whereas the master's offer not to beat his slave in return for such service was coercive. Putting the homicide case into the two conditionals required by Rhodes's analysis, we have: (1) If the defendant pleads guilty to homicide, then the DA will not seek the death penalty and does nothing; (2) If the defendant does not plead guilty to homicide, then the DA will seek the death penalty. The first conditional is then neutral in Rhodes's terms, and the second is a threat, which is to say that the whole proposal is a threat, or coercive. Thus, Rhodes would arrive at a similar conclusion to Edmundson, and probably Nozick, though without incorporating at the outset views about the wrongfulness of the DA's proposal.

Edmundson contends that the plea bargain case raises questions about a matter which loomed large in Nozick's account of coercion, namely the recipient's moral baseline, or rights he understood as background to the proposal. Indeed, as we saw, Nozick distinguished the morally expected course of events which supposedly reflected B's moral rights from the so-called normal course of events, and which was the background or baseline against which we measure whether A's proposal constitutes an improvement in, or worsening of B's lot. When the moral course of events diverges from the normal course of events, as it did in Nozick's slave and addict cases, the recipient's preference will be a guide as to which course of events represents for him an offer or a threat.

To clarify the importance of the moral baseline, Edmundson cites two further cases; first, where A proposes for a significant sum to help B overcome some transportation problems which would otherwise result in a huge loss for B. Here Edmundson returns a verdict of hard bargaining, as opposed to coercion, since A's action would leave B no worse off than he had a moral right to be. This case is contrasted with another where a company under contract to supply parts attempts to vary the terms mid-stream, thus coercing the second company, since these components were crucial for the latter to meet its own contractual obligations, thus resulting in their being worse off than they had a right to expect in custom and law (1998, 75, 81).

### 2.2.2 Sea Rescue and Coercion

Edmundson's version of the sea rescue case largely parallels that of Nozick, who also specified that both P and Q were aware that Q's only hope was to accept P's proposal. Under these circumstances, Nozick's concern is whether P's proposal constitutes an offer to rescue Q, or a threat to let him drown, if he does not agree to P's terms. Nozick's *normal course of events* is the baseline from which he makes just such a determination, but as we noted earlier it seems more reasonable to equate the baseline with the status quo ante, ante, that is, any proposal by P. From such a baseline it would seem easier to determine whether P's proposal is likely to improve Q's situation or worsen it. As we pointed out, the notion of the *normal course of events* is itself quite unclear. Q, being in the dire straits he is, would, in at least one obvious sense of the *normal course of events*, drown. Now that P has happened upon the scene, Q's chances of rescue have improved substantially, especially if Q can count on P's doing what would be normal and moral under such circumstances, namely effect a rescue if that can be done without P's endangering his own life. Indeed, in this case Nozick considers that the normal thing to do is the morally expected thing, namely, to rescue Q, in which case demanding payment is wrong and amounts to a threat to let Q drown.

Edmundson agrees that part of what makes the sea rescue case difficult is that it is not clear whether the baseline for judging P's proposal[19] includes a duty to be a good Samaritan. Indeed, the problem of deciding which duties are included in the moral baseline appears to prevent Edmundson's attempting to offer any final resolution of the sea rescue case, consoling himself with the fact that Nozick has similarly avoided doing so. However, as I suggested earlier, Nozick does tell us that most readers are likely to believe that exacting a high price from a drowning man is a threat.[20]

Although Rhodes does not discuss the sea rescue case, we should perhaps see whether he could offer us a more definitive verdict than Edmundson, who contents himself with the rather lame observation that any conclusion will be a function of the facts and one's moral convictions. As we saw, Rhodes did discuss Nozick's drug addict and slave cases, rejecting Nozick's finding of coercion in the former, but agreeing in the latter that the master's proposal not to beat his slave was a threat. The sea rescue case comes closer to the addict case, which Rhodes resolved into two conditionals:

If addict does base deed, then dealer gives addict drugs. (=offer)
If addict does not do base deed, then dealer does not give addict drugs. (=neutral)

According to Rhodes's analysis the combination of offer + neutral = offer. The sea rescue case could be similarly analysed:

If A pays B a huge sum, A will rescue B. (=offer)
If A does not pay B a huge sum, A will not rescue B. (=neutral)

So, it seems that applying Rhodes's analysis to this case would again overturn Nozick's verdict, since like the drug addict case, it would be an offer not a threat. If Rhodes's findings differ from those of Nozick, at least in the drug addict case, and as I have suggested, also in the sea rescue

[19] Or in Edmundson's terms, what P declares he intends to do (1998, 81).

[20] Nozick suggests that one way to turn it into an offer would be for Q to be the sort of moral monster who deserves to drown (1997, 27).

case, Rhodes believes this may have to do with the tendency of theorists like Nozick to include background threats such as those of drug withdrawal, or being beaten, as a baseline from which to determine whether a proposal is a threat or an offer, rather than correctly focusing on the relevant conditionals, as in Rhodes's model (2000, 375).

Nozick is not the only theorist to think that we need some sort of baseline in order to decide whether the proposal constitutes an improvement or a worsening of the status quo, which is to say, whether it amounts to a threat or an offer.[21] As Wertheimer also noted, the verdict we reach may further depend on the perspective from which we assess the baseline. Wertheimer's statistical test focuses on what is normal in a given society, which might include longstanding customs about rescue at sea. The moral test would attempt to decide whether Q has a moral right to be rescued by P, and if so, P's proposal is a threat (1987, 218). Wertheimer's phenomenological test refers to Q's preferences, which could rest on the mistaken belief that P has a duty of rescue.[22]

Further, with respect to P's duties in cases of private necessity and what Q may have a right to expect, Epstein thinks it's instructive to note that customs about rescue at sea have led to admiralty courts refusing to enforce salvage contracts where salvors have taken advantage of those in distress to drive a hard bargain (1993, 55). Thus, Nozick may be right to hold that proposal to charge a substantial rescue fee is coercive. On the other hand, Epstein does not favour enforcing a duty of easy rescue. Most people are willing, often to the point of futility, to come to the aid of others, while compulsion may only result in people leaving the scene to escape liability (2003, 100).[23]

As we saw, Edmundson does not offer any verdict about whether there is a duty of rescue in the celebrated sea rescue case. However, he does propose a conclusion in his opening chapter on coercion which he thinks many will find repugnant, namely that the law is not in

[21] cf. Narveson (2001).

[22] What P says he is prepared to do may rest on the belief that he is entitled to exploit his position as a monopoly carrier.

[23] Similarly, Epstein considers that tort jurisprudence may offer hope for resolving trolley problems; strict liability will prompt the trolley driver to ensure that his vehicle is in proper working order and to take evasive action to reduce loss of life (ibid., 101–102).

fact coercive. He is led to this view by two cases considered earlier in the chapter, namely the highway robbery case and the robbery statute which provides for imprisonment upon conviction. While Edmundson agrees that highway robbery is obviously coercive, in that it is immoral, he denies that the statute threatening sanctions is also coercive (1998, 82).[24] But of course coercive proposals are not simply those that propose immoral acts. Threats which do seem necessary for coercion may or may not involve something immoral, though they do introduce departures from the way events might have been expected to unfold in their absence. According to Nozick such a course of events might on occasion be the normal one, or on the other hand the morally expected one. However, contrary to Edmundson, we can still hold that the state acts coercively in threatening the robber with punishment but does not automatically act immorally in doing so. This is not to say that all uses of state coercion can be excused under the same rubric as its attempts to prevent robbery.

Edmundson nevertheless remains convinced that the cases he has presented are a serious embarrassment for the view that the law is coercive, one of those fallacies to which unfortunately not only anarchists are susceptible, but others of various political persuasions (1998, 3). Like other definitions we have considered, for Edmundson coercion consists in the attempt by A to bend B to A's will on pain of some consequence if B does not comply (1998, 86). While there is nothing very remarkable about this definition, there is also nothing in it which would rule out the coerciveness of law, that is of A being a placeholder for law or the state, something which Edmundson is anxious to do. On the contrary, as Huemer reminds us, states are coercive and in the habit of attaching punishments to their laws (2013, 9).

Although Edmundson thinks that the coerciveness of law tends to be assumed rather than argued for, he cites an argument by Bayles to the effect that a legal prohibition of some action is coercive since it results in our not performing an action we might have performed prior to the enactment of the prohibition. However, Edmundson considers this a bad argument because it assumes coercion consists in making a course

---

[24] Edmundson claims that the threat embodied in the robbery statute is no more coercive than if the traveller were to repel the attempted robbery with his own weapon. Our view is that both self defence and the statute involve coercion which may well be justified.

of action less palatable. But it is not altogether clear what Edmundson's objection amounts to; coercive acts are those where P makes certain alternatives less desirable for Q. On the other hand, Nozick did not want coercion to simply apply to any act resulting in Q changing course; he thought that some ways of getting someone to do something were coercive, namely threats, while others were not, namely offers (1997, 37–38). Though Nozick's point may not quite be what Edmundson had in mind either, since like many other eminent theorists, Nozick subscribes to the widely held view that law is coercive (1997, 89).

## Edmundson's Possible Allies

In addition to Nozick, Edmundson includes people such as Hart, Rawls and Dworkin among the many theorists who share the popular understanding that the law is coercive, a thesis which Edmundson insists will not stand up to serious reflection. To illustrate the broad nature of this attack on law he cites MacCormick's claim that the very existence of law itself with its prohibitions and punishments is an essential feature of state coercion where sanctions are threatened to secure the obedience of the citizenry (1982, 243). If we took this characterization at face value, we might assume that MacCormick is a proponent of the coerciveness of law, whereas in fact it turns out that he is not, but rather holds a view like that of Edmundson.

Indeed, with respect to popular view that what distinguishes law is not just that it reflects longstanding custom, but that it does so in a uniquely coercive manner, MacCormick's aim is to show that it is false (ibid., 236). To do that, he first examines civil law proceedings to see in what sense they might be considered coercive. He admits that at least at the sentencing stage, coercion may well be evident when the defendant is ordered to prison or has his property seized under a bench warrant, though he claims that such coercion is in the background as opposed to being constitutive of legal orders (ibid., 238). Rather it is typical of a civil law doctrine that it provides for reparation when rights are infringed, and as such may give rise to disputes requiring authoritative settlement.

Similarly, in the case of criminal law, MacCormick claims that while coercion is often present, it is not essential (ibid., 241). Although he agrees that states are not voluntary associations, one can imagine a world where defaulters might not have to be coerced into accepting penalties, just as happens with club members (ibid., 242). MacCormick's point seems to be that if the law is coercive, as it invariably appears to be, it is only contingently, and not necessarily, so (ibid., 244). Perhaps, then, it is not surprising that Edmundson did not lean more heavily on MacCormick for support since what sounded at the outset like a strong denial of the coerciveness of law proves on closer inspection difficult to distinguish from qualified assent.

However, given that deniers of legal coercion seem to be in the minority, it should be noted that Morris also appears to share MacCormick's view that coercion is not essential to the definition of the state and its laws and that we can imagine an ideal state whose citizens are only too happy to obey its just laws, with the result that coercion is not necessary. We could of course concede the conceptual point, since MacCormick and Morris are not the only ones to imagine that the coercive state as we know it might in the fullness of time wither away. Morris understandably does not want to make too much out of what we might or might not conceive but claims to be more concerned to determine the extent to which laws are correctly described as coercive, even as a matter of contingent fact (2003, 13). According to Morris, it was Hart's critique of Austin which drew attention to fatal flaws in the latter's account of law as coercive sovereign orders. Hart did indeed question whether laws command or threaten in the way a gunman does, when he orders his victim to hand over his money, or else. He thought that while penal statutes came closest to the coercive model, they did not entirely fit the notion of orders given to others because legislators were also subject to their provisions (1961, 25, 48). Of course, the fact that politicians are liable to be hoist by their own petard need not imply that laws are any less coercive, as perhaps noted in Hart's reference to the law's coercive underpinnings (1961, 48). While Hart certainly thought that the notion of law as threats issued by a sovereign was largely limited in its explanatory power to the fairy-tale kingdom of Rex, it nevertheless serves as a salutary reminder to the proverbial man in the Clapham omnibus, that his non-compliance could result in arrest and imprisonment (1961, 60).

Moreover, a legal system as we know it will for Hart be characterized by primary rules such as those restricting force and fraud, along with secondary rules which tell us how the former become law in the first place, or cease to be so, and what it is for them to be infringed (1961, 92). Hart may well be providing a more subtle and nuanced account of the coerciveness of a legal system than Austin, but law is still very much in the business of telling us what we or some official must do (1961, 113). Again, Hart reminds us in his Preface that his aim was to better understand law, coercion and morality (1961, v), while in his penultimate chapter, "Law and Morals", Hart speaks of the forbearances common to law and morality, which consist, for example, of prohibitions on violence towards others. While most will freely subject themselves to coercive arrangements, sanctions will be required to coerce the free riders (161, 193). Any doubts that Edmundson was right to place Hart in the camp of those who subscribe to the coerciveness of law should be set aside by Hart's later verdict that legal coercion like any coercion requires justification (1963, 20), and to which we are entirely sympathetic.

However, Morris claims that his particular concern is with the fact that coercion is front and centre, something he takes to be evident in Rawls's observation that politics is inseparable from coercion backed up by punitive measures (1993, 136). Morris responds to Rawls that law may be coercive but isn't always so, for example, the legal duties of officials (2003, 17). Again it isn't clear why such laws would count as examples of laws not backed by sanctions, since the duties of officials, like any other legally imposed obligations, are at least in theory subject to enforcement.[25] Morris thinks that in emphasizing the extent to which liberal states rely upon force and sanctions, we may overlook other resources at their disposal, of which the principal one is authority, about which we shall have more to say in the following chapter. States may also lead

[25] Whether or not officials are sanctioned for their dereliction of duty is another question. Milke suggests that much bureaucratic malfeasance passes "under the public radar" (2006, 123).

their citizens to modify their behaviour by taxes and licensing, exemptions for charity[26] or recognition for public service (2003, 23). Such a view echoes MacCormick's claim that many government inducements are non-coercive, or enshrined in the social order, reinforced by softer incentives (1982, 246).

Although the state may have various ways of ensuring compliance, as Morris and MacCormick suggest, that does nothing to diminish the coerciveness of its orders. Those orders may ensure compliance without the use of force, but the threat of force is never far away, and such threats are coercive. Non-compliance may very well be met with various levels of force, as someone who attempts to ignore a tax assessment, or practise medicine without a licence may very soon discover. Nevertheless, Morris insists that the state is often in the business of offering the proverbial carrot rather than a stick, a view for which he finds support in Mill. But while Mill allows that government might provide advice and information, rather than issuing commands and penalties, this is something it rarely does, if for no other reason than that Mill thinks it improbable that government should prove a useful repository of knowledge (1970, 305, 317).

While Mill thought that government did not necessarily meddle, nor did it trust that goods could be reliably supplied privately, it often set up a parallel arrangement, which eventually crowded out individual initiative. Thus, as Holcombe comments, the libraries once built by Carnegie are now supplied by government (2000, 259). Seldon argues in a similar vein that the welfare state was primarily a political contrivance serving the state and its employees rather than, as is often thought, a rescue service for the working classes adrift on the sea of the Industrial Revolution. By the early twentieth century most workers were insured privately against unemployment and sickness; it is thus a historical fiction to claim that they lacked such benefits until the state ensured compulsory enrolment (2002a, 62–63, 67). As for other public works such as bridges and railways, for which a reasonable business case might be made, based on the tolls or fares to be collected, Mill noted again that compulsion is

[26] Holcombe argues that while charitable exemptions might look relatively benign, decisions about awarding tax-free status are typically arbitrary and bureaucratic (2000, 247).

never removed entirely, because governments typically resort to taxation to finance such projects, along with the panoply of regulations required to prevent tax evasion (1970, 307).

Thus where government is concerned, supposed carrots look upon closer inspection to have a distinctly wooden character about them, a fact which Morris appears to recognize towards the end of his argument, where he notes that it is reasonable to assume that laws will be backed by sanctions to ensure compliance (2003, 27). Moreover he seems to assume that a government monopoly is required to restrain the recalcitrant and that the preferences of such a monopoly can be equated with those of society. On the other hand, like MacCormick before him, Morris wants to maintain that it is simply a contingent fact about laws that they tend to be backed up by sanctions rather than that they are necessarily so. MacCormick doesn't say whether he considers it logically necessary that a legal order determine rights and define offences for the members of a society, perhaps because that is what it means to have a legal order, or whether that is just what as a matter of legal history it happens to do. Nor is it clear whether he thinks some necessity attaches to the rights and offences which loom large in our system, or whether they are simply those we happen to think important. If sanctions are not exactly necessary, Morris thinks that they are a virtually universal accompaniment of legal orders, given that humans are the way they are, or as Raz put it, laws without sanctions are logically possible, but humanly impossible (1990, 158–159).[27]

### 2.2.3 The Coerciveness of Law and the Presumption of Liberty

Undeterred by the fact that writers such as MacCormick and Morris offer less than resounding support, if indeed they offer any at all, for his attack on the coerciveness of law, Edmundson insists that the rhetorical purpose of the received or, as he calls it, pre-reflective view, is to shift the justification of coercion onto the state and its legal apparatus. He argues that

[27] Raz also goes on to point out that he considers the claim that resort to sanctions is not part of our concept of law to be controversial (ibid.).

it therefore serves a similar function to its near relative, the presumption of liberty, which has likewise suffered from a dearth of critical scrutiny. In the hope of remedying this deficiency as well, Edmundson asks in what sense we are entitled to make any presumption in favour of liberty in the first place. Indeed, he considers Rawls, for example, to have definitively rejected any such presumption. However, while supposedly not assigning any special value to liberty, Rawls supports the view that restricting behaviour, legally or otherwise, requires justification (1993, 292).

Even Edmundson admits that Rawls's formulation sounds a lot like a presumption of liberty, if there were indeed any such thing (1998, 92). Indeed, according to Feinberg, if there were, it would shift the burden of justification onto those favouring coercion (1973, 22). Edmundson of course thinks that Rawls has simply affirmed the consequent without having established the antecedent (ibid.). Moreover, Edmundson takes Rawls's supposed failure to establish a strong presumption of freedom as indicative of the fact that this presumption has disappeared from serious political philosophy. One of the arguments that might be offered in support of such a presumption is that liberty is a good, to which Edmundson responds that this would not accord priority to liberty since it is only one good among many (1998, 93). One might contend that liberty is at the top of the heap of goods; Rawls seems to have thought that once the needs of the less fortunate had been attended to the golden age of liberty would eventually be ushered in (1971, 543). However, since for Edmundson such arguments have failed to clearly establish any abstract presumption of liberty, he claims that liberalism has turned to something more concrete, namely the coerciveness of law, which will in turn prove as otiose as the presumption of liberty.

Of course, there is just no reason to think that liberty qua good is simply one good among many. Liberty is more appropriately seen somewhat negatively, as the absence, rather than the presence of some quality or other. Thus, Lester sees liberty, at least of the interpersonal variety, as a matter of costs *not* imposed on others (2000, 59). Force and fraud typically impose such costs, as in Jasay's robbery example, where one is coerced into handing over the wallet one would rather keep, which is to say the handing over of one's wallet is imposed (1991, 19). Rather than a value in and of itself, Narveson reminds us that the lack of things standing in our way is a precondition to doing what we value (2002b, 38).

While Edmundson claims to have shown that the truism of the coerciveness of law should now be discounted as beneficial to political philosophy, like the presumption of liberty before it, upon closer inspection he has offered no convincing grounds for revising the thesis that the law is coercive. For that matter, nor does it seem that the presumption of liberty, from which such a thesis flows, has vanished from serious political philosophy. With respect to Rawls, for example, it may be that his ideas about the priority of liberty have shifted, perhaps due to Hart's criticisms.[28] In any case Rawls revised the first of his two principles of justice to the effect that everyone should be entitled to a similar schedule of fundamental liberties (1993, 291).

Even in Rawls's revised standard version it hardly seems to be the case that the presumption of liberty has vanished, any more than it has from other writers who are much clearer about the role of liberty than he is: Hospers thought that equal freedom for all could only be secured by recognizing limits, so as not to violate the freedom of others (1971, 12), while Narveson speaks of a sphere of liberty, whose limits are determined by what would infringe upon the rights of others (1988, 7). Dworkin also points out that he understands liberty in the negative sense of freedom from legal constraint, particularly in matters of great importance (2002, 120). If Dworkin's aim is to subsume liberty under equality of resources, this is to better reflect the status we accord it (ibid. 183). As for Edmundson's claim that the coerciveness of law and the presumption of liberty from which it is derived no longer have anything to offer to political philosophy, this is just false. Rumours as to the demise of both the presumption of liberty and the coerciveness of law appear to have been greatly exaggerated.

[28] See Lomasky (2005, 181). Rather than despairing of establishing the priority of liberty, as Edmundson argued (1998, 92), Hart thought that Rawls had failed to do so (1985, 247).

## 2.2.4 Malum Prohibitum v. Malum in Se

For most of his discussion of coercion Edmundson claims to have proceeded on the assumption that the law's proposals are not wrongful. He also argues that if also we assume a moralized view of coercion, as Nozick does, we will find it harder to reject the conclusion that the law is not coercive. Edmundson contends that a robbery statute, for example, will make it more difficult to adhere to the thesis that the law is coercive, because those who think that the law should punish robbers will not believe that such a law is coercive. We have denied all along that there is any such difficulty, something Edmundson himself appears to recognize when he agrees that finding the law coercive is not necessarily to condemn it (1998, 106). Moreover, he thinks that at the very least a finding of coercion places a burden of justification upon the law, which in our view is as it should be. However, in his final chapter on coercion, to test the assumption that the law's proposals are not wrongful, Edmundson does not just address the subject of criminal law which provides the most plausible examples of the non-wrongfulness of law by outlawing behaviour generally considered morally wrong, or *malum in se*.

Edmundson instead turns to *malum prohibitum* cases or those where the act is not wrong in and of itself, or not *malum in se*, but wrongful, if at all, only because illegal. Indeed, such laws constitute the bulk of modern statutes, but are a likely source of the coerciveness of law, since their proscriptions appear to lack any independent moral warrant and should therefore be more difficult to justify (1998, 110). Edmundson responds to the view that there is a class of laws which exceed their moral warrant by appealing to the principle of fairness, to which he already had occasion to refer in his opening chapter, and which can be traced to writers such as Hart and Rawls. According to this principle, if others have contributed to some aspect of the common good, it is unfair of us not to do likewise, since, as Hart points out, we benefit from restrictions others have imposed on themselves for the general welfare (1984, 85). Indeed, Edmundson claims that failing to do one's bit, although a *malum prohibitum*, is morally wrong (1998, 111), which if true appears to collapse the distinction between the two classes of wrongs.

In fact, Edmundson assimilates the *malum prohibitum* cases to the rules of the road, which are paradigmatic of those regulations necessary for coordinating the actions of a diverse populace (1998, 110). With the benefit of hindsight, he professes to have become persuaded of the fundamental truth of the principle of fairness, when he was upbraided by a fellow pedestrian for having disobeyed a crossing light. Although he apparently thinks this a good example of what Hart had in mind, it remains unclear how Edmundson is supposed to have benefited at the expense of the other's compliance, particularly in view of his own earlier remark that jaywalking is unlikely to herald the decline of civilization (1998, 28).

Moreover, the principle of fairness has been attacked, most notably perhaps by Nozick, when he asks us to consider whether we are obliged to take our turn in providing neighbourhood public entertainment simply because others have agreed and already done so. Nozick thinks that even if we add a rider to the effect that the benefits accruing from the performance by others were greater than the costs of your doing your share, it would still have to be the case that there was nothing you would rather do than stand at the microphone on the day in question.

Edmundson responds that Nozick's attack might be less compelling if it were to involve something less frivolous, such as monitoring the city's water supply (1997, 112, n.22). No doubt there are many ways of managing water and sanitation, ranging from the fully private to the socialized systems of recent years, but given the predominance of the latter, we could respond that it was too risky to be left in the hands of volunteers, and it wouldn't be efficient to provide adequate training for one day's work. In cases where volunteer labour is something of a tradition, such as jury duty or blood donation, possible undersupply could be met by increasing compensation, where it is poor or non-existent, bearing in mind that others such as lawyers and bureaucrats live quite handsomely off the avails of such industries.[29] Nozick again reminds us that the fact that we live in societies and benefit from the contributions of countless others who have gone before us does not mean that we have amassed a debt to "society" which can be called in whenever

[29] cf. Rothbard (1978, 90).

its self-appointed spokesmen decide (1974, 90). Thus, we would submit that Edmundson's strategy of showing that laws of the *malum prohibitum* variety turn out to be indistinguishable from those that more clearly track morality, or *malum in se*, fails; the former do indeed constitute paradigm cases of the coerciveness of law, and if wrongful, it is only because they are illegal. They can therefore be expected to present acute difficulties for the state's carrying its burden of justifying them.

## 2.2.5 The Coerciveness of the state's Monopoly on Enforcement

Finally, Edmundson takes up the question as to whether the state's assumption of a monopoly on punishment itself constitutes a classic case of wrongful coercion, as some have argued. Such writers contend that the state is acting immorally when it abridges our right to self-help, to punish those who have wronged us. Appealing to Hohfeld's distinction between liberty and claim rights, Edmundson contends that there is no such right, which theorists from Locke to Barnett have defended.[30] While individuals may have a claim to punish their wrongdoers, in respect of others they only possess a liberty, which the state may override without prejudice to any strong rights individuals have.

In response to Edmundson, the distinction between claim rights and liberties is not altogether clear, any more than it is clear which of the two best accounts for a supposed natural executive right to punish. It may even be some mixture of the two, as seems to be the case with property, where an owner's liberty to use a piece of property derives from a claim right to the property in the first place involving proper transfer of title. Indeed, Edmundson appeals to a property example to clarify the right to punish, suggesting that if all you have is the liberty to use my car on occasion, you have no right to complain if my need to use it conflicts with yours (1998, 121). If, as Jasay points out, the basic example of a claim right is your typical contract to sell, rent or borrow (1991, 48), those are

[30] See Locke (1960, 208), Rothbard (2002, 89–90), and Barnett (1998, 214).

the ways I acquire a stronger claim right to your property, including the liberties of use or disposal.

If liberties tend to ride on the back of claim rights, at least when it comes to property relations, Edmundson's example doesn't really explain why punishment functions differently. It seems essential to Edmundson's account that we be able to detach liberties from their underlying rights to allow for the fact that the right to punish did not entail that others, especially the state, not interfere in the exercise of your right. Edmundson does not seem to have noticed that in thus removing a major obstacle to the state's assumption of a monopoly on punishment, it is unclear how the state itself could ever acquire more than an unprotected liberty to punish. A central claim in Edmundson's argument for the authority of the state, which we shall take up in the next chapter, consists in reducing the burden of the duty incumbent upon its subjects to one of non-interference in the administration of the law. It is not clear what the source of this duty of non-interference is, unless the state, unlike individuals, has a claim right to administer the law including punishing offenders.

Nevertheless, Edmundson appeals to Nozick to shore up his view that our liberty to punish is not protected from interference by others, notably the state. Although Nozick is inspired by Locke, who held that individuals possessed a natural executive right to punishment (1960, 271), Nozick does in fact think that confusion and disorder, which Locke himself anticipated as an objection, would indeed follow a regime of "open" punishment to which all hold a strong or claim right. Nozick therefore suggested modifying Locke's view, so that unlike compensation, punishment is not owed to the victim, and is not subject to his authority (1974, 138). But as Rothbard has written, there is no reason to distinguish punishment from compensation; punishment or compensation is owed to the victim rather than "society", though the victim may waive his right to punish for suitable compensation. Indeed, for Rothbard, there might be more than one ground for compensation: the thief would be liable to restitution not only for the property wrongfully taken but for an amount equal to the value of the property for personal distress caused to the victim (2002, 86, 89).

In fact, it may even be that double compensation falls short of the mark, a suggestion Rothbard thanks none other than Nozick for (2002, 89, n.7). However, the Nozick of *Anarchy State and Utopia* thought that to avoid some of the hazards of leaving punishment up to victims or their agents, punishment should be a collective enterprise, which the agent chosen by the majority would eventually come to dominate. Accumulating as it does the entitlements of its subscribers apparently entitles the dominant protective agency to deny independents the right to act against its members, thus paving the way for the agency to gain a monopoly on protection. Moreover, the prohibition of behaviour which might set its subscribers at risk will itself call forth compensation, to the extent that such prohibition sets the independents at a disadvantage.[31]

Again, it is not clear why the protective association can only aggregate the entitlements of its subscribers[32] and not the hazards which supposedly attend individual enforcement. Moreover, the sum of what both Edmundson and Nozick claim are unprotected liberties is still an unprotected liberty, which is to say, as Schmidtz observed, the dominant protective agency fails to gain a claim or strong right to punish which is not subject to interference (1991, 36). Thus, if there is a way of demonstrating that the state's monopoly on punishment is not wrongful, which is what Edmundson hoped to show, neither he nor Nozick have produced it. On the contrary, the independents do not act wrongfully if they decide to pursue their own wrongdoers, though as Rothbard pointed out, victims will likely, even under a libertarian dispensation, resort to other party private enforcement and adjudication services (2002, 90; also n.10).

However, Edmundson thinks that few are likely to agree that an independent who had not surrendered his Lockean executive right could rightfully punish O.J. Simpson if he were found guilty of murder as charged. Indeed, not only is there much theoretical interest in legal traditions which predate the state's monopoly, one suspects that the proverbial man in the Clapham omnibus might well find it preferable to exercise

[31] One suspects that this compensation may not be as generous as that supposedly suggested to Rothbard: cf. Nozick (1974, 81–84, 110–113).

[32] Nozick appears to think that the sum of all the entitlements is somehow greater than the sum of its parts (1974, 140).

his natural executive right, at least on occasion, to sitting on a jury for months on end, only to have the likes of O.J. walk away scot-free. If terrorist events in recent years are any guide, the man in the bus may have to be a good deal more proactive, since the authorities typically only arrive in time to pick up the pieces.

Self-help, subject to differing degrees of control, goes back at least to the Twelve Tables of Roman Law dating from 450 BC, which according to Cicero, boys learnt by heart at school. Nicholas writes that one might punish a thief on the spot, provided one called out, or one might haul him and his stolen property before the magistrate who would order him scourged before handing him over to the victim (1984, 209). In fact, Edmundson's conclusion that the coerciveness of law may be difficult to uphold (1998, 123) is somewhat less grandiose than his earlier claim that it is a fallacy typical of those who think, for example, that government is not entitled to a monopoly on punishment. If it were really a fallacy to hold that the law is coercive then one wouldn't have thought that it could be sustained at all, but rather ought to be consigned to the trash bin of history, along with its cousin, the presumption of liberty, as he himself earlier recommended. However, as I trust I have shown, it is Edmundson's case which is much harder to sustain than that of his opponents.

Indeed, in so doing I have responded to Edmundson's challenge to produce argument to support the view that the coerciveness of law requires justification, rather than simply adopting it without question. I have argued that the law is coercive, and that this fact does place a burden of justification upon the state and its law. Moreover, as Benson points out, many areas of contemporary law appear to have little justification, having begun as attempts to consolidate royal power, a project which has continued unabated under representative democracy (1990, 87). Although Hart believed that the simple doctrine of sovereignty could have benefited from radical surgery, Rex still appears to be alive and well: the absolute or democratic sovereign, obedient only to divine or earthly fictions, happily commands obedience from his subjects (1961, 73, 49).

On the other hand, under the decentralized legal system envisaged by Benson, there is no question of protection firms arrogating to themselves rights not held by individuals (1990, 294), or to paraphrase Nozick, having more entitlements does not mean being more entitled (1974, 190). As David Friedman emphasizes government is synonymous with coercion which it declares lawful (1989, 112), a view echoed by Rothbard, who reminds us that only the law and order provided by government legitimizes coercion; in the absence of a state apparatus supported by coercive taxes, there would be no levers of power for private protection agencies to seize hold of and transform themselves into something more nearly resembling a state (1977b, 7).

## 2.3 Summary

We reviewed several prominent accounts of coercion, beginning with Nozick's well-known essay, where he proceeds from the necessary and sufficient conditions for standard cases of coercion to the more difficult ones of distinguishing threats from offers or warnings. In the second part we took up the question of whether the state and its law were coercive, by way of response to Edmundson's claim that they weren't. Edmundson admits to being in the minority on this view, since most political philosophers would deny Edmundson's contention that the coerciveness of law is a fallacy. We introduced Edmundson's distinction between laws that are *malum in se* and the great majority of statutes and regulations that are *malum prohibitum*. Having little or nothing to do with obvious moral questions, the latter are more difficult to justify, and we rejected the attempt to do so by appealing to fairness. Finally, we rejected the state's monopoly on coercion as simply an example of the sovereign prerogative which did not die out with absolutism, a question we return to in a further chapter.

## Works Cited


Barnett, Randy E. *The Structure of Liberty.* New York: Oxford, 1998.

Benson, Bruce L. *The Enterprise of Law.* San Francisco: Pacific Research Institute, 1990.

Brubaker, Elizabeth. *Property Rights in the Defence of Nature.* London: Earthscan, 1995.

Coase, R.H. *The Firm, the Market, and the Law.* Chicago: Chicago U. Press, 1988.

Dworkin, Ronald. *Sovereign Virtue.* Cambridge: Harvard U. Press, 2002.

Edmundson, William A. *Three Anarchical Fallacies.* Cambridge: Cambridge U. Press, 1998.

Epstein, Richard. *Bargaining with the State.* Princeton: Princeton U. Press, 1993.

———. *Simple Rules for a Complex World.* Cambridge: Harvard U. Press, 1997.

———. *Scepticism and Freedom.* Chicago: Chicago U. Press, 2003.

Feinberg, Joel. *Social Philosophy.* New York: Prentice-Hall, 1973.

Feinberg, Joel. *Harm to Others.* New York: Oxford U. Press, 1984.

Friedman, David. *The Machinery of Freedom.* La Salle: Open Court, 1989.

Gwartney, J. D., and R. L. Stroup. *What Everyone Should Know About Economics and Prosperity.* Vancouver: Fraser Institute, 1993.

Hart, H.L.A. *The Concept of Law.* Oxford: Oxford U. Press, 1961.

———. *Law, Liberty and Morality.* Oxford: Oxford U. Press, 1963.

———. "Are There Any Natural Rights?" In *Theories of Rights*, ed. J. Waldron, 77–90. Oxford: Oxford U. Press, 1984.

———. *Essays in Jurisprudence and Philosophy.* Oxford U. Press, 1985.

Hayek, F.A. *The Constitution of Liberty.* Chicago: Chicago U. Press, 1978.

Henderson, David. *Joy of Freedom.* Upper Saddle River: Prentice-Hall, 2002a.

———. "Myths about US Health Care." In *Better Medicine*, ed. David Gratzer, 175–195, Toronto: ECW Press, 2002b.

Hobbes, Thomas. *Leviathan.* Oxford: Oxford U. Press, 1909.

Holcombe, Randall G. *Writing off Ideas.* Oakland: Independent Institute, 2000.

Hospers, John. *Libertarianism.* Santa Barbara: Reason Press, 1971.

Huemer, Michael. *The Problem of Political Authority.* Basingstoke: Palgrave Macmillan, 2013.

Jasay, Anthony De. *Choice Contract and Consent.* London: Institute of Economic Affairs, 1991.

Lester, Jan. *Escape from Leviathan.* London: St Martin's Press, 2000.
Locke, John. *Two Treatises of Government*, ed. Peter Laslett. Cambridge: Cambridge U. Press, 1960.
Lomasky, Loren E. "Libertarianism at Twin Harvard." *Social Philosophy and Policy* 22, no. 1 (Winter 2005).
MacCormick, Neil. *Legal Right and Social Democracy*. Oxford: Oxford U. Press, 1982.
Milke, Mark. *A Nation of Serfs.* Mississauga: Wiley, 2006.
Mill, J.S. *Principles of Political Economy. Books IV and V*. Harmondsworth: Penguin, 1970 [1985].
Morris, Christopher W. "Are States Necessarily Coercive?" [unpubl.] 2003.
Narveson, Jan. *The Libertarian Idea.* Philadelphia: Temple U. Press, 1988.
———. *Ethics in the Business and Professional Life.* Waterloo: U. Waterloo, 1998.
———. "Libertarianism." In *The Blackwell Guide to Ethical Theory*, ed. Hugh LaFollette. Oxford: Blackwell, 2000b.
———. "Coercion: A Few Obvious Things." [unpubl.] October 2001.
———. *Respecting Persons in Theory and Practice.* Lanham: Rowman & Littlefield, 2002a.
———. "Liberty and Equality: A Question of Balance." In *Liberty and Equality*, ed. Tibor Machan, 35–59. Stanford: Hoover Institution Press, 2002b.
Nicholas, Barry. *An Introduction to Roman Law.* Oxford: Oxford U. Press, 1984.
Nozick, Robert. *Anarchy, State and Utopia.* New York: Basic Books, 1974.
———. *Socratic Puzzles.* Cambridge: Harvard U. Press, 1997.
Olson, M. *The Logic of Collective Action.* Cambridge: Harvard U. Press, 1965.
Rawls, J. *A Theory of Justice.* Cambridge: Harvard U. Press, 1971.
———. *Political Liberalism.* New York: Columbia U. Press, 1993.
Raz, J. *Practical Reason and Norms.* Princeton: Princeton U. Press, 1990a.
Rhodes, Michael. "The Nature of Coercion." *The Journal of Value Inquiry* 34, [ 2000].
Rothbard, Murray, "Robert Nozick and the Immaculate Conception of the State." *Journal of Libertarian Studies* 1, no. 1 (1977a): 45–57.
———. *Power and Market*. Kansas City: Sheed Andrews & McMeel, 1977b
———. *For a New Liberty.* New York: Collier, 1978.
———. *Making Economic Sense.* Auburn: Mises Institute, 1995.
———. *The Logic of Action Two.* London: Edward Elgar, 1997.
———. *Man, Economy and State.* Auburn: Mises Institute, 2001.

———. *The Ethics of Liberty.* New York: New York U. Press, 2002.

Schmidtz, David. *The Limits of Government*. Boulder: Westview, 1991.

Seldon, Arthur. *The Dilemma of Democracy.* London: Institute of Economic Affairs, 2002a.

Skoble, Aeon J. *Deleting the State: An Argument about Government*. Chicago and La Salle: Open Court, 2008.

Sowell, Thomas. *Basic Economics.* New York: Basic Books, 2000.

Viminitz, Paul. "Coercion." [unpubl.] July 2001.

Wertheimer, Alan. *Coercion.* Princeton: Princeton U. Press, 1987.

Woods, Thomas. *The Politically Incorrect Guide to American History*. Washington, DC: Regnery, 2004.

# 3
# Authority

I trust I have clarified somewhat the notion of coercion, if only to re-affirm that *pace* Edmundson, one can coherently speak of the state as a coercive order. Some writers who do not necessarily share my scepticism of the state and all its works, nevertheless record the fact that modern democratic states compel uncritical obedience from their citizens (Dunn 2005, 19). Even Edmundson appears to acknowledge the power of the state to push people around, so let us now turn to the question of its authority to be the bully it is. According to Edmundson, we should find it difficult to reconcile the bullying nature of law with the fact that at least at times its demands largely overlap with those of morality (1998, 34).

However, those of us who are interested in advancing liberty while constraining coercion are probably much less concerned with the convergence between morality and law than where there is little or no such convergence. To use Edmundson's terminology again, we find the class of *malum prohibitum*, or conduct wrong merely by virtue of being prohibited, which apparently constitutes the bulk of the state's legal and

© The Author(s), under exclusive license to Springer Nature Switzerland AG 2022
G. Booker, *Coercion, Authority and Democracy*, Palgrave Studies in Classical Liberalism, https://doi.org/10.1007/978-3-031-16883-3_3

regulatory endeavours,[1] more troublesome than that of *malum in se*, or what most agree to be wrongful and typically oppose at least in principle.

Even where the state touts its intervention as some sort of moral crusade, it is unlikely that it represents much of a departure from *malum prohibitum*. For example, the US Dept of Justice was at one point pursuing a criminal investigation of the Mercedes division of Daimler-Chrysler for having paid bribes as part of its overseas operations in Africa and Latin America. What isn't at all clear, however, is that bribes are morally wrong. While we might all prefer a situation where governments or firms were not powerful enough to grant favours, various writers have argued that bribes of one sort or another may be simply a cost of doing business in many foreign countries.[2]

About *malum prohibitum* cases in general, Edmundson observes that since we are not necessarily duty bound to obey the law, it is not surprising that many conclude that its dictates are coercive and in need of justification (1998, 110). In our view, legal orders in general are coercive; what is peculiar to the class of *malum prohibitum* is that the burden of justification will be much more difficult to discharge than those where they incorporate an extralegal moral duty. With respect to the latter, the *malum in se* class, which are directly derived from moral duties, such as refraining from force, theft or fraud, is in fact legitimate, either on the part of the individual resorting to self-help, or as Simmons reminds us, on the part of states to which a similar right of punishing wrongful acts may be extended (1993, 265).

Given that the state appears to lack moral authority for much of its legal coercion, we shall see what sort of argument Edmundson is able to offer in favour of the state's legal reach extending far beyond the narrow band of *malum in se* cases. Edmundson's opening salvo is in fact directed

---

[1] Newspapers regularly report such interventions, such as that of *La fromagerie Boivin*, a fourth-generation cheesemaker in Quebec, who fell afoul of federal regulations when they decided to depart from time-honoured methods for ripening cheese by deep-sixing ten barrels to the bottom of the Saguenay River. Since this technique is largely untried it lacks the requisite bureaucratic approval (*Globe and Mail*, July 29, 2005). cf. Epstein (2003, 57).

[2] Rothbard (2002, 129–130) holds that it is not wrong to offer bribes, though depending on one's employment contract, it may be wrong to take them; cf. Rockwell (1997), Lemieux (2005) Machan and Chesher (2002, 152).

against those of us who have succumbed to the siren song of philosophical anarchism led by writers such as R. P. Wolff, in the hopes of rescuing political philosophy from slipping once again into obscurity, as it had supposedly done at the hands of the positivists.

In fact, Edmundson has set himself the task of explaining how we can have a legitimate political authority, if as Wolff and other philosophical anarchists have argued, we have no general obligation to obey the law. Edmundson finds it particularly troublesome that it has now become quite fashionable in influential centres of learning to hold that there is no such obligation (1998, 31–32). Godwin, for example, had argued that neither morality, justice nor common sense could justify doing the bidding of something calling itself the government (1976, 228–229). More recently, Wolff has written that the authority of the state, entailing a duty of obedience, is in direct conflict with the autonomy of the individual (1970, 18).

As a prelude to showing how we might ground legitimate political authority in the face of attacks by philosophical anarchists such as Wolff, Simmons and Green, Edmundson begins by reviewing some of the arguments which have been deployed to defend political authority, most of which have proved unsatisfactory for one reason or another. Perhaps the best known of these is that found in Plato's *Crito*, where Socrates's interlocutor, after whom the dialogue is named, encourages Socrates to escape rather than submit to the death sentence. Socrates believes that he is obliged to abide by the laws, rather than follow Crito's suggestion, which Socrates considers the sort of behaviour one might expect from a slave, rather than a citizen. Socrates believes he is beholden to the well-governed city which has nourished him from birth and would rather suffer at its hands than bring the law into disrepute by going into exile.[3]

With respect to the question of emigration from an unjust regime, Nozick asked why that should be necessary, rather than staying and simply being able to opt-out of collective orderings (1974, 173). Socrates, of course, doesn't think that either option is open to him at this stage because of the contracts and agreements implied by his long residence in Athens. However, it is not at all clear what is reasonably required

[3] see "Crito," *Dialogues of* Plato (1953, Vol. 1, 382–384).

by such contracts, implied or otherwise. Socrates apparently believes that they place us under an obligation to obey the laws, whatever they happen to be, and although he also held that injustice was an evil, he thought that fleeing would amount to returning evil for evil. But as Narveson has rightly pointed out, while martyrdom might be a useful way of drawing attention to injustice, it hardly seems reasonable to think we are duty bound to follow Socrates's example (2000b, 4).

Recent history has not lacked for unjust regimes, and among the most widely discussed is that of Nazi Germany. Concerning the duty to obey the law, Edmundson wants to argue that indeed we have one, but unlike what Socrates was proposing, it is less than absolute. As to the sort of duty residents of Nazi Germany could have been under, for example, to report their Jewish fellow residents to the authorities, Edmundson understands the notion of a prima facie duty to be one of obeying just laws, rather than of obeying the law, period (1998, 10–11). The implication is that Nazi laws, to the effect that citizens of the Reich had a duty to inform on their neighbours, or that it was wrong of them to flee the Fatherland, are not sufficiently just as to impose even prima facie duties, but, if anything, are plainly unjust on the face of it. Indeed, as Dworkin remarks, those who claim that Nazi laws were just a mockery mean that they lacked the properties of legal systems which would justify coercion (1986, 103–104).

## 3.1 Consent

But even in the case of less wicked states, it is not clear in what sense we have consented to obey the laws, as Socrates seems to have thought he did. Edmundson notes that giving express consent can, under certain circumstances, give rise to a duty, though he is less sure that, for example, traditional pledges of allegiance to God, King and Country can reliably bind those they are supposed to (1998, 16). As well as forms of express consent, there are hypothetical varieties where it is supposed that X is the sort of thing that the reasonable and informed individual would consent to. Thus, a doctor may proceed to treat an unconscious patient, believing that the reasonable patient would consent to such treatment if he were able (1998, 17).[4] Moreover, hypothetical consent arguments have been appealed to in justifying the state, claiming that it would be rational to consent to the state if that is the only alternative to the Hobbesian war of all against all. Though, as Schmidtz points out, the proposition that the state is the only alternative is the only one doing any real work in this argument and it is irrelevant to the justification of the state whether rational bargainers would consent to it or not (1996, 87).

Leslie Green considers the problem of political authority to be one of deciding whether there are any valid reasons for wanting to bind oneself to the state (1988, 158). Of the three sorts of reasons he thinks the most interesting, namely convention, social contract and consent, for him the last is the most promising as a source of political authority, though even here he concludes with the caveat that in the absence of any compelling account of its validity, it will fail to provide any general justification (ibid., 185). Before addressing the question of the validity of consent, Green however attempts to clarify what is or is not involved in consenting, especially the sort of consent that might be appealed to in justifying political authority, where consenting is typically seen as a way of undertaking an obligation (ibid., 162).

Plamenatz once remarked that consent had been used with many meanings (1968, 1), a fact also noted by Green. We referred above to the question of consent to medical treatment, and we might well wonder in what ways this sort of consent is or is not like consent to the state's authority. Raz, for example, claimed that the fact that we readily granted authority to professionals such as doctors meant that we were not precluded at least in principle from doing likewise with governments (1990b, 12). If the case of medical consent is unlike consent to government, it is that the former would appear to place much less onerous obligations on the consenter. Another important feature of medical consent is that it can be withdrawn, even in the middle of a procedure, and as Hebert points out, the onus is on the doctor to show that halting the procedure would cause serious harm to the patient (1996, 99–100).

[4] cf. Waldron (1993, 49) and Schmidtz (2006, 98, n.39); of course, the doctor's belief about hypothetical consent could turn out to be mistaken, as in Malette v. Shulman (1987), 63 O.R. (2d) 243. (H.C.J.), cited in Hebert (1996, 28–29).

However, in the case of government, Plamenatz concluded rightly that, despite their insistence that they acted with the consent of the governed, present-day governments were more oppressive than any in history (ibid., 181). Green also acknowledges the ultimate authority which the state claims over people's lives (ibid., 169), while Dunn reminds us that, as we concluded in the previous chapter, coercion being the defining characteristic of states, they have little interest in allowing their subjects to follow their own inclinations (2000, 117–118). Whereas doctors may well have authority over people's lives, it stops short of being all-encompassing and ultimate, with obligations incumbent upon the laity mostly amounting to advice, which they may ignore to the possible detriment of their health. We can fire our doctors, seek a second opinion or opt for alternative therapies, or even if we consent to treatment,

we may be less than compliant. Only in cases of mental illness involving clear risk to the patient and others can doctors order us to undergo involuntary psychiatric assessment, which they do *qua* agents of the state.[5]

Or as Green puts it, while most of us know what counts as consent to the use of one's organs for transplantation, it is far from clear what counts as consent to the authority of the state (ibid., 169). He further argues that whereas medical consent guarantees the patient's say in his own well-being because of general presumptions of liberty and autonomy, political consent is largely about obedience to higher authority (ibid., 181). Indeed, it is typical of governments that they enforce compliance by threats, with the result that, as Plamenatz claims, the government of the free may not be less coercive than one of the slaves (ibid., 175). With political consent largely in mind, Plamenatz defines consenting in terms of conferring a right on someone, which he would not normally possess (ibid., 167). Such a definition could even account for the case of medical consent, where in the absence of consent, treatment may constitute battery.[6] However, Green objects to identifying consent with its normative consequences, such as the rights or immunities it confers;

[5] cf. Hebert (1996, 162–164).

[6] cf. Foot's discussion of the anthropologist who wishes to photograph for scientific purposes an unwilling native servant (2001, 48).

in his view, by incorporating normative consequences into the definition, as Plamenatz has proposed, we are as it were begging the question as to whether there is a satisfactory theory of consent which would underwrite the state's authority (ibid., 163).

While Green's point is well taken, it perhaps should also be said that Plamenatz has little to add to Green's comparative study of consent. Plamenatz's interest is a somewhat different one, namely distinguishing what he considers the synonymous notions of government by consent or responsible government from other types of government (1968, 167–168). As to the relative merits of such a form of government, Plamenatz is of the opinion that representative, or government by consent, is better than its alternatives, given the quality of life available under modernity (ibid., 166). For the purposes of his inquiry, Green recommends looking at consent as a way of acquiring obligations, rather than the resulting obligations themselves. Plamenatz does not deny that one could look at consent in the way Green suggests; it is just not relevant to the task he has set himself (ibid., 172). Simmons, on the other hand, with respect to consent as strictly understood, speaks not only of the consenter's handing over of certain rights to act but also of agreeing not to interfere in the exercise of such alienated rights (1979, 77).[7] Indeed, as we shall see later, Edmundson will argue that the burden of political obligation needs amount to nothing more than some such special obligation not to interfere in the administration of government. Of course, there are those who think that the duties owed to legitimate authorities are not just negative ones of non-interference. Just how onerous those positive duties are is partly a function of how closely consenting is seen to resemble promising. While Edmundson notes, for example, that promising is a good example of how express consent can give rise to duties (1998, 15), Simmons argues that the sort of consent he is interested in differs from promising in several ways. For him, the primary function of consent is authorizing, with obligation upon the consenter playing only a secondary role (ibid., 77). Raz, on the other hand, thinks that political consent to the state entails, among other possible duties, a promise to obey (1988,

[7] One is reminded of Stanley Baldwin's supposed promise on giving up the premiership in 1937 not to spit on the deck or talk to the man at the wheel.

83). How much of an obligation is however quite unclear, though it is likely at most to be one of non-interference. But while Green thinks that we require actual consent of an individual to the state's authority (ibid., 162) in order to become subject to any duties flowing from the principle of *pacta sunt servanda*, in Raz's view, unlike promises, consent need not be identified with specific acts of individual consent to obligations. Indeed, on this account there are other ways to incur duties or confer rights, short of specifically consenting to do just that (ibid., 83), such as, after deciding to fly, one finds oneself obliged to submit to a search and obey the cabin crew during the flight. Nevertheless, Green thinks that the justification for these sorts of obligation which come by way of doing something else is different from those where we have voluntarily assumed an obligation (ibid., 164).[8]

### 3.1.1 The Appeal to Estoppel

Adopting forms of non-intentional consent can give rise to an appeal to the legal doctrine of estoppel to ground obligations to political authority, a move which Green understandably wishes to block. According to Lord Denning in reference to Charles Rickards v. Oppenheim ([1950]1 KB 616), the term is promissory estoppel, by which an agreed waiver to a contract may be considered binding. In the case cited by Denning, Oppenheim encouraged Rickards to continue working on a project, even though it was likely to take much longer than provided for in the original contract (1979, 206, 208). Thus, his conduct, if not his words, implied that he would not enforce his rights under the contract, including refusal of delivery.

Of course, we then need to ask whether this principle has any relevance to obligations we may or may not have to political authorities. In fact, I suspect, it does not. As an example of estoppel, Green offers the case whereby sitting down at a restaurant, I agree to pay for any food

[8] Then again it seems that in contracting with an airline for their services, we contract into a bundle of obligations with them and their regulators, as they do with us, some of which is no doubt spelled out in the fine print. The question is whether anything like that happens with states.

ordered, even if I intend to leave without paying (ibid., 163). It would seem closer to the case cited by Denning if the restaurant informed me, for example, that there would be some delay in my being served, to which I responded that I was not in a hurry, thanks to my attractive date and had even accepted consideration in the form of free drinks while waiting. The principle of estoppel, at least as understood by Denning, would then suggest that I had agreed to the revised terms of my contract with the restaurant and would not be entitled to deny that I had done so and leave without paying.

The case as envisaged by Green is perhaps closer to those who drive off from a gas station without paying, for which a proprietor may seek an appropriate remedy such as a charge for theft. In his discussion of democracy, to which we shall have occasion to refer in greater detail in the next chapter, Singer also appeals to the doctrine of estoppel, at least as it is more loosely understood, to elucidate his account of quasi consent. True to his Australian origins, Singer draws a moral lesson from a time-honoured social custom, the pub *shout*, where those in a group take turns buying drinks for all, with each member obliged to do so at the appropriate time (1974, 49). No doubt much is to be learned from such traditions of mateship and a *fair-go*, and perhaps less from ancient legal principles. However, someone inclined to try his hand at free riding, or not giving his mates a fair-go, should doubtless place himself at the end of a large shout, when with any luck his mates will no longer be in any position to notice whether it was his turn or not. For that matter, nor will he, probably.

However, as to the value of any such appeal to a rather recondite legal doctrine, we seem to have moved too far from the details of the case presented by the Master of the Rolls for it to be at all clear how instructive it may prove in the question of political consent. The point of the legal case was that we were not entitled to return to the terms of the original contract when there was evidence of our having waived them, or given our quasi-consent, as Singer would have it. In the case of the state, assuming the initial agreement involved obeying the laws, it is not clear what variation to that agreement the state is at estoppel entitled to hold us to. While Raz allows Singer's appeal to estoppel to deny our right to ignore the results of a vote in which we participated, this would be to assume that only democratic enthusiasts vote in elections, which Raz thinks is false (1979, 241).

Further, as Green reminds us, since the state has no interests of its own, but instead serves the interests of its citizens, an argument claiming harm to the state or its authorities resulting from rejection of obligations is entirely without merit. Moreover, if any non-compliance could be shown to harm other individuals, in that they rely on my compliance, this does not mean that I should be estopped from not doing my bit and failing to acknowledge the state's authority (1988, 165). Or as Raz points out, the problem of basing a general obligation to obey on the supposed harm to any individual caused by one's non-compliance is that often one's failure to obey does not affect anybody, or if it does, it is not something we or others are necessarily aware of (ibid., 239–240).

### 3.1.2 Possible Salvation in Associative Obligations

In the face of such difficulties, others, such as Dworkin, have suggested casting the net a little wider to derive a form of obligation which might guarantee the compliance on which it is believed others depend. Dworkin recommends taking a second look at associative or communal obligations which in his view display considerable moral complexity. These communal or family associations are typically not overtly consensual, which is one of the reasons Dworkin thinks philosophers have tended to shy away from them. Even those associations, where there is an element of choice, such as our friends, do not in Dworkin's view involve the formal commitment typical of membership in a club (1986, 197).

One of the important features of such associative obligations is that they are typically reciprocal, which should lead to a much higher degree of compliance. Their reciprocity seems to result from their being special to a particular group, as well as personal, with duties being owed to particular individuals, who have a sense of what may reasonably be expected from one another (ibid., 199). Not only do the members of such groups evince fraternal concern for their fellow members, but Dworkin also thinks it important that such concern be equal for all members, which he takes to mean that no one's life is more important than someone else's, a fact which will be reflected in the group's structure (ibid., 200–201). This equality requirement apparently rules out, for example, caste systems, as genuine fraternal communities.

By way of comment on Dworkin's proposal, let us work back from the last point about equal concern. Given the less formal nature of associations and the relationships they give rise to, as compared with, say, contractual relationships, I would have thought it difficult to be sure that concerns were always equal in the requisite sense. No doubt caste systems more or less by definition consist of groups with rather rigidly defined boundaries, but presumably within the caste itself concern could reflect the equality Dworkin thinks is important. In that sense, castes don't seem very different from any other association, where personal reciprocal relationships are confined to members rather than non-members, a fact which is probably true of fraternal associations with which we are more familiar, such as unions or professions.

Here Dworkin's response seems to be that our obligations are not simply confined to the associations we happen to consider primary, but that obligations, such as those of reciprocity and equal treatment are owed in the end to all and sundry, since there are manifold ways in which we are associated with the rest of humanity, to say nothing perhaps of animals and the environment. Dworkin of course does not wish to be so enthusiastic about associations as to ignore their downside, namely discrimination in favour of their members, which he thinks will likely conflict with their duties to treat non-members fairly (ibid., 202). Dworkin has thereby produced a *deus ex machina* for ramping up obligations, beginning with those at the level of a small association, until by a process of intertwining and ever more complex and larger associations, we reach the *polis* or governing association, where anything resembling a genuine association may well have disappeared.

Nevertheless, Dworkin insists on the hypothesis that political obligation is best construed as associative, and that rather than trying to find a contractual basis for collective decision-making we would do better to look to the obligations generated by our fraternal and communal associations (ibid., 206). With respect to our obligations to macro-entities such as the political community, Dworkin distinguishes the nominal community from the fully fraternal one which exemplifies more ideal qualities such as reciprocity. The bare community of Canada would in the first instance consist of the piece of real estate which standard atlases identify as the country, along with certain minimal beliefs about the structure and functioning of the state. Dworkin thinks that our associations may function at a higher level than mere history and geography might suggest where we respect the rules which govern political outcomes. At a higher level still we understand the principles, such as those of integrity, which underwrite those rules, with the result that our associative community achieves moral legitimacy (ibid., 213).

Let us now look a little more closely at Dworkin's proposal to see whether associative obligations could offer any sort of satisfactory solution to the problem of political authority and legitimacy, or whether he has simply side-stepped the issue, a criticism he denies. Dworkin claims his opponents have two choices: reject associative obligations or show why political obligation cannot be associative (ibid., 207). Of course, there is no reason to assume that these are the only alternatives open to us. We first must ask whether Dworkin has given us a satisfactory account of associative obligations, before attempting to see whether they prove a more fruitful source of obligations supposedly arising from collective decisions. One important feature of associative obligations, at least as Dworkin understands them, is that contrary to the tradition of voluntarism quite widespread in political philosophy, they are often not a matter of choice. In fact, Dworkin claims that we cannot account for associative obligations if we accept the view that the only way we can incur obligations is by choosing to do so (ibid., 197).

So, what about the popular wisdom that, although we don't get to choose our family, we do at least choose our friends? Even in the case of family, there is a considerable choice, such as when to leave the family into which one was born, perhaps to follow one's career or set up one's own family elsewhere. Perhaps Dworkin would not deny these choices, but as we develop a shared history, we assume the obligations that arise during it, mostly without being aware that we have done so. Dworkin's organic account perhaps picks out some features of our associations with family and friends but says nothing about the fact that like all such associations they presumably evolve, or are shed, along with any obligations possibly incurred in their wake. Further, one might wonder how closely many of these familiar relationships exemplify the equal concern and reciprocity which Dworkin seemed anxious to see in them. One suspects that some contractual relationships, which Dworkin contrasts less favourably with associative ones, may well at times exhibit more of the properties he considers typical of the latter.

Moreover, we would have thought that one of the more obvious features of such familiar associations is that they presupposed emotional bonds of one sort or another. Immigrants, including myself, have found themselves at too great a distance to maintain much by way of reciprocal relationships with families and friends at different ends of the earth.[9] This still leaves the question as to what sorts of ties remain between the black sheep of the family and his far-flung relatives, for lacking the requisite propinquity, there is little question of authentic associative obligations. Many have thought that some sort of connection remains, as suggested by the 1902 photo, included by Blainey in his *The Tyranny of Distance,* of members of the Melbourne stock exchange giving a spontaneous rendition of the Old Hundredth after hearing of Britain's victory in the Boer War (1966, facing 293).[10]

While Dworkin acknowledges that emotional ties are widely thought to be important, he does not consider them to be an integral part of associative obligations, since this would suggest, even at the level of large communities, that we had such ties with every member, which of course we don't (ibid., 196). For similar reasons Dworkin insists that in close relationships such as those with a sibling, the primary feature is reciprocity rather than anything of an emotional sort, which just seems wrong on the face of it, whether we are speaking of close or distant relatives. As we saw, Dworkin had hoped to show that fraternity was a more promising source of political obligation than the domain of contracts favoured by philosophers. However, to do that, he has found it necessary to give a less than plausible account of the more familiar associative obligations, ignoring some of the obvious features of their dynamic structure,

---

[9] Dworkin remarks that, if nothing else, distance may stand in the way of my becoming a citizen of Fiji, since I don't meet the bare requirements of geography which would form the basis for richer associations (ibid., 202).

[10] Ties were apparently still strong enough a dozen or so years later for 60,000 of their compatriots to die for King and Country.

such as voluntariness and emotions, in order for them to fit the mould of any recognizable political obligation. With respect to the dilemma presented by Dworkin, rather than denying all associative obligations, we have suggested that his characterization of them is less than convincing.

If we are correct, we have shown that political obligation cannot be associative, at least as understood by Dworkin. Even if he could show that political obligations could be fashioned out of more mundane associative obligations of one sort or another, others have rightly questioned whether polities are in any important sense associations. Rawls, for example points out that unlike the political, the associational is indeed characterized by voluntariness and affections (1993, 137). Narveson has also observed that in forming associations people do come together to pursue some common goal. In the case of societies people just happen to be together, often as an accident of birth, rather than having joined it for a purpose. This of course has never prevented politicians from expatiating upon the purpose which society patently doesn't have and from ensuring that we shall never lack for guardians who will diligently attend to its pursuit (2002a, 165). However, Dworkin seems to think that the virtues of the ideal association can somehow be replicated at the political level. He asks us in fact to consider three models of society in ascending order of virtue. At the lowest level is the one corresponding to the bare association mentioned earlier, where citizens see their association as the sort of geographical and historical accident which Narveson thought was typical of a society, as opposed to an association. The next step up from this most rudimentary and inauspicious social arrangement is for Dworkin a society of rules, which sounds much like the political society we are familiar with, where we generally agree to abide by the patchwork quilt of rules produced by legislative compromises (ibid., 210). What we should be aiming at is the society of principle, rather than compromise, bearing the hallmarks of an association whose aim is reciprocal and equal concern for its members.

While Dworkin insists that by equal concern, he stops short of asking that we love our neighbours, this might be of little comfort, for example, to the attorney whose reaction to a possible forced evacuation from his home in a well-to-do part of New Orleans relatively untouched by Hurricane Katrina was that he would strongly resist any such attempt on the part of the authorities. Instead of equal concern, he claimed that the state owed him nothing but benign neglect, a duty which he for his part would no doubt be only too happy to reciprocate. The fact that most states have not reached the level of principled rather than pragmatic politics, and as I have argued, are unlikely to ever do so, implies in Dworkin's terms that they lack legitimacy and represent nothing but power masquerading as fraternity (ibid., 214). The recalcitrant lawyer from the Big Easy would probably be rightly suspicious of the descendants of Citizen Robespierre invoking the name of fraternity, thus rejecting any attempt to remove him from his property as nothing more than the exercise of bare power.[11]

Dworkin, of course, thinks that if we could usher in the reign of a community of principle rather than compromise we would achieve that unanimity of purpose which characterizes associations, though apparently we would still disagree about justice and fairness (ibid., 214). However, if it is true that we disagree about justice and fairness, and I think he is probably right about that, then I am not sure why we would agree about what it was to have an association based on principle, even if that were possible at the level of a polity. On the other hand, we find his description of the run-of-the-mill political society all too familiar, with its patchwork of ad hoc statutes on everything from divorce to bankruptcy drafted in response to the demands of particular interest groups. While Dworkin thinks that by becoming an association of principle we could promote legal integrity, Leoni thinks that we would do better to abandon politically created statutes and return to a tradition where law had arisen as the result settling countless private disputes over many generations (1991, 88).[12]

---

[11] Some 60 years after The Revolution, Bastiat wrote that no end of troubles resulted from founding the law upon fraternity, genuine or otherwise, most notably the destruction of liberty (2001, 81, 39–40).

[12] cf. Barnett (1998, 124) and Tamanaha (2006, 42).

## 3.2 Fairness as a Possible Foundation of Political Obligation

Before looking more closely at Edmundson's account of legitimacy, let us briefly examine another quite influential argument for political obligation, namely the argument from fairness. There is to be sure some connection between obligations arising from some sense of fairness and Dworkin's associational variety, characterized by equal concern and reciprocity, but which Dworkin in fact sees as improving on obligations derived from fairness. One of the best-known proponents of fairness as a ground of political obligation was Dworkin's predecessor at Oxford, H. L. A. Hart, who was concerned that some might free ride on others' respect for the law (1961, 213). In the context of arguing how political obligation differs from other rights creating transactions such as consenting and promising, Hart held that those who have obeyed the rules governing some cooperative venture have a right to expect that others similarly restrict their liberty, a right which may be enforced by authority (1984, 85).

Hart's formulation raises obvious questions about the sort of venture he had in mind, and what it means for it to be conducted according to rules, since considerations of fair play need not be confined to organizations with rather formal sets of rules. Perhaps the rules determine how one becomes a member, and what is expected of members vis-a-vis other members. The rules may vest authority in officials, though one's obligation to do one's share may remain a moral one over and above anything the rules may call for. Acknowledging his debt to Hart, Rawls similarly emphasizes the moral nature of obligations of fairness which are incumbent on all participants in a joint venture, none of whom wish their compliance to be taken advantage of (1962, 144). Although, as we saw, the later Rawls claimed to distinguish the associational from the political, the fact that this obligation applied to anyone who stood to gain from a regulated group effort would appear to cover just about any such venture along that continuum. Rawls goes on to explain that a paradigm case of the special prima facie duty which arises from voluntarily accepting benefits, and which he claims to have borrowed from

Hart, is in fact political obligation. In opposition to some social contractarians, Rawls points out that political obligation does not presuppose an actual promise or contract. Although it may be overridden by mitigating circumstances, you cannot simply refuse to do your duty when the time comes but need to declare conscientious objector status early on (ibid., 145–146).

Indeed, what Narveson calls particular rights, of which a typical example is the right that other parties fulfil their end of a bargain (1988, 56), appear at least initially to have something in common with Hart's special rights. However, as we noted, Hart seemed to think it important to show how the rights and obligations peculiar to politics differed from those arising from promising or consenting. In this context, I may be bound whether or not I have specifically agreed, though Rawls apparently allows for some process of opting out, depending on the benefits which have supposedly accrued under any such tacit contract. In this sense, political obligations, although Hart contends that they are special, appear to impose general duties or restrictions on all and sundry.[13]

However, to return to the question of special versus general duties, it seems that Hart's example of political obligation, since it is apparently incumbent on large numbers of people, comes much closer to a general than to a special obligation. However, Hart insists that while special rights, of the sort that supposedly gives rise to political obligation, justify an individual's interfering with another's freedom, we appeal to general rights to ward off such interference (ibid., 87). To the extent that such general rights imply duties of non-interference on the part of all, they amount to what is more often called negative rights, which on a libertarian view, such as mine, constitute our fundamental moral rights. Special rights would then be a variety of positive rights which give rise to positive duties, and which you may be coerced if necessary into performing. When we ask how it is that I acquire such duties, it is because I have promised or contracted to perform some service to the

[13] Similarly, far from implying a right to do whatever you please, which as Narveson writes, is tantamount to no rights at all (1988, 45), libertarianism involves mutual restrictions on the exercise of liberty, so much so that Freeman (2001) considers libertarianism in fact a rather illiberal doctrine, at least in his sense of liberal.

individual to whom it is owed, or for Hart, it is a duty I have chosen to lay upon myself (ibid., 88).

Preferring not to be confined to promises or contracts, Hart and Rawls claimed there was another way of acquiring such positive duties, namely by their being collectively or mutually imposed, where those who first submitted to the necessary restrictions can insist that others do likewise. Leaving aside the question of who gets to decide that something is a required limitation on freedom, presumably those who first agreed to do so, it is not clear why their choosing prevents others from choosing not to if their priorities are different. To hold otherwise is to say that citizens of the Third Reich had a duty to report dissidents to the Gestapo, and that they did not have the option of choosing otherwise because that would be unfair to those who had performed their duty. On the other hand, Narveson reminds us that promising in fact illustrates quite well how positive duties may be derived from more fundamental negative ones. One is not obliged to promise or contract, but once having done so, one has a positive duty to fulfil it. Not to do so is to interfere in the ability of others to do as they wish, since you have failed to do what you said you would do, whereas in the case of Hart's mutuality of restrictions you have not agreed to anything, which is to say the restrictions are unilateral rather than mutual (ibid., 60).

What is also clear is that Dworkin's construing of political obligation as associative owes much to his illustrious predecessor. As observed earlier, Dworkin similarly held that political association has it in common with other associations like family and friendship that the more you associate the more likely you are to find yourself incurring obligations (1986, 206–207). Indeed, the first criterion of such associative obligations was just as Hart saw them, namely that they must be special to the group rather than general duties owed to outsiders (ibid., 199). However, as Green pointed out, one of the more obvious difficulties in attempting to piggy-back political obligation onto family associations is that it suggests that the authority of the state is something akin to *in loco parentis* rather than a doctrine which applies to mature adults (2004, 272). The standard reply has been something to the effect that even mature adults occasionally need information which only the state can provide to ensure that decisions are taken in the public interest, a view which it is the aim of this chapter to reject. As to the state's being uniquely able to coordinate more efficiently the actions of large numbers, Barnett has argued that this sort of centralized ordering of widely dispersed knowledge is largely a myth, and gives rise to intractable difficulties (1998, 46). Even if the state could perform such wonders on occasion, as Green observes, this would not constitute grounds for binding anyone. Indeed, a duty of obedience seems superfluous when the state's armamentarium already includes various weapons ranging from persuasion to coercion (ibid.).

Moreover, Green rightly reiterates his view that consent is necessary for the obligation to obey, which is to say we cannot back into such an obligation without really trying, as Hart and Dworkin would have us believe. If we reject the possibility of unconsented obligations, whether they result from association or not, it may well turn out, as Green claims, that people are under no obligation to obey, even if we were not dealing with Stalinist Russia, but one of Dworkin's true communities of principle (ibid., 280). Green further suggests that one thing we might expect a theory of law to do is to explain how it is that law obligates. Dworkin seems to agree that it is worthwhile to ask how law justifies state coercion, except in cases where there are overriding arguments, (ibid., 190) to which Green responds that it is a bit odd to simply assume that political obligation is justified except when there is some stronger argument against it.

To decide whether the law is or is not justified in using force, Dworkin appeals to both individual rights and past political decisions (ibid., 93), holding in an earlier work that individual entitlements are a function of the just quality of any political order (1977, 87). While past and present political decisions may in practice dictate the justification of coercion and entitlement decisions, we are interested in the normative question of how such measures ought to be justified. If they are justified, it is because they are morally justified, a fact which may in turn be reflected in political or legal decisions. Governments forever have decided that they are justified in collecting taxes and have produced mountains of law to back up their claim. The right to tax is typically justified, according to Murphy and Nagel, in the name of government services and distributive justice

(2002, 3). However, following Nozick who observed famously that taxation amounted to forced labour (1974, 169), and Rothbard, that it is a coerced levy (1977b, 83), we are much less likely to hold that taxes are a justifiable method of paying for government services, if for no other reason than that, as Seldon points out, forced payment for such services prevents their ever being put to the test of seeing whether those for whom they are supposedly provided would pay for them (2002a, 77). As to how much we might be inclined to contribute to ensure the continuance of some service will doubtless be a function of our estimation of its importance in the light of our financial means.[14] With respect to the alleged authority to redistribute wealth, as Nozick and Rothbard suggested, those from whom wealth is seized to give to those whose need is greater, at least in the eyes of the Central Committee, are condemned to slavery. Yet as Rand claimed, no one can possess the right to impose duties, costs or obligations on another (1967, 325). Indeed, as Lester has explained, the absence of such impositions is the essence of liberty (2000, 59) and, with medieval tenure now a thing of the past, when it comes to you or your property as Narveson reminds us, any use of either is up to the owner (2008a, 90).

We noted earlier that Dworkin's doctrine of associative obligation owed much to Hart's account of political obligation, as did that of Rawls. However, it should also be said perhaps that Dworkin claims not to be sympathetic to the popular defence of legitimacy, such as that of Hart and Rawls, which is based on some notion of fair play. According to Dworkin, such an argument makes the unreasonable assumption that people can have favours and their resulting obligations thrust upon them. Moreover, the argument from fairness is ambiguous, since it is not clear in what sense people can be said to benefit from political organization. One typical answer, Dworkin suggests, is that someone can be said to benefit if they are better off under a particular regime than they would otherwise be, though he admits measuring any supposed improvement may prove difficult (1986, 194). Dworkin's criticisms are reminiscent of those of Nozick who held that we should be careful of any attempt to

[14] cf., Narveson (1988, 239).

premise a right to prohibit free riding on the supposedly joint enterprise to which Hart referred. Nozick offers a couple of reasons for such scrutiny, first that unanimous consent to coercive government in the state of nature appeared to be unnecessary. Second, such a joint enterprise was contrary to Nozick's rejection of group rights, to the effect that the sum of individual rights did not create new ones. Nozick then proceeds to examine the two options open to Hart for grounding any right of enforcement, namely that it flows from the nature of obligations in general, or from the obligation of fairness, both of which he will eventually reject (ibid., 90–91).

Hart for his part seems to have thought that in the paradigm case of promising the right and obligation has to do with the voluntary transaction between the parties, rather than that there is some moral quality peculiar to promising itself (1984, 84). However, more important for this discussion are the special rights which do not result from voluntary action, such as those involving mutuality of restrictions thought essential to a joint enterprise. In this case, since the defence of voluntariness would appear unavailable, Hart simply asserts that the initial cooperators are due obedience by late-comers (ibid., 85), a view which Nozick observes is notable only for its lack of argument (ibid., 91). Since Hart fails to show how a right of enforcement derives from supposed non-voluntary mutual restrictions on liberty, Nozick explores the option that such a right is a formal characteristic of all genuine obligations, finding that obligations do not invariably go hand in hand with any such right and do not need to be understood against the background of a natural right not to be forced to do something, as Hart argues. For Nozick I may waive my right not to be forced to do A, which is to say that I release P or the state from their obligation not to force me to do A, yet this does not create in me an obligation to do A (ibid.).

Hart had claimed that the self-professed social cooperators had a right to enforce cooperation from those who might think it in their interests not to do so, but as Nozick observes, since the converse does not hold, we may consider the obligation to do something as separate from the right to force you to do it. To illustrate the fact that obligations are one thing and rights of enforcement another, Nozick offers the example where A's promising B that he will not murder anyone, while not conveying to B the right to force A not to, since that is a right B already has, does place A under an obligation to B (ibid., 92).

Having successfully driven a wedge between obligations and their enforceability, Nozick also rejects as objectionable the celebrated principle of fairness. To support this verdict Nozick offers his equally celebrated counterexample of a joint enterprise consisting of a neighbourhood entertainment system where each listener is supposed to take a term as DJ and do his bit to entertain his neighbours as per the roster. However, Nozick does not think you are obliged to take your turn at the microphone; you may prefer to do other things than get on board the neighbourhood scheme, which raises the question as to how others can put you under an obligation by setting up a venture themselves. Perhaps any such demand should have to meet a cost–benefit test to show whether the costs of contributing to the community venture are outweighed by the benefits from the contributions of others. Even if we conducted such a test, and assuming that costs are subjective and unmeasurable, Nozick concludes that the so-called principle of fairness would remain objectionable as it would if you were to dump unsolicited books on people's doorsteps and later demand that they pay for them (ibid., 95).

### 3.2.1 From Fairness to Prima Facie Obedience

Like Nozick and Dworkin, Edmundson also claims to have some reservations about the principle of fairness touted by Hart and Rawls, since there does seem to be a gap between a supposed natural duty to support just constitutions and a duty to comply with the laws that happen to be on the books. By way of illustration, Edmundson recalls an incident from his student days at Berkeley where he crossed a deserted street on the outskirts of the town against a traffic signal. Although he was not putting himself or anyone else at risk by doing so, another pedestrian waiting patiently to cross scolded him for his illegal behaviour. Although Edmundson now finds himself occasionally thinking it unfair that he observes the speed limit while others rocket past him on the freeway, he is still uncertain whether he or the scolding pedestrian have any real reasons for complaint, at least any that are grounded in fairness. Edmundson remarked earlier in the chapter that there may be other grounds for complaint, if one believes as he apparently does, that exceeding the speed limit can endanger lives. Indeed, he seems to believe that the highway code offers much useful instruction on the question of obeying the law, having begun his first chapter with the question of whether one had a duty to stop at a traffic sign in the middle of the desert where there is good visibility in all directions. In this case, he considered that he had both a reason and a duty to stop just because the law says so (1998, 12). Such a duty is to be sure prima facie rather than absolute, which is to say that the duty to obey the law may be set aside in the face of more weighty moral considerations, such as those that would rank refraining from murder as more important than not jaywalking. In any case, if there is some such prima facie duty to obey the law, various theorists have asked whether we are to say about Germans in respect of Nazi law that they had a prima facie duty to report the whereabouts of Jews to Nazi authorities, but that, given Nazi policy towards the Jews, there was in fact no moral reason to comply. Edmundson modifies his original claim of a prima facie duty to obey the law to read a prima facie duty to obey sufficiently just laws. Since the Nazi state could not reasonably be described as sufficiently just, it would therefore seem to follow that its citizens did not have any such duty (1998, 111).

On the other hand, Dworkin thinks that we need not deny that Nazi Germany possessed a legal system, since it obviously did, though we can well understand someone claiming that Nazi law was not really law, or a degenerate form of it (1986, 103–104). Dworkin still wants to allow that even in this context a German judge could make a true finding, especially in a case with few political overtones. Even in a case where statutes discriminated against a Jewish defendant, it might be possible to justifiably, if only weakly find in favour of the Aryan plaintiff (ibid., 106). Edmundson, of course, does not favour Dworkin's more nuanced approach, believing that the case of Nazi law not only serves to clarify what it is to have a prima facie duty to obey the law, but also that the

Germans quite clearly did not have any such duty because of the absence of justice in the Nazi state.[15]

With respect to the question as to whether coercion, which is supposedly justified by appeals to fairness, is prima facie wrongful or not, Edmundson suggests asking a further question he thought relevant to determining what prima facie duties Germans had *vis-a-vis* Nazi laws, namely to ask whether it would be appropriate to feel badly about any coercion used in enforcing such laws, perhaps to the point of awarding compensation to those on the receiving end. However, if it turns out that Nazi or any other coercion was not justified, it isn't clear what such a test of remorse is supposed to accomplish—some may or may not feel remorse, regardless of whether coercion was justified or not. Edmundson nevertheless concludes that prima facie duties are only owed to a sufficiently just state, and not to a state ruled by gangsters, where scruples about disobedience are entirely inappropriate. Of course, he thinks it a relatively easy matter to decide what will count as a just state, such that it may be reasonably thought to attract prima facie obligations. No doubt Canada, or the US, qualifies, given a greater reluctance, for example, to consign fellow citizens to concentration camps.[16]

On the other hand, Dworkin thinks we need to allow for contexts where we find significant parts of our own law morally reprehensible, where there are only relative differences between ourselves and the Nazi state (1986, 107). Edmundson considers it obvious that we live in sufficiently just states, such that it is not prima facie wrongful to coerce those who have benefited from a cooperative scheme from doing their fair share. The question, of course, is who gets to decide that this is the cooperative scheme we are involved in and that it is indeed fair, though it is doubtful that Churchill, Roosevelt and Mackenzie King

[15] Perhaps Edmundson would have shared Churchill's recently revealed opinion that Hitler merited the fate of a gangster rather than a sovereign, which is to say being put to death in the electric chair, something Churchill apparently thought could have been arranged through Lend Lease.

[16] Churchill, for example, at the 1943 Quebec conference felt compelled to declare that by comparison with the fascist dictatorships of Europe, Canada was a bastion of freedom. If Stalin was not *persona non grata*, Gilbert reminds us that it was because considerations of prudence prevented the leader of one of the Allied Powers from being added to the list of dictators (2006, 105).

worried much about it in 1943, if only because they too probably considered the answer self-evident. Among the long list of potential candidates for calling the shots are the state, the government, the House of Commons, whose servant, as Gilbert reports, Churchill claimed to be (ibid., 104), the people, or some segment thereof, such as the neighbours who have already contributed. If we are less hasty to rush to judgement, in the manner Dworkin recommends, we might try stepping into Judge Siegfried's shoes, which might in turn encourage us to be more sceptical about the supposedly obvious justice of our own states.

## 3.3 Edmundson's Response to Philosophical Anarchism

Having canvassed various sceptical views about political obligation in his opening chapter, which Edmundson admits, raises genuine doubts about any duty of obedience (1998, 31), he goes on to argue why any such doubts stop short of the philosophical anarchism which is now typically thought to follow from a rejection of political obligation. The first element in Edmundson's account of legitimacy is what he calls the simple correlativity thesis, namely that a state's legitimacy only is contingent upon its imposing on its subjects at least a prima facie duty to obey its laws (1998, 36). However, he agrees that sceptical views about political obligation which have become widely accepted in political philosophy in recent years, together with his correlativity thesis, tend to undermine the claim that there is such a thing as a legitimate state.

Since Edmundson is greatly troubled by the prospect of philosophical anarchism, dropping the correlation between legitimacy and a duty to obey might look like a promising strategy. On the other hand, he notes that Raz, for example, holds that having authority, de facto or otherwise, is not just a matter of influencing people, but also one of issuing authoritative commands, since justifiable coercion is not the same thing as authority (1990, 118). Political authorities do indeed resort to coercion and threats, but for Raz, legitimate authorities do more than that, since they claim to impose duties on their subjects, and to the extent that this claim is justified, they are owed obedience. For Raz it just seems to be a matter of our social history that our governing institutions are believed to issue lawful orders to their citizens (ibid., 118).

As to the question of justifying a claim to legitimate authority, Raz argues that we are more likely than not to act according to right reason if we accept authoritative directives as binding rather than trying to reason things out for ourselves (ibid., 129). Anarchists such as Wolff were wrong in thinking that the only way to preserve autonomy was to consent to every act of government; for Raz this is going too far, since it rules out the possibility of legitimate authority (ibid., 11–12). To do otherwise is to undercut our reliance on authority in the everyday world where we depend on the advice of people such as doctors and financial planners. The fact that we do delegate authority to others shows that it is beneficial to do so, since we can then concentrate on doing what we do well. For Raz, the paradigm case of authority is taking advice from friends or fiduciaries, and if we deny acceding to government authority, then we shall have similar qualms about doing so in the case of other more limited authority (ibid., 12).

By way of response to Raz, we reject the view that the authority exercised by governments is just the authority we regularly delegate to others writ large. The whole point about governmental authority is that we have not delegated it, we have not consented. To the extent that others, such as a doctor, can order our detention, they do so as agents of the state, which has almost unlimited power to coerce and confine. This power was assumed by the medieval monarch to protect his subjects, and as Hogue notes the king's peace considerably extended the royal writ (1966, 149). Even if we accept that rights pertaining to such a doctrine be reserved to the sovereign, the reach of government has long since ceased to confine itself to breaches of the king's peace, such as murder, rape and robbery. As Higgs writes, not only is protection much more likely to be provided privately rather than publicly, suggesting that the sovereign has neglected his longstanding duty,[17] government functionaries go to great expense to prosecute people for offences that are in no sense breaches of the peace, such as using unapproved recreational or therapeutic drugs (2004, 104).

[17] Benson estimates that US private sector expenditures in criminal justice are several times greater than those of the public sector (1998, 80).

Another part of Raz's response to anarchism is the claim that legitimacy enables people to conform to right reason (ibid., 13). Indeed, he thinks that anarchism derives much of its popular appeal from a rejection of rule by others, whereas we are more likely to do what is really in our interests if we follow the directives of legitimate authority. Hand in hand with this view is the sovereign's claim to serve the people, a notion perhaps captured in the royal motto *ich dien* and in the doctrine of *noblesse oblige*. The denial of the view that the business of authorities is to serve the governed has been typical of philosophical anarchism since Thrasymachus, who famously held that the ruling class typically legislated in their own interest.[18]

Having noted, then, that Raz, for one, might not be inclined to support Edmundson's decision to uncouple a duty of obedience from legitimacy, let us press on with Edmundson's case to see why he favours such a move. In so doing, of course, he wants to be able, like Raz, to reject philosophical anarchism, which he thought might prove irresistible, if it were true that a state's legitimacy depended upon its imposing a prima facie duty to obey the laws, and it was also true that there was no such duty. According to Edmundson, a satisfactory theory of the state will include an authority thesis and a legitimacy thesis, and that the true account will avoid the errors of philosophical anarchism by combining the appropriate version of each thesis. To be an authority entails that one's directives create enforceable duties of obedience, while legitimacy is seen to impose somewhat more modest requirements, namely that duties of obedience are reduced to duties of non-interference in the administration of justice (1998, 43). The idea seems to be that while the anarchist might quarrel with a fully fledged doctrine of political obligation, he cannot really object to a duty of non-interference. Indeed, at first sight this sounds like something that might even appeal to a common garden variety libertarian anarchist since the only duties owed to authorities are negative ones of non-interference. However, we need to ask exactly what it amounts to not to interfere with the reach of the long arm of the law, particularly when that arm

[18] cf. Narveson (2000a, 7). In addition to setting their own remuneration and benefits, many modern rulers do not seem to be wanting for further means of self enrichment: cf. Schweizer (2019).

reaches in our direction. Or as Edmundson points out, it is one thing not to stop for the proverbial traffic sign in the desert, but quite another not to stop for the traffic cop who happens to be watching that sign.

Edmundson considers it philosophically distressing that the fortunes of legitimacy are tied to those of political obligation (1998, 50). Then of course there are those of us who are more likely to find the possibility of a legitimate state an embarrassment to political philosophy. In any case, to insulate the legitimate state from Edmundson's worries, he argues that we should instead attend to administrative prerogatives which are supposedly less worrisome. Edmundson seems convinced there is a difference that matters between a duty to obey the law and a duty not to interfere in its administration, but it is far from clear why he thinks so, for even on his own account, there is considerable overlap, since a duty of non-interference also generates obligations (ibid., 52). Edmundson claims that other considerations, such as those of utility, can be appealed to in support of the latter, by which I take it that he is referring to the fact that while we can ignore the stop sign in the desert with impunity, we cannot so easily ignore the traffic cop who happens to be there to enforce it, because of the direct consequences that are likely to follow. So, in this sense it is better for all if I don't complicate matters by running from the police. It is less clear why I might find myself duty bound to do so, unless he has in mind that the aim of such a directive is to limit my options as to whether or not I choose to obey, that is, to provide me with what Raz called exclusionary reasons to obey, where authority overrides our right to act as we see fit (1979, 27). With reference to necessity, which Edmundson also thought backstopped a duty of non-interference, one very clear way in which it becomes necessary for us not only not to interfere, but even to assist with the administration of justice is that such a duty is itself clearly expressed in law.[19]

Edmundson focuses his attention on resisting arrest, since that particular response to the reach of the law offers the most flagrant example of not complying with its administrative directives, one that marks a more radical departure from social norms than breaking some law or other.

[19] e.g., The Canadian Criminal Code prohibits not only obstruction of, but also failing to assist a peace officer in the performance his duties. cf. Martin (1971, Sect. 118; Sect. 246).

While we have a weightier duty to avoid murder than not to jaywalk, which is to say the strength of the legal prohibition is relative to the moral quality of the action proscribed, Edmundson holds that both murderer and jaywalker are subject to the same duty not to resist arrest, a duty which is legally and practically advisable (ibid., 53).

However, Edmundson further claims that submitting without resistance isn't simply a counsel of practical wisdom but is in fact a moral duty. This is evident, he argues, from the fact that while I might run a light because I am in a hurry to get my wife to the hospital, I have a clear duty not to ignore the police cruiser which attempts to pull me over, as well as to explain to the officer why I was in such a hurry. There might be other situations, such as my slipping away after being detained by mistake, where Edmundson thinks that people's moral intuitions might differ as to whether I had a duty to explain myself first. As to his remark that moral philosophy might not be of much help in sorting out such conflicting intuitions, he himself claims to be arguing for a view which is true, (ibid., 47) and which suggests there is something by way of a moral argument to be given and a correct answer to the question as to whether I have a duty to explain myself to those charged with the administration of justice even when they make mistakes. As for what we may or may not feel any compunction about is, as he points out, a somewhat unreliable guide.

Edmundson also thinks that immunity from interference may extend to someone, who, for example, decides to direct traffic at an intersection after the traffic lights have failed, though that person in turn will need to hand off the task to more competent authorities. According to Edmundson, the latter, including those exercising de facto authority, have a *de jure* monopoly on administrative prerogatives, underwritten by the presumptive legitimacy of the state.[20] To further illustrate the way in which he believes that the presumption of legitimacy supports a general duty to respect administrative prerogatives, Edmundson returns to the question of the legitimacy of the Nazi state. We are asked to imagine ourselves towards the end of the war in Nazi Germany and to contrast

[20] One is reminded here of the criminal law requirement that a citizen who arrests someone on grounds of having committed a criminal offence has to hand them off promptly to a police officer: cf. Martin (1971, Sect. 449, 359–360) and Edmundson (1998, 53, n. 6).

the duties we would have to assist in the apprehension of a fugitive from the American military police versus a fugitive from the German police or from a German civilian. Edmundson trusts that if we could somehow influence the outcome of the pursuit, we would agree that while we have a prima facie duty not to mislead the MP, we have no similar duty not to obstruct the German policeman or civilian. The reason is that the MP is acting on the authority of a legitimate state, whereas the German policeman and civilian are not (ibid., 55).

Edmundson contends that the nature of this supposed prima facie duty not to interfere in the administrative prerogatives of a just state is especially evident in cases of civil disobedience, e.g., the landmark case of Walker v. The City of Birmingham, which involved an injunction prohibiting Martin Luther King and associates from holding a demonstration against segregation. After proceeding with the rally in defiance of the injunction, King was found in contempt, a verdict later upheld by the US Supreme Court, even though the ordinance under which the injunction was granted was unconstitutional. Edmundson claims that his doctrine of administrative prerogative helps clarify the fact that although Dr. King had no moral duty to obey the ordinance, he did have at least a prima facie duty not to resist the court's administrative prerogative (1998, 56). On this matter Edmundson finds himself in full agreement with Bentham to the effect that under a government of laws the good citizen, although being free to speak his mind, ought to obey lawful orders (1994, 10).

Edmundson contrasts his view that we have a general prima facie duty not to resist the administrative prerogatives of a just state with that of Hobbes who appears largely to hold the opposite view, namely that I cannot be required not to resist the imposition of force upon myself, or to incriminate myself (1909, 107, 167). On the other hand, we are not free to interfere in the sovereign's attempt to bring another to justice because this prevents the sovereign from exercising his right of protection, one of the main reasons we submitted to the sovereign in the first place. In support of his view that we have no duty not to resist the king's men, Hobbes observes that condemned men are led to the gallows by armed guards, even though they have consented to the law, by which they have sentenced (ibid., 108). However, Edmundson believes that rather than showing that there is no duty not to resist, Hobbes's condemned man example shows at most that it is understandable that we would try to avoid long sentences or execution (1998, 61). However, Edmundson considers the condemned man example to be a case where not resisting is tantamount to obeying, which is to say that the only way not to resist the order to put your head on the block is in fact to obey it. Thus, there will be cases where not interfering in administrative prerogatives amounts to obeying them, though Edmundson claims that in the end fewer duties will be imposed than under a traditional account of political obligation.

So it seems that at least sometimes the distinction between not resisting and obeying, which Edmundson thinks is so important for his case against anarchism, is virtually non-existent. Indeed, he has thus far failed to convince us that this distinction ever amounts to very much, and as a result it will be unable to perform its expected function. For the proverbial man in the Clapham omnibus, obeying the law simply amounts to obeying the endless dictates of this or that official. Rather than worrying about some abstract duty to obey, the average citizen is more likely to be concerned about what someone on the endless list of government officialdom can do to him if he doesn't comply with this or that order.

Of course, Edmundson thought that the disposition of Martin Luther King's civil disobedience case provided a good illustration of his distinction. While King had no duty to obey an unconstitutional city ordinance, Edmundson thought King had a duty to comply with the relevant administrative procedures, even if the ordinance on which they rest is null and void (ibid., 56). But, if we are talking about a moral duty first and foremost, it seems odd to claim that we are morally required to do something which is a moral nullity.[21] Edmundson, however, insists that while there may be no legal or moral reason to comply with the unconstitutional ordinance, there may be a good reason not to resist its administration. If he thinks we have a moral, as opposed to a legal or prudential one, it seems he has yet to tell us clearly why he thinks so.

[21] Aquinas held that unjust laws were more like acts of violence, and do not bind in conscience, quoting Augustine's view that an unjust law is no law (1953, 72).

Indeed, one of the central problems with state enforcement is that much of the time the state acts morally *ultra vires*, that is, it quite typically requires us to perform duties which are either moral nullities or morally wrong. Simmons, for example, cites laws which prohibit harmless behaviour, require military service or demand payment to finance all manner of government operations (1993, 264). More specific examples are not hard to come by: for example, Prairie wheat farmers had been jailed for ignoring the erstwhile Canadian Wheat Board monopoly, and privately selling their wheat south of the border where it could fetch a better price than in Canada. As Epstein points out, such farmers could be forgiven for thinking that a supposed right to farm, such as that touted by Roosevelt in 1944, implied at least two correlative duties: (1) nobody can block one's entry or exit from farming and (2) one can sell produce to anyone willing to buy at whatever price can be agreed upon (2005, 29). However, some farmers had found a ready ear in government for a more positive doctrine, namely a right to be insulated from the vagaries of the market. In the case of the Wheat Board, what began in 1935 as a voluntary marketing organization, became a state backed monopoly with considerable control over prices as well as insulation from commercial risks. Such state sponsored cartels are also, as Epstein observes, immune from the scrutiny to which private cartels are regularly subject (ibid., 32). Nor are government prohibitions having little or nothing to do with morality confined to big government, for as Spooner argued, one need appeal to nothing more than the majority principle to justify takings, with the majority typically being influenced by envy and ambition (1992, 321). Local government also offers fertile ground for the arbitrary will of a majority and is thus the source of many similar unwarranted curbs on individual freedom. Bolick notes that cities frequently use powers of eminent domain not only for public projects like roads, but also for seizing property which they consider under-utilized, such as low-income housing, but which could produce more tax revenue if redeveloped.[22]

---

[22] What Bolick calls a reverse form of Robin Hoodism (2004, 84–85). One is reminded of the plan of the City of Toronto to prosecute those attempting to supplement their incomes by collecting bottles and cans from blue boxes to recoup cash deposits. The City considers the

However, according to Edmundson, the fact that a particular law is void of moral worth does not mean that we can ignore directives issued under its warrant. In fact, as we noted, Edmundson held that just such a distinction helps explain what otherwise might appear to be the incongruent findings in the case of Martin Luther King, that while on the one hand he had no duty to obey the ordinance requiring permission to hold a demonstration, he did have a duty not to disobey an injunction upholding that ordinance (1998, 56). On the contrary, while we are quite happy to leave the determination of legal sense to those who happen to make a career out of such questions, we deny that King had any moral duty to obey either the ordinance or the court order deriving from it. Edmundson claims that King had a prima facie duty to obey the court order simply because it constituted an administrative directive of a just state. One would have thought that an obvious earmark of such a state was that it did not require obedience to laws, whose moral and for that matter, legal pedigrees were, in Edmundson's words, nullities. It seems that a state which requires such obedience has begun the descent into tyranny, which is to say, its justness is far from a foregone conclusion. Perhaps we shouldn't be inclined to follow Bentham's advice to obey punctually, not that Edmundson ever makes it clear whether any such exhortation derives more from prudential, rather than moral considerations. More germane, perhaps, is the celebrated dictum of Junius, that the subject who is truly loyal to the chief magistrate will neither advise nor consent to arbitrary measures, or, as Zakaria has written more recently, liberty has primarily meant freedom from arbitrary authority, especially that of the state (2003, 31–32).

Edmundson re-affirms his contention that one can somehow sidestep the anarchist's concerns about political obligation by focusing instead on the supposedly less demanding obligation of not interfering in the law's administration (1998, 61). On the contrary, I have attempted to show that even if one could distinguish not interfering with administrative prerogatives, as Edmundson is wont to call them, from obedience to the law in a wider sense, it is not clear how this is going to allay

contents of blue boxes to have escheated upon being placed at the curbside. With respect to eminent domain seizures, Greenhut considers them legalized theft (2004, 190).

the fears of those whose enthusiasm for government is under fairly tight control. Indeed, as Edmundson himself acknowledged, those who speak of a broad consensus that there is no such duty are not cranks but hold positions in prestigious centres of learning (ibid., 33). However, crank, or academic, someone from the government, claiming no doubt that he is here to help you, will tell you that under C circumstances you are required to do A, failing which you will be subject to penalty P. Thus, obeying the executioner by putting one's head on the block is the rule, rather than the exception, as Edmundson claimed. Obeying the sharp end of the law may constitute a narrower duty, but it is no less objectionable than political obligation as traditionally conceived.

Nor for that matter did Edmundson's distinction appear to be of any great use in clarifying Martin Luther King's treatment by the courts. Of all the administrative hurdles placed in King's way by the supposedly just state, it isn't obvious why disobeying the court injunction should rank as the paramount instance of such disobedience. The fact that a court thought so probably has more to do with the fact that the bench and its jurists such as Edmundson are likely to be more sensitive to cases of contempt than that it was morally the most egregious of King's failures to obey the magistrates.

### 3.3.1 Authority Indistinguishable from Arbitrary Rule

For Edmundson political authority largely amounts to believing that we best obey the commands of government because it knows what is good for us. He further comments that although the political machine does not possess superior knowledge, the populace is nevertheless better off heeding its *ex cathedra* pronouncements (ibid., 63–65). While for Edmundson political authority is not epistemic, we may recall that Raz, for example, held that important forms of authority were in fact epistemic and that the anarchist was guilty of an overstatement to the extent that he denied this; if we can grant authority to a professional there is nothing in principle wrong with doing so to a government (1990, 12). However, as noted earlier, forming a contract with some sort of professional to handle aspects of one's affairs because of their superior expertise or knowledge bears little resemblance to the coercive relations most people have with government. The latter is more reminiscent of Faust's pact with Mephistopheles than anything else. What Raz should have said is that there might be such a thing as a legitimate limited governmental authority, provided we could fire our government with the same ease that we do an accountant. The fact that we cannot do so has forced voters to resort to other exit strategies such as escaping by affluence, or to the underground economy.[23]

Of course, there are those who believe that we consent to be governed, and that we receive a goodly measure of peace, order and good government in return. Others, such as myself, tend to hold that mostly what we get in exchange for our birthright is a mess of potage, and that central government can in no way approximate the precise knowledge held by individuals or small groups. Barnett notes that centralized decision-making could work if it had access to that widely decentralized personal and local knowledge; in fact, knowledge is widely dispersed, implying similar decision-making (1998, 61). Leoni makes a similar point about legislation, namely that its centralized production makes it impossible to reflect local conditions and the wishes of a dispersed citizenry (1991, 22), which would seem to support Edmundson's view that legislative compromises do not constitute a superior form of cognition. While for him political authority is mostly not epistemic in nature, it can provide good, if not always clear reasons to obey and although many interests have been weighed in reaching a particular legislative compromise, we would do better to accede to that result than not.

According to Edmundson, we must take their word for it that whoever did the weighing and balancing, if not getting it right, at least reached a decision, and it is best if we just obey. This sounds more like an instance of no reasons at all than one of their being less than perspicuous, thus lending weight to Leoni's claim that the dominant mythology of our age is political rather than religious, where the reigning myth is of a people being represented by rulers with privileged access to the truth as well as the ability to follow it (ibid., 23). Of course, in other respects such

[23] cf. "The escapes from over-government" in Seldon (2002a, Ch. 3).

mythology is not entirely confined to the present era, since Plato also hoped to have political leaders in possession of the truth, which would be ensured by having only those fit by birth and philosophic training assume command of the republic (1941, XXII, 208).[24]

Moreover, Plato argued that those who failed to acknowledge that expertise was required to take charge of the ship of state were like sailors fighting over who should be at the helm, while failing to understand that navigation requires special expertise (ibid., XXI, 195–196). Similarly, as Raz pointed out, legislators may have reason to impose a certain tax, as well as the way it is to be paid. In so doing, he claims, it is not unlike our deciding to buy a particular loaf of bread after considering various options. The authorities have matters which they are competent to decide, just as we have ours. On the other hand. authorities are to be obeyed even if they are mistaken, since for Raz the whole point of authority is to preclude individual judgement (1990, 126–127).

Hobbes thought that while bees and ants could live peacefully together without any governmental structure, mankind could not do likewise but required the great Leviathan who would protect them from one another, as well as from foreign invasion (1909, Ch. 17). The latter justification is particularly ironical, since, as Porter reminds us, if it is monumental violence in recent centuries we are talking about, Leviathan is not called great for nothing (1994, 299). Thus, Horace's famous line *Dulce et decorum est pro patria mori* is characterized by the Great War poet, Wilfred Owen, as a noble lie no longer appropriate for children. No doubt acknowledging that dying for one's country can be a tough sell, particularly during an election, Roosevelt promised in 1940 that the sons of America would not be sent to fight in foreign conflicts, but as Higgs pointed out, for close to half a million who never returned, this proved as much of a lie as Horace's (2005, 135).[25]

---

[24] By dint of possessing knowledge inaccessible to the denizens of Walmart, the philosopher is thought fit to receive the orb and sceptre, or to sit at the right hand of him who does; cf. Carter (1979, 35). As to Oxford's producing those fit to rule, cf. Symonds (1991, Ch. 2, "Prophets, Classics and Philosopher Kings").

[25] Faust has reminded us that foreign conflicts may pale by comparison with domestic ones when we recall that for the US the well over half million soldiers who perished in the Civil War is roughly the same as the fatalities in all other wars from the Revolution to the Korean War (2008, xi).

Other writers since Hobbes have elaborated on the doctrine of sovereignty, particularly with respect to those it supposedly protected. For example, Heinrich von Treitschke remarks that there is a gulf fixed between rulers and ruled with the State alone being sovereign, which in turn implies a right to arms and resources sufficient to pursue its self-determined interests (1963, 77, 18–19). A generation or so later, Harold Laski observed that the authority of the state depended on its power to coerce its opponents and force them into submission, using the armed forces if necessary (1935, 14). More recently, anthropologist Harold Barclay, has written that a democracy does nothing to alter the time-honoured hierarchy between rulers, consisting of a small elite, and the ruled (2003, 23–24). Boetie reminds us, however, that it is not the legions at the command of the sovereign who keep him in command, but rather a small number at the top of the hierarchy who maintain control through iterated pyramids, the main outlines of which seem common to various command structures (n.d., 22).[26] Molinari on the other hand sees the notion of governors as a modern manifestation of the doctrine of divine right, a fiction which one would do well to dispel, whereupon their aura of authority will disappear and the governors will be seen to govern no better than the governed (1977, 10–11).

### 3.3.2 Moral Discovery as a Possible Source of Authority

Unlike Molinari, Edmundson, as we saw, has not lost faith in the authority of government, holding that government can provide us with better solutions to coordination problems than if we were left to our own inclinations. One of the ways in which it might do that is that the law is supposedly capable of what Hurd calls moral discovery, where from coordinating action on relatively straightforward moral questions it might provide solutions to questions with several right answers and do so in a way that is morally authoritative (1999, 174–175). As a possible example, Edmundson mentions a statutory rape law, which widens the

[26] cf. Grazia (1952, 116).

definition of rape to include cases of what could be innocent mistakes (1998, 65). Of course, to the extent that such a statute proposed to enlarge upon moral prohibitions against force and fraud, it may well risk harming the innocent, and thus represent a significant departure from customary moral norms. Although this does not seem to be what Hurd, for example, had in mind, she believes that law makers are uniquely placed to develop solutions which are thought to possess considerable epistemic authority (ibid., 176).

Of course, there is still a question as to whether the ability of legislators to develop yet more laws or find ways to tweak old ones to please certain constituencies really amounts to some sort of moral discovery. The minorities who simply go along with a statute are as unlikely to feel that it represents a genuine moral discovery as they are to believe that the solution reached by legislators possesses any authority akin to that possessed by other professionals with whom they might have a fiduciary relationship.[27] Moreover, the fact that law is able to make some solutions both salient and widely accepted as authoritative, tells us little about what law really ought to be doing and why it should have the authority it is often believed to have.

While Edmundson does not think that the law overall offers fresh evidence of antecedent moral obligations, he allows that it does provide for moral improvisation by making salient a solution to a coordination problem such as which side of the highway to drive on, thus generating a rule which supposedly has moral force because it delivers otherwise unachievable advantages (ibid.). While he appears to believe that traffic laws are an obvious example of the law's facilitating a wide range of exchanges, we saw earlier that he had some trouble convincing himself that he really should stop at the traffic sign in the desert, where there was no opposing traffic, or that it was wrong to disobey a "don't walk" crossing light, and right for another pedestrian to reproach him for doing so. He correctly concludes that not a lot hangs on relatively trivial cases of disobedience and that they don't offer great prospects as a foundation of some general duty to obey (1998, 28, 31). On the other

[27] cf. Leoni reminds us that minorities are unlikely to mistake democracy or supreme rule of the majority for freedom from coercion (1991, 101).

hand, Edmundson contends that the law which solves such an important problem as which side of the street to drive on clearly has moral import.

Hardin also finds it a compelling example of real-world coordinations but reminds us that law only later reinforced coordinations which road users had already worked out among themselves. Indeed, what is noticeable about such a solution is that it worked for a long time without authoritative enforcement. This sounds like a different and more plausible tale than that told by Edmundson. According to Hardin, early road users did not need officials to tell them that everyone could benefit by keeping to one side while going in a particular direction (2003, 13–14). While law did as it had always done, it did not invent the coordination, but formalized established custom. Nor did the law bring moral obligation in its wake, since the custom arose by trial and error and proved an effective method of reducing harm. There will no doubt always be risk takers, just like those who run remote stop signs or disobey pedestrian signals. Methods of enforcement range from the informal scowl of Edmundson's critical onlooker to hefty penalties which may accompany formal law and adjudication following the original coordinations.[28]

So, Edmundson's claim that it is the job of law to solve a coordination problem, if not wrong, is an unfortunate oversimplification. He further argues that this solution just must be one that people accept, not necessarily the best one, morally or otherwise (1998, 65). One might wonder why people should adopt a solution which is not necessarily in line with their preferences, nor is it morally the best. Perhaps that isn't something they should even worry about, since we saw that in Edmundson's view solutions were best worked out by the state, and it is best that loyal subjects take the state's word for it. Those of us not inclined to blind obedience can offer a more plausible criterion of optimality, namely that suggested by Pareto, which will allow us to make up our own minds about a proposed government intervention. According to Pareto a social solution is optimal if no further improvements can be made to A's lot

[28] Not that formal law invariably follows such coordinations, even when as DeSoto argues, it might assist the development of, e.g., real estate capital markets in third world countries (2000, 156–157).

without worsening B's. Further, a solution Y is an improvement over, or Pareto superior to Z if at least one person is better off in Y than in Z.[29]

Edmundson, on the other hand, thinks that the most we can ask of legislative compromise is that various goals and interests are weighed in the balance and that whatever decision is arrived at politically is better than no decision at all (ibid., 66). Governments have little interest in applying the Pareto yardstick, which sets clear limits to what they can do. Indeed, responding as they do to all manner of pressure groups and lobbies just about guarantees that modern governments will not be shining examples of Pareto in action. They are only too happy to improve A's lot at the expense of B and countless others besides. As Tullock points out, concentrating benefits and diffusing the costs ensures that while it will be in A's interest to pursue the benefits, it will not be worthwhile for B and his fellow taxpayers who bear the small individual cost to oppose the levy. Tullock cites the interesting case of a small firm of manufacturers of violin chin rests for whom it was worthwhile to lobby for a protective tariff, whereas for the small amount it added to the cost of a violin, it would not have been worthwhile for a purchaser to travel to Capitol Hill to oppose it (2002, 38).

However, as Seldon notes, one way to end the granting of favours is to remove that power from the armamentarium of government, something it has shown little interest in doing (2002, 46). He argues that what we need is a public philosophy which would hold that it is immoral to seek favours at the expense of others and of our own real interests (1990, 121), since all producers are ultimately consumers. Indeed, the Pareto criterion is a move in the right direction, since, as Narveson contends, it suggests some rough and ready way of deciding whether a change is better for some, and no worse for anyone (1988, 184).

[29] cf. Narveson (2002a, 79); improvement by incremental adjustments, as suggested by Popper (1961, 65–66), perhaps sounds a little dull by comparison with many of the grand schemes touted by politicians.

### 3.3.3 Law and Morals Do Not Necessarily Overlap

A common assumption among those interested in the interface between law and morality is that both inquiries generally head in the same direction.[30] Indeed, as far as Edmundson is concerned, the degree of overlap between the two is such that law can reinforce any moral requirement and thus overcome the hazards allegedly inherent in private enforcement. Not only can it do so, but it rightly possesses a monopoly of doing so (1998, 157). However, as we have already noted, there seems to be an abundance of cases where the government has no business presuming to monopolize compulsion, which is to say it all too often exceeds its moral warrant. In fact, as Epstein has observed, frequently the law not only fails to improve upon customary orderings, but may have the opposite effect, such as when the state intrudes on the workplace and undermines such orderings (1998, 60).

An example of such unwarranted government intrusion is the at-will labour contract where one party is free to quit just as the other party is free to fire, with no questions being asked on either side. If arbitrary behaviour is permitted on both sides, there seems little reason to intervene to head off the capricious behaviour supposedly confined to management with its attendant regulation of wages and hiring. According to Epstein the attack on at-will contract fails since it is not plausible to think that the average employee contracts to become worse off than he was before (2005, 44–45). Further, Hasnas has shown how in the ramping up of white-collar offences post-Enron, legal requirements can only be met at the expense of what business ethicists had traditionally held to be the important moral principles governing business practice. US legislation, for example, has significantly broadened the definition of white-collar crime, while weakening many of the traditional safeguards at criminal law such as the *mens rea* requirement, the ban on vicarious criminal liability, the presumption of innocence, and proof beyond a

30 Edmundson also assumes that coordinations backed by law typically bring moral innovation in their wake, though as Hardin reminds us, some coordinations are less than felicitous, such as those with respect to US slavery and later Jim Crow laws (2003, 14); similarly with respect to the Balkans, where coordination for group advantage broke down informal relations between ethnicities (1995, 29).

reasonable doubt. In addition, new sentencing guidelines place a heavy premium on corporations going out of their way to comply, both before and after any investigation, to reduce draconian fines. Although ethicists have traditionally taught that corporations are bound by the same moral rules as the rest of us,[31] Hasnas points out that corporations simply cannot afford, for example, to respect promises of confidentiality, despite loss of employee trust, because of the huge liability that might result. He concludes that failure to recognize the significance of such perverse legal incentives has rendered much contemporary business ethics beside the point (2006, 10, 15–16, 19–20).

On the one hand then, Edmundson seems to think that the law generally tracks morality, though in providing solutions to certain coordination problems it may give rise to further obligations having a moral as well as a legal force. On the other hand, he also contends that such a solution may be much less than the morally best and that we should console ourselves with the thought that the use of political authority leads us to believe that some decision is better than no decision. However, why the exercise of political authority gives us any such reason is far from clear, and if Edmundson's argument so far was intended to establish that, he has failed to do so.[32]

### 3.3.4 The Morality of Taxes in Particular

While, as we have seen, Edmundson believes that the law incorporates morality into it and may often secure further benefits conveyed by legal rules, he also holds that a given coordination may fail to be optimal, either with respect to individual preferences or morality, or both. For example, Hurd notwithstanding, he finds it hard to believe that what governments tax and spend would necessarily correspond in any way with what we might be inclined or feel bound to do with our money (1998, 65). Well, if it is so very hard to believe, one might well ask

[31] cf. Narveson (1998, 73).

[32] Indeed, Jasay has argued just the opposite, namely that if political authority is tempted to use coercion to impose value choices on society about which there is some doubt it should refrain from doing so (1997, 151).

why we should believe it, unless we happen to subscribe to Tertullian's dictum *Credo quia absurdum est*. If that seems to be leading the witness, Edmundson does hold that our belief that government gives us good reason to obey its laws is on a par with that of scientists being able to provide an authoritative account of the universe (ibid., 66).

However, much of the point of our discussion is whether there are any legitimate political authorities, at least, morally speaking, and, contrary to Edmundson, the answer appears to be that there are not. As for any supposed similarity between those and scientific authorities, besides the question as to whether *legitimate* is being used the same way for both, I am not really sure what a legitimate scientific authority amounts to, but it seems that government authorities would have much to learn from the humility of the physicist who said about quantum theory that it was the best theory they had at the moment and they hoped that it was approximately true. Of course, while not a lot by way of public policy generally hangs directly on the truth of the quantum theory, in the case of climate theory, the hypothesis that there is measurable global warming has been pressed into the service of yet another political crusade. Politicians and their scientific lobbyists, who are convinced that such increase in global mean temperature over the past century or so as it has proved possible to record is moreover anthropogenic,[33] can be expected to ignore Jasay's warning and employ the full coercive apparatus of the state to correct heresy.

With respect to our duty to render unto Caesar, however, Edmundson was of the opinion that this may well be at variance with what we would probably think was our duty to do with our money. There also appears to be little doubt in Edmundson's mind that the government is quite correct in asking us to hand over tribute, which left to our own devices we may not have been inclined to do, at least partly because we thought we had no moral duty to do so. Edmundson on the contrary clearly

[33] Essex and McKittrick refer to this hypothesis as the Doctrine of Certainty, which in their view is simply wrong (2002, 17–18). With respect to post Maunder Minimum warming, Plimer reminds us that there is no hard evidence about the amount contributed by humans as opposed to what is nonhuman. As for whether carbon dioxide emissions drive climate, the evidence points in the opposite direction (2014, 26–29).

thinks we have a duty to do so, paying taxes being one of the obligations the state may impose on us (1998, 157). Taxes are doubtless one of the least welcome of such impositions and as Bovard remarks, they serve as a continual reminder of state paternalism (1999, 21–22), which Edmundson thought definitive of political authority. Rothbard further noted that the government was peculiar among human institutions in acquiring its revenues coercively, a fact which the display of sovereign legitimacy has for the most part managed to conceal (1978, 25–26).[34]

Apparently, the libertarian indictment of taxes[35] is now thought to be so influential that those who favour what they style as an egalitarian redistribution of wealth have been moved to challenge the view that all taxation is legalized theft: thus Murphy and Nagel deny that anyone seriously believes all taxation is illegitimate because it takes property without consent. According to these writers, many people make noises that sound like this because of the wide appeal of popularized libertarianism, which misleads people into thinking that they have a moral property right in pre-tax income, when what they have is a legal right to their net or after-tax income. Murphy and Nagel claim that the belief that we are morally entitled to our pre-tax incomes results from some sort of conflation of what we are legally entitled to, namely our post-tax incomes, with what we may think we have a deeper moral claim to, namely our pre-tax incomes (2002, 33–34).

In response to Murphy and Nagel's claim that no one really believes that taxation is illegitimate, I very much doubt that most people have trouble distinguishing legal from moral claims, especially anyone who has had a friendly encounter with the tax authorities. Presumably, Murphy and Nagel are also aware that a claim about the morality of taxation may well be true, regardless of the number of those who do or do not believe it. As for the rhetoric about everyday libertarianism, if the notion of strong property rights has proved harder to banish

[34] As for Canadian taxation, in 2006, according to Veldhuis and Palacios (2006), it took Canadians till June 18 to pay off their tax bill, close to 2 months later than when calculations were first made in 1961. The OECD (2006) found that Canada consumed a higher proportion of GDP, and had higher corporate rates than the US or Australia, with the CTF (2007) finding that only China had higher corporate rates.

[35] For Rothbard they were nothing but government grand larceny (ibid.).

from everyday thinking than Murphy or Nagel would like, this may be evidence that such a view is also more widely held than they would have preferred. Nor is it obvious why everyday libertarianism need be any more confused than the everyday equivalent of Murphy and Nagel's claim that a fair society would be one of equal opportunity for all (ibid., 55), which already bears most of the hallmarks of your average confused platitude. In fact, when Murphy and Nagel do consider libertarian views proper, rather than their popular coinage, what we have are fundamentally opposing views, rather than one clear and right view versus one confused and wrong view. Although it is not a view they share, Murphy and Nagel concede that libertarianism is one to be reckoned with, citing its defence of property and contract, opposition to redistribution and individual sovereignty as severely constraining the right of government to interfere in our lives (ibid., 65–66).[36]

However, Murphy and Nagel argue that libertarianism, at least in its popular manifestations, confronts a conceptual problem when it claims that taxes constitute a taking which requires justification. On their view our income is only post-tax income, which is to say, there is no income prior to taxation. On the other hand, if there were no pre-tax income, there is nothing on which to base taxes, and no post-tax income either, suggesting that even popular libertarianism has little to worry about. Indeed, as Brennan argues, there is nothing illogical in claiming a right to one's gross income, and to the extent that Murphy and Nagel think there is, they are mistaking a matter of accounting for one of logic (2005, 212).

To Nozick's celebrated equation of tax with slavery (1974, 169), latter-day liberals, such as Ignatieff, have responded that while we may not be fond of tax, it is not morally wrong (2004, 17). To be sure, Murphy and Nagel also hold that there can be no principled objection to enforcing payment of taxes (ibid., 123). As they argue, laws of any sort, such as criminal, traffic or zoning laws and the myriad other forms of regulation, all constrain what we can do. But on the libertarian view, a much narrower band of activities are subject to enforcement, namely those that

[36] In view of Murphy and Nagel's claim that libertarianism attracts considerable attention one should not be surprised at its influence on everyday thinking, something Macey (1998, 373) found sadly lacking in earlier years.

cause wrongful harms to others. Indeed, Rothbard proposes replacing the vague concept of harm with the more precise one of invasive violence against the person or property of another (1997, 127, 128). If any taxes at all are legitimate this would only be, as Jasay reminds us, if it is necessary to prevent the state's subjects from harming one another, though even here there will be some unpleasant facts of life, such as the fact that you cannot have what I already own, which do not constitute compensable harms (1991, 24, 27). In support of his claim that taxation amounts to forced labour, Nozick argues that the redistribution which is the rationale for much taxation results in arbitrarily subsidizing certain individual preferences at the expense of others. Some choose to work longer hours for more pay, while others prefer less pay and more leisure. If it would be wrong to take leisure from the man with more of it because that would amount to forced labour, it is not clear why we can take money from the man who happens to have more of that good (ibid, 170).

Despite having claimed that no one really believes that taxation amounts to legalized theft, Murphy and Nagel admit to having a hard time convincing people that if they own anything it is only through the good graces of the state and should not resent having a goodly portion of their pre-tax income escheat to the state (ibid., 176–177).[37] Graetz and Shapiro admit to similar difficulties in understanding how the estate tax first introduced in 1916 could have been repealed in 2001 with broad bipartisan support. They surmise that robber baron envy could no longer be counted on to carry the day as it was in the early days of the last century. Perhaps voters had come to realize that the real robber barons are, as DiLorenzo points out, those who live off the avails of government (2004, 133). In any case, as Citizen Gates claimed, if you work hard to set up a lucrative business, paying taxes along the way, it is not obvious why your death generates further tax obligations. Indeed, if Bill Gates is not seen as another Rockefeller, despite attempts of various governments to have Microsoft suffer the same fate as Standard Oil, maybe, as Graetz

[37] As an expatriate Australian, Murphy might be distressed to learn that in recent years the Australian government has levied no tax on retirement income. There are doubtless pensioners in that country who believe, contrary to Murphy and Nagel, that in leaving their gross incomes intact, the government has finally acted justly.

and Shapiro suggest, it is because Americans, contrary to Marx's predictions, rather than overthrow capitalism, have become paid-up members as property holders and investors (2005, 8).

Thus, the belief in private property may not be as much of a myth as Murphy and Nagel would like to think. While they seek to remind us that property is a mere convention, for Hume, convention is central to stability in possession which can only be achieved by wide social agreement to let its members enjoy what they have acquired through diligence and hard work (1960, 489). Such *mere* conventions, or spontaneous ways of coordinating divergent interests, being basic rules concerning property and its exchange are prior to the state rather than creatures of it (ibid., 541). Robb writes, for example, that long after the advent of central government in France, many communities remained beyond its reach, with the result that self-rule was not a libertarian pipe dream but the order of the day (2007, 34). The hamlet of Goust in the Pyrenees was just such a community, remaining an autonomous republic till the twentieth century, where among the interesting features travellers were pleased to observe was an apparent absence of taxpayers (ibid., 19). The residents of this rocky platform high above the spa of Eaux-Chaudes appear to have led lives of reasonable quality and order without the ministrations of the Republic, no doubt as the result of conventions, such as a council of elders, about which Murphy and Nagel would have little to say, other than perhaps noting their mere conventionality.

Moreover, with respect to the egalitarian theories of justice to which these authors seem partial, Stone remarked some years ago that the presumption of equality is beset by many hazards, not the least of which seems to be the conflation of equality with justice, which only diverts us from the task of deciding which facts of entitlement are relevant to justice (1978, 1019). As Narveson has more recently pointed out, once we have settled on the appropriate characteristic according to which people are to be treated, then they will get whatever it supposedly calls for (2002a, 61), which might not be the same as someone else. But, as Lucas reminded us, while we may secure some measure of equality in some respects between some individuals, we shall never achieve it for everybody under all circumstances (1971, 150). Again, it is most encouraging to think that supporters of redistribution such as Murphy and Nagel face an uphill battle in getting a hearing in the marketplace for their theory of justice.

Benjamin Franklin is recorded as having famously pronounced in a letter to Jean Baptiste Le Roy in 1789 that in this world nothing can be said to be certain except death and taxes. While death has remained an abiding feature of the human condition, to speak of the certainty of taxes and leave it at that is to beg the sorts of questions that we have been raising about them and the governments which institute them. First, given that governments in the eighteenth century mainly confined themselves to duties and excise taxes on imports and exports,[38] Franklin probably did not have to spend most of the first six months in any given year rendering unto Caesar. Second, it suggests that like the poor taxes have been with us always, which of course is not the case. Richard Pipes writes that for most of the recorded history tax was reserved for conquered peoples or the socially inferior (1999, 238).

Further, according to Pipes, the US continued to meet its financial needs for the first half of the nineteenth century by customs duties and sales of land. However, as Van Creveld has written, the Civil War occasioned the imposition of the first income tax in US history (1999, 232). The move to progressive taxation, which takes an increasing proportion of income as income rises, appears to have been staved off for much of the nineteenth century by those who protested that the only just principle was to extract the same proportion of income from everyone.[39] The first to overcome such reservations about progressive income taxes was apparently Prussia under Bismarck's successor Caprivi, which in 1891 ordered the Kaiser's subjects to render taxes from less than one to about 4%.[40]

Canada's story on taxes is in fact worth noting, particularly because of the determination of its leaders of the late nineteenth century to keep taxes low to encourage immigration and investment. The first post-Confederation Liberal Finance Minister, Sir Richard Cartright, expressed views on taxation in his 1878 budget speech unlikely to be heard from

---

[38] cf. Milke (2002, 4).

[39] cf. Hayek (1978, 308).

[40] Hayek notes that the modesty of such proposals would have rendered any attempt to oppose them unlikely to succeed (ibid., 310).

any finance minister in more recent years, namely that since tax constitutes a loss, for the government to take more than what was necessary, would be for it to engage in theft.[41] Rothbard has in more recent years explained how taxes are a loss, namely that they diminish the production base and act as a disincentive, causing people to spend more time on leisure or take tax-supported employment (2001, 797).[42] As for the myth that taxes are voluntary, and not robbery, Lysander Spooner, a contemporary of Richard Cartright, reminds us that if, unlike a highwayman, government does not literally hold a gun to our heads, at least the highwayman, unlike government, does not pretend that his robbery is anything else (1992, 84–85).

Some present-day politicians might still claim that deep down they agree with such views, but that what has changed since the days of Cartright and Spooner is the scope of the public service. Spooner would still reply that determining that scope is a rather one-sided business, and when the government comes to collect its bill to meet the expenses of protecting life and property, it will not do to say that you never asked them to do that in the first place (ibid., 85–86). Moreover, lest we think that the promotion of life, liberty and the pursuit of happiness was more appropriate to the US than Canada, Sir Wilfred Laurier's speeches on the campaign trail in 1894 suggest that there was at least a period when there was something distinctly liberal about the Liberal Party in that it supported freedom in all its manifestations including freedom of commerce.[43] However, the rejection of direct federal taxation which characterized the first 50 years following Confederation was finally overcome in 1917, and as in various other taxes Canada seems to have been inspired by American precedent. Further to Franklin's dictum that there is nothing as certain as death and taxes, Hospers replied that this did not imply that we should be taxed to death, as the saying goes (1971, 322). When income taxes have risen in the course of the last century

---

[41] cf Milke (2002, 9).

[42] Arthur (2007, 79) has estimated that about two thirds of the tax deduction is directly lost to the economy before the tax contributes to any spending, from which a further 20% is lost to government overheads and waste.

[43] cf Milke (2002, 10).

from around 5% to anywhere from 20 to 70%,[44] Hospers argues that the government seizure of our means, although gradual, appears to have no limits, and simply constitutes a transfer of wealth and power to the bureaucracy who are convinced they know better than we, the people, how to put our money to the best use (ibid., 322–323).

## 3.4 The Public Goods' Defence

Again, with respect to the goods which government has come to believe it must supply from what many claim is its only source of income, namely taxes, Seldon has argued that we need to separate those goods that are truly public from those that are not. Public goods *proper* are *non-excludable*, meaning that those who don't want them can't be excluded from receiving them, and *non-rival*, meaning that those who use them without paying do not reduce the supply available to those who do pay. By this criterion, Seldon concluded that most so-called public services are not public goods proper, and thus, contrary to widespread belief and practice, do not in fact have to be supplied by government (1990, 169, 174). Jasay offers further comment on the nature of public goods and why it has been traditionally thought that the government must provide them and that they must be compulsory. On his account such goods are characterized by similar properties to those of Seldon: *non-rivalry* or *jointness* (greater use of the good by one user does not reduce the benefits available to others) and *non-excludability* (a member of the public cannot be denied access to the good). Goods having both properties are *pure* public goods. However, according to Jasay the traditional theory also recognized that the class of such pure public goods was small or non-existent. He cites the interesting example of a private good such as club membership which permits a member to make greater use of the facilities than other members at no additional cost, with any increase in costs being spread over the whole membership (2002, 19, 20).

Even though the traditional theory allowed on the one hand that there were few if any genuine public goods, some goods having the

[44] Veldhuis and Palacios (2006, 8) report that Canadian tax rates for 2006 are around 45%.

above-mentioned properties will fail to be produced. To ensure that they are, coercion is necessary, though as Jasay rightly observes, if a good failed to be produced because it was irrational for anyone to contribute, contributing little makes no more sense than contributing much (ibid., 20). On the other hand, Hayek seems to have accepted the traditional wisdom that the government ought to supply such goods as health, sanitation and roads because it would be difficult to charge for them (1978, 225). Here Hayek apparently takes himself to be following Adam Smith who wrote that it would be necessary for the commonwealth to supply those public works which no person or group could be expected to profit by building and maintaining (1976, Vol. 2, 723).

However, while Smith thought there might be some case for public works, he was less convinced that any deficiencies in the private management of turnpikes, for example, would necessarily be remedied by state management. Because toll revenues tended to outstrip expenses there would be a strong temptation to use them as a cash cow, as Smith found in the case of the post office (ibid., 727). Smith thought that one solution for local public projects unlikely to be self-sustaining is for them to be placed under local or provincial, rather than state administration. He cites the example of street lighting in London which would not be nearly so efficiently run if it were up to Whitehall; since the inhabitants of London are the prime beneficiaries, it makes sense to pay for them out of local taxes. Not that Tammany Hall is immune to corruption, but Smith thinks differences in scale are likely to minimize such problems (ibid., 731).

But, it seems, more recent writers are not as likely to share Smith's view that local government constitutes less of a threat. Bolick thinks that if the country declares war, we will know whom to blame, whereas finding out who is responsible at the local level may be more difficult, whence the adage: "You can't fight city hall" (2004, xiii). A much-criticized instrument of local government power is eminent domain seizure, which many see as a glaring affront to property rights and nothing more than government sanctioned theft. Greenhut reminds us that many corporations have only been too happy to benefit from such seizures, offering increased revenues to the city fathers in return (2004, 191).[45] Perhaps it should be noted that occasionally eminent domain has also worked against corporations, such as when it was invoked to prevent Walmart from setting up in Hercules, California, on the grounds that the corporation was not a good fit for city *smart growth* policies. Of course, this raises the question as to whether planning should be subject to enforcement since writers such as Jacobs were sceptical that most city governments possessed the resources for understanding the enormous complexities of urban life (1992, 417).

Not that governments necessarily confine themselves to planning public works but are all too often directly involved in putting them into effect, and thus may be responsible when such projects go awry. For example, a report of the US Army Corps of Engineers has admitted that much of the havoc caused by Hurricane Katrina could be attributed to poor engineering.[46] On the other hand, if past government behaviour is any guide, what we will probably never hear is that someone has been personally held to account for policy and implementation failures stretching back over 40 years, as in the case of the New Orleans levees, not that government would display a similar reluctance to investigate if it involved a non-government agency. Thus, Seldon has noted that government externalities are very hard to correct, if only because the byzantine political chain of command proves difficult to uncover (1990, 176).

Even when government does reluctantly investigate, as in the case of 9/11, the National Commission report simply records the fact that there were widespread policy and management failures involving the various bureaucratic silos such as the CIA and FBI (2004, xci, xciv). The 9/11 Report acknowledges that many of these agencies were formed in response to another famous surprise attack on the US, Pearl Harbor, with the presidential biographer claiming that both events were evidence of similar human failures related to empire building (ibid., xlix). The authors of the 9/11 Report thought it important to enter the caveat that they were writing with 20/20 hindsight as did one commentator

[45] For further ramifications of eminent domain see Fitzgerald (2003, 29), Jacobs (1992, 311) and Sandefur (2006, 96).

[46] Cf. "Army Corps admits design flaws in New Orleans levees," Ralph Vartabedian, *LA Times*, June 2, 2006.

on Pearl Harbor (ibid., 485). In the case of the latter event, there is now evidence to suggest that Roosevelt was aware of an impending attack. He ordered a build-up of Red Cross resources to handle the expected casualties, explaining that American isolationism could only be ended by the direct attack his intelligence had warned of. Perhaps not surprisingly, Denson finds the inscription "I hate war" on Roosevelt's monument in Washington to be somewhat hypocritical (2006, 196). But as Machiavelli pointed out, in order to preserve the state, the prince may often have to do the opposite of what he said he would and offend many of the principles his subjects hold dear. He must focus on the result, and if the outcome is favourable, the masses will overlook the methods taken to achieve it (1992, 49). Denson, on the other hand, seems less inclined to believe that Roosevelt's ends justified the means, but proposed that a recording be played every hour at the Roosevelt Memorial, re-creating the sounds of the men who banged on the hull of the partly submerged USS Oklahoma in the hope of being rescued (ibid.).

Despite its manifold failures, our habit of relying upon the omnipotent state dies hard. As Skoble writes, we just get used to having the state do certain things and find it hard to imagine how they might get done without the state's help (2002, 86); if we have trouble imagining a post office not run by government, it may be because we are concerned that this might be the end of mail service. But although in some Commonwealth countries the monopoly government post office was also responsible for telecommunications, most of us have gotten used to the fact that we can now choose from various providers of such services, and that mail itself did not become a thing of the past, once Fedex and UPS got in on the act. According to Creveld, war provided much of the impetus for the centralization of power in the monarch and for the expansion of services to encourage subjects to put on the king's uniform (1999, 336). Other writers such as Porter have also remarked on the connection between war and the welfare state, whose foundations were laid during the age of imperialism which preceded World War I. Those foundations continued to be built on between the Wars with the structure of the welfare state being completed in the aftermath of World War II (1994, 179–180).

With respect to the war economy as it were spilling over into peace time, Gilbert has noted Churchill's interest in harnessing the energy used to fight the Great War to build a better Britain, including such policies as nationalizing the railways, progressive taxation and state supported housing (2006, 55, 67). One might well wonder why Churchill, who at one time had supported free trade against protectionism, would advocate state monopolies to remedy the supposed faults of private ones. Mavor claims to have witnessed similar enthusiasms in Ontario politicians who in the same era advocated public ownership of Ontario Hydro, a fact which he attributed to politicians creating and managing an electrical monopoly to reinforce their own political control (1925, 240–241). Nor would this be the last time that government in Canada would try its hand at business. Foster reminds us, for example, of the case of Petrocan, the main result of which was a $10 billion increase in the country's debt, requiring about $1 billion a year to service, or the equivalent of the income tax from 100,000 average families. While government may claim that welfare redistribution will result in fewer driving Porsches so that others can eat, Foster contends that ventures like Petrocan will result in less for everybody (1992, 300–301). The more recent policy fad of subsidizing electric vehicles in the name of an imaginary climate crisis is likely to mean that more are going hungry while others drive Teslas.

Thus, it is not surprising that Churchill believed that the methods of the wartime economy could be applied to peacetime, and that lessons learnt in recycling spent shell casings to overcome a shortage of brass could help create public housing. Total war thus brought about the total ascendancy of the state, with the result that by the end of World War II, Creveld can characterize its role as one of increasing its control over all aspects of society, undermining the many institutions not made in its own likeness (ibid., 354).

While the relief of civil disasters is a natural enough extension of the all-encompassing role the state can be seen to have arrogated to itself, Hurricane Katrina and other calamities have led many to question just how effective the state really is as a relief agency. One of the problems with state intervention is that it tends to crowd out private initiative and cooperation, as Taylor has noted (1987, 168). Moreover, it is often claimed, for example, that Canada's social safety net is more extensive than that of the US. However, instead of comparing how much our respective governments are willing to redistribute to the less fortunate, when we look at how much individuals give privately to charity, Leroy has shown that every US state except for West Virginia is considerably more charitable than Canadian provinces (2004–2005, 9–13).

Of course, others have thought that the state and its tax apparatus were necessary to guarantee rights to life, liberty and the pursuit of happiness, characteristic of a liberal society. Thus, Holmes and Sunstein cite the example of the 1995 fire in Westhampton, NY, which took three days to extinguish. The fact that there was no loss of life and minimal property damage is attributed to the spending of upwards of $2,000,000 in public funds to achieve that outcome. I would have thought that firefighting was not the most obvious example of state intervention to prevent losses to life and property, since throughout much of its history it has been largely voluntary. Indeed, Holmes and Sunstein themselves concede that 1500 local volunteer firefighters participated in Westhampton. Bush fires typically occur in less densely populated areas and are largely fought by volunteers. Volunteer rural fire brigades are responsible for about 90% of the land mass of the state of New South Wales, Australia, for example. The fact that paid services may add to the cost of anything contributed by volunteers, as in the case of Westhampton, is no guarantee that those services were necessary or that the money was well spent.

Indeed, Skoble cites the rebuilding of the city of Chicago largely through private charity as evidence that government is not necessary for disaster relief (2002, 88). McChesney notes further that only about $50 million of the $200 million losses incurred in the Chicago fire of 1871 were recouped through insurance, with many of the insurance companies being bankrupted as a result (1986, 71). McChesney goes on to show how we got from firefighting being universally a volunteer activity in nineteenth-century America to the government monopolies now common in larger urban areas. Traditional wisdom has it that direct municipal control of fire services was occasioned by market failure, notably where competition between rival volunteer brigades impeded efficiency. However, McChesney concludes that paid fire departments are much better accounted for by political payoffs than market inefficiency (ibid., 92). The fact that much of North America and Australia, for example, is still served by volunteer fire brigades shows that government is no more necessary now than it was a century or so ago to ensure the service, thus supporting McChesney's argument that the reason for municipal takeover is probably not one of public interest. It seems that in rural areas there is less chance of Tammany Hall being confused with public interest, with firefighting being seen on a par with barn raising. As McChesney notes, the fact that the most famous boss of Tammany Hall was William Tweed, whose notoriety as one of the more aggressive volunteer fire captains seems only to have helped his later political career,[47] lends further support to the view that municipalization had little to do with public interest and everything to do with the interests of firefighters, insurance companies and politicians (ibid., 83–84, 88). In the case of the latter, public employees offered more scope for patronage and voting influence, and it is probably not a coincidence that the change from private to public fire departments occurred during the era of *machine* or *boss* city government. Nor was this change confined to protection agencies. Publicly financed education arose at about the same time, and according to West, once again was largely dictated by self-interest (1967, 128).

As to why we should not be surprised that those claiming to act in the public interest are in fact acting in their own, Jasay explains that in contractarian theories of the state, the state is not a contracting party, but rather is the agent of the principals to the contract, with the intent being that it acts impartially on behalf of the principals (2002, 51). Jasay suggests that such an intent would acquire copious amounts of virtue to be vaguely credible, if only because of a lack of any self-enforcing structure. Of course, he doesn't think any more than I do that there will be sufficient virtue to go around, which would ensure that the state not only delivered on formal equality, but that it could somehow avoid the temptation of acting like one of the principals, and the *primus inter pares.* The likelihood of its not succumbing is considerably reduced by the fact that although the government of the day may change, the state and its bureaucracy are permanent (ibid., 50). Thus McChesney recommends that we treat the bureaucracy simply as other actors or stakeholders with

[47] see Ackermann (2006, 18).

their own interests, which would explain why it is to their advantage to continually expand the public sphere at the expense of the private while pretending that it is in the interest of society to do so (ibid., 81).

On the other hand, Holmes and Sunstein claim that libertarians talk rather glibly about the minimal state, when the cost of policing and corrections in the US amounted to some $13 billion in 1992. Given that much of this amount was supposedly directed to protecting private property, then even the so-called minimal state could run up significant costs as it did in the Westhampton fire. In response, it is difficult to conclude much at all from government expenditures, as the Auditor-General for Canada is fond of pointing out. In the case of policing and corrections costs, we need to know whether law enforcement was directed towards removing serious threats to life and property, which we might think should remain the concern of even a minimal state. Browne, for example, has suggested ending the so-called war on drugs and the prosecution of other victimless crimes, allowing us to concentrate on genuine crimes against the person and property of others (2000, 188).[48] To avoid the inefficiency and corruption common to public authorities he encourages greater use of private companies in crime detection (1995, 137). That is to say, the costs of law enforcement which Holmes and Sunstein thought libertarians were so cavalier about could be reduced by about 45% by giving up the war on drugs alone. Bergland suggests eliminating at least 17 US federal departments, including FEMA, notorious for its failures in responding to Hurricane Katrina, to produce a government only a fraction of its present size and more appropriate to its constitutional mandate (2005, 163). In fact, Otteson argues that the all-pervasive welfare state Leviathan has exceeded its moral mandate as well, in that its interference is incompatible with treating its citizens as persons, who should be free to make bad choices and suffer the consequences (2006, 78–79).

Thus, it seems somewhat beside the point to pronounce with Holmes and Sunstein that the truly liberal state will ensure that coercion will only be used for truly liberal ends (1999, 64). No doubt a government

[48] See also Bergland (2005, 88, 98); cf. Block also foresaw retailing recreational drugs in the same way we came to sell liquor post-Prohibition (2007). It took some years for those retail outlets to appear, at least in Canada, but Covid lockdowns have proved an opportunity for those merchants as they have to online retail.

that confined its responsibilities to the prevention of force and fraud, might be welcomed, even by some libertarians, and it would doubtless be a good deal smaller than it is today, but as we have been pointing out, government typically does not confine itself to those tasks. In fact, if such a prospect is not embraced by all libertarians, it is because they see little likelihood of ever reducing the writ of government to that understood by classical liberalism. Because the governors of the republic do not confine themselves to their moral mandate, namely the protection of individual liberty, it becomes much harder to avoid arbitrary and authoritarian measures. As McChesney pointed out, there is little chance of getting officials to wield their authority in the public interest, even though most claim to be doing just that, namely improving social welfare, when they are calculating their own expected personal gains.

One of the rights which the governors reserve unto themselves, if not exactly in themselves, is that of deciding, for example which uses of resources, such as land, are in the public interest and which are not. Thus, they reserve such rights as those of planning, zoning or eminent domain. Whereas the latter, for example, was traditionally mostly invoked for public works such as roads or bridges, it is now often used to assist private developers in projects politicians favour.[49] Following McChesney's analysis, the governor is first and foremost helping himself, by consolidating or even expanding the reach of the state at whose trough he feeds. Other options were clearly theoretically open, requiring little or no government action, such as leaving the developer to assemble the required real estate by making deals with the individual owners. Respecting the rights of individual property holders could well prove more costly, than if the developer were subsidized by state coercion in the form of eminent domain, which is why he will likely choose the latter method.

In his essay on the history of property Richard Pipes discusses a related assault by government on private property undertaken in the name of affirmative action, supposedly to reduce discrimination of one sort or another, especially in the workplace. In terms of public goods, the claim is that, left to their own devices, the unregulated interactions of ordinary people will fail to produce the good of non-discrimination. Not

[49] Cf. Stossel (2004, 149–150).

only is there the question whether it is anybody's job to produce such a good,[50] as Pipes points out, attempting to do so discriminates against those not singled out for preferential treatment (1999, 270). Richard Epstein similarly notes how little anti-discrimination legislation has to do with upholding freedom of contract and prohibitions against force and fraud. Under a liberal dispensation individuals decide with whom to do business and on what terms, while the state's role at most is one of securing a social space free of force and fraud for conducting such transactions (1995, 3–4). Like the many government interventions already mentioned, such policies rest on all manner of assumptions which have rarely been put to any sort of empirical test.

Sowell concludes after close examination of such initiatives in a variety of countries that despite claims made in their favour there is little or no evidence of their effectiveness (2004, 198), if only because we cannot rewrite the past, but should instead see how we can improve the present and future (2018, 127). Moreover, it is interesting that Sunstein also thinks that the futility of many government programmes could be avoided by engaging in detailed cost–benefit analysis, including qualitative and quantitative estimates of expected outcomes (2002, 20). Perhaps a cost–benefit analysis might address some of the defects Sowell found with respect to affirmative action programmes, though something like his ex post facto investigation is also needed to see whether a programme lived up to its expectations. Of course, the politician is likely to respond that he has his own cost–benefit analysis to conduct, and it is quite unlikely his reading of the political tea leaves will bear any resemblance to the sort of findings Sowell or Sunstein would have in mind.

Sunstein does indicate some awareness of the pitfalls of government regulatory policy, foremost being the inability to decide what is important and see that it gets funded appropriately (ibid., 4), noting that legislators have difficulty keeping problems in perspective, often because of a welter of details, and can be swayed by influential colleagues and officials (ibid., 28). Despite such reservations, Sunstein reports that the Office of Management and Budget's accounting of the costs and benefits of regulation generally show benefits to be in excess of costs. While he

[50] Cf. Narveson (2002a, 203–224).

admits that such figures are probably self-serving, he believes we need to start somewhere, and that in the case of most government interventions, benefits exceed costs. To arrive at the latter conclusion, he apparently takes the government's word for it, though he does admit that regulatory policy involves compliance costs of at least $400 billion a year (ibid., 4). But even here Sunstein may be underestimating compliance costs by about 75%, since Blundell and Robinson report another study where they are estimated at $700 billion, of which only 2% falls on the regulators. Indeed, the fact that the great bulk of estimated compliance costs are externalized explains the great growth of regulations, whose supposed rationale was of course to overcome externalities (2000, 5–6).

Holmes and Sunstein were indeed right to say that at least in an ideal world a supposedly liberal government would use the funds extracted in a fair manner from the populace to produce something useful, whereas we contend that the reality is mostly otherwise. While the existence of taxes is one of the more obvious examples of the government's extracting resources, and the clearest sense in which it is liberal is that it is liberal with other people's money, I continue to maintain, *pace* Edmundson and others, that there is no warrant for its doing so. On the contrary, to the extent that the myth of authority persists, as Mencken pointed out so aptly, it has to do with the view that government is not a mere human institution but rather one not subject to the errors of ordinary mortals, whereas such places are often populated with those who lack even a modicum of good sense and behaviour (1958, 179–180). If government is not entitled to extract the resources in the first place, then the fact that it does so fairly is of little interest, though, as Narveson points out, governments which insist on providing services have a duty to distribute them impartially (1999, 303). Moreover, the fact that one's resources are supposedly redeployed in the efficient production of public welfare is also beside the point, since the taxpayer is no doubt capable of finding his own pet projects to spend money on, rather than have them dreamed up by the bureaucracy, whose schedule of socially useful public goods will likely be different from that of the taxpayer. Of course, there is a good chance that Joe Public's schedule of goods will include the deterrence of theft, which is doubtless why Holmes and Sunstein present it as a paradigm case.

On the other hand, Mencken would have found it somewhat ironic that deterrence of theft should be placed in the hands of those who in his view, have about as much public spirit as so many burglars or streetwalkers and are about as useful to the commonwealth as an abundance of circus performers or card sharks (ibid., 180, 181). As David Friedman reminds us, since government consists largely of legalized theft, we find the same principles operating as with private theft, notably that whatever is taken should be considered a loss, not a gain for some other purpose. Further, those competing for government handouts may invest close to the expected payoff to secure them, just as a thief hopes to profit by his act, not just to break even, or less. Indeed, as with the latter, resources are required to minimize depredation, such as tax avoidance strategies, with the result that the total social loss likely exceeds the amount plundered (1989, 153–154).

Not only do governments claim the authority to take possession by force, which is to say they have the right to do what is forbidden morally and legally by others, they similarly claim the high moral ground when dealing with fraud. The same hypocrisy is evident here as in other government enthusiasms. According to Bennett and DiLorenzo, governments have responded to demands for accountability by moving more and more of their expenses offline or off-budget. They concluded for example that local government, the sector supposedly most responsive to its citizens is in fact much less so (1983, 122). In the case of national governments, Bennett and DiLorenzo cite well-publicized loan guarantees made directly by the US Congress, such as those to New York City and to the Chrysler Corporation. However, governments of all stripes seem to have a knack for bailing out failing enterprises, and in the view of Bennett and DiLorenzo substitute political allocation for more efficient market use of capital (ibid., 142).

Nor does Canada lack for similar examples which are short on economic rationale but long on political. As Foster records, there is a long list of disastrous government interventions from the Bricklin car to Mirabel airport, to say nothing of Petrocan, which left the country with little other than an enormous debt (1992, 297, 301). Bennett and DiLorenzo further observe that it is not even necessary to vote appropriations to generate funds for pet projects. Lawmakers can simply create various forms of regulation to achieve the same effect, such as import quotas on automobiles which subsidize local producers at the public's expense. Another form of tariff which also restrains trade on behalf of producers is a licensing requirement on all manner of jobs from taxi drivers to funeral directors (ibid., 165). As Milton Friedman once remarked, the only way to prevent these restrictions on economic activity is to create a general presumption that the government simply has no business licensing anything (1982, 144).

Further, on the matter of regulation, McChesney reminds us that politicians often stand to gain by merely threatening to regulate, which he characterizes as a form of political extortion. The threat might also involve the deregulation of hitherto cartelized industries, which can generate large political contributions from cartels, such as the dairy or medical industries, anxious to head off such a threat. Interestingly, McChesney does not necessarily oppose such *milker bills*, because politicians would find a way around any attempt to get rid of them, and possibly inflict greater harms than the present forms of rent extraction. In his view the obvious way to minimize the latter is to prune back the power of the state to coerce and confiscate, which is much of what it typically does. That is of course exactly the solution we are proposing here, since we have the luxury of setting aside the real world of politics, where the chances of reducing the ability of politicians to enrich themselves by taking and threatening, McChesney observes, are slim indeed, and the attempt to do so might only result in more of the same (1997, 169, 170).

### 3.4.1 Public Goods Via Decentralized Coordination

With respect to the normative theory of the state, as opposed to the sordid realities of everyday politics, it has become something of a commonplace for the authority of the state to be seen mostly as one of solving both coordination problems and prisoners' dilemmas, of seeing that public goods are produced which individuals left to their own devices will fail to provide. Thus, Edmundson notes that by solving such problems the state may make an important moral contribution to society

(1998, 69), while Raz holds that such solutions are fundamental to the state's authority (1990, 132). Although Edmundson does not elaborate upon prisoners' dilemmas, he does discuss the matter of coordination, principally that of the necessity to coordinate on the side of the road we drive on, a matter Hume himself had seen as relevant in the eighteenth century, including the need to prevent pedestrians colliding on the sidewalk (1975, 210). Raz for his part stressed the right of the competent authority to back up such conventions by coercion, since some would be tempted to free ride on the cooperation of others (1990, 15).

Hardin also considers coordination as central to the maintenance of social order. For him, much coordination occurs spontaneously, founded no doubt like the principles of Hume's coachmen and postilions on its ability to make life easier for all. Such rules, as Hume observed, may well be somewhat arbitrary like the rules of a game, with Hardin agreeing that there may be no ex-ante reason for choosing one coordination over another (2003, 14). Hume in fact thought the doctrine of first possession, while somewhat arbitrary, once settled upon would provide a way of resolving disagreements (ibid., 195–196).

The industrial age brought further developments in transportation technology with the need for other coordinations such as those on railway gauges. Standard Gauge (1435 mm) is used in about 60% of the world's countries, including most of North America, where the occasional departure is limited to closed systems like the Toronto Transit Commission (1495 mm) or tourist operations. The main impetus towards eliminating the variations dating from the beginning of railways, which is to say coordinating on the gauge which became standard in Britain by the end of the nineteenth century, was economic. Interoperability allowed for much easier transfer of freight over the large distances in North America, for example, whereas the persistence of different gauges likely proved economically costly in a country such as Australia. While Iberian gauge (1668 mm) at one time made integration with the rest of Europe more difficult, Spain is now making greater use of standard gauge as is Australia.

Not only do coordinations arise for the most part spontaneously, but they are also largely self-enforcing, which as Hardin points out, is different from the answer traditionally given, namely that it is authority.

We keep ourselves in order because it is in our interest to do so, and such coordinations may just evolve, as they did with rules of the road (ibid.). If we settle on a particular railway gauge for a given system, variability between systems need not be a problem unless we require interoperability. Ellickson also emphasizes the fact that order often arises quite independently of the state, contrary to the belief of statists who fail to appreciate informal ordering systems (1991, 4). As a result of his study of how ranchers in Shasta County, Calif., got along with one another, solving various problems such as straying cattle and boundary fences, Ellickson observes that Hobbes was a little too ready to assume that order required government. Rules and entitlements can often arise spontaneously, supplementing or pre-empting those of the state, including enforcement by gossip and occasional resort to violence (ibid., 143).

In their study, Anderson and Hill report that cattlemen's associations found more productive ways of enforcing grazing limits than the range wars often depicted in films, such as excluding non-cooperators from the economic benefits of the round-up. Even the great and famous were not immune from such sanctions. When Theodore Roosevelt expanded his herd well beyond the range rights associated with a new ranch, another leading rancher informed him that if he did not resolve his cattle's trespass by acquiring additional grazing rights at a substantial premium, he should leave, a warning which Roosevelt apparently heeded (2004, 164–165). Anderson and Hill conclude that while the American West provides ample illustration of the use of property rights to encourage responsible development, there are other cases, such as water shortages in Oregon, to which the government responded with fiat property assignments, which in the view of these writers dissipated rents and failed to promote cooperation (ibid., 211–212).

As further examples of non-hierarchical processes of coordination, Ellickson mentions language and cities. In the case of the former, he cites the English language which developed into the pre-eminent world language, shaped by millions of speakers, without the need for any analogue to the *Academie francaise* (ibid., 5). As an example of a city whose development was largely managed in the absence of a master overseer, Ellickson cites Chicago, which resulted from the coordinated efforts of a few million people in the Midwest. Chicago's rapid growth paralleled that of famous medieval European cities such as Venice, Genoa and Antwerp, which historically played an important role in creating a class of citizens independent of feudal lords. They became important centres of commerce and wealth, and as Richard Pipes records, they were instrumental in creating a class of property owners who possessed political, personal, economic and legal freedoms.[51] Among those freedoms were the right to self government, the right to own and alienate property, exemption from external taxes and the right to due process including freedom from arbitrary arrest and searches (1999, 108–111). Finally, another institution of non-hierarchical coordination is the free market which for example enables food to get from the farm to the kitchen, employing thousands of people along the way, most of whom only contribute to solving a small piece of the market puzzle. Rather than being more efficient to have a market czar in charge of the whole operation, as Ellickson contends, the opposite is more likely (ibid., 5).

So, the answer to the question as to who will keep us in line, is as Hardin pointed out, that we will do so ourselves, because it will be in our interest to follow the coordination that we have settled upon. We are all the authority that is needed and are quite capable of taking on the Teddy Roosevelts of the world when required. One of the benefits of coordinating one's own solutions is that one can tailor them to local conditions which may require coordinating upon different rules. Anderson and Hill note for example that the west required a different approach to water use from the common law tradition of landowner riparian rights which held in the east where there was no shortage of water. In the west they opted for a prior appropriation doctrine which permitted diversions of less abundant water for farming and mining, as well as tailoring rules to fit the conditions faced by people such as trappers, ranchers and wagon train travellers (2004, 10).

However, while Hume clearly thought that there was a place for non-hierarchical orderings, such as those of the waggoners, coachmen and postilions, for the appropriate use of the road, he seems at the same time

[51] Thus, the slogan *Stadtluft macht frei*, which the Nazis famously mocked with their version over the gate to Auschwitz. With coercive medical treatment back in fashion, yet another variation suggests itself: *Impfung macht frei.*

to have thought that only government and the magistrates could ensure that justice and equity prevailed over the temptation to seek short-term advantage (1975, 205). However, as we saw earlier, the waggoners and coachmen are apparently smart enough to realize that they need rules of the road at least for their own safety and convenience, so it is not clear why Hume thinks we now need the state's help to do what it is plainly in our interest to do. Indeed, he contends that if we could have depended on natural law to reign in our impulsive actions, we would not have needed positive law. However, customary rules of trade are a form of positive law, so it isn't just a matter of choosing between positive rules handed down by government and natural justice, as Hume implies. Non-hierarchical rules can apply the broad doctrines of natural justice and liberty to everyday issues, such as right of way on the road, or as Hume reminded us, avoiding bumping into one another on the sidewalk.

It seems reasonable to assume that if the principles of natural liberty and justice were just part of the human stock in trade and existed prior to government, at least as Hume understood it, detailed rules to coordinate other human activities could be developed by those whose mutual ease and convenience depend on them. It isn't obvious why we need Hume's vast apparatus of government to develop positive rules, though one could imagine that decentralized law making might need to recognize concerns such as Dworkin's about a patchwork of laws or those where an individual law might make sense but does not form part of a principled whole (1986, 184).

One might respond to such a claim by observing that the lack of principle and coherence which Dworkin finds in the multitude of statutes is apparently the best that two or three centuries of parliamentary rule have managed to produce. Perhaps it is time to abandon the political machinery of government which Hume thought essential, and McChesney second best, and draw upon earlier common law traditions which seemed more faithful to principles of natural justice and liberty. Although this is probably not what Dworkin had in mind, it is not necessarily incompatible with his call for greater legislative integrity, which he thinks encourages the citizenry to apply a similar standard to their dealings with one another (ibid., 189). However, to the extent that for

Dworkin integrity implies some sort of top-down uniformity of principle, for example that government uniquely creates and enforces a property regime (ibid., 296), as we saw in the case of riparian rights, local conditions may dictate considerable variation in customary rules which have often developed quite independently of government intervention.

However, the role of citizens in developing rules for everyone, as touted by Dworkin, has diminished with ever-expanding government. Indeed, as Hazlitt wrote a generation ago, we are accustomed to an endless torrent of statutes with the US Congress at the time having enacted some 40,000 laws, which Hazlitt thought could be reduced to a fraction of that number, if government confined itself to preventing violence and keeping the peace (1997, 41). As Hasnas points out, those who took their disputes to the early moots were simply seeking a better alternative to blood feuds, which the moots provided by at times levying heavy fines against wrongdoers, rather than imprisonment (2005, 128). Further, Rothbard recommends returning to a system where restitution is paid to the victim of crime, rather than having the victim pay taxes to keep his attacker in prison, as at present (1978, 45–46). Successful resolutions by the moots eventually built up a body of customary law or morality, which as Hasnas writes, served as the basis for the English common law. Such decisions established payments due in damages as well as rights and behaviours necessary in a peaceful society (ibid., 129–130).

Hasnas also records an important development in customary law, namely the Law Merchant in medieval Europe, which provided the assurance necessary for trade both within and beyond state borders. Merchants at first devised their own informal tribunals to settle disputes because national courts lacked expertise and efficiency in this area. These merchant courts eventually developed into a system of commercial courts which applied the principles of the Law Merchant throughout Europe (ibid., 130–131). Benson writes that one of the significant contributions of the Law Merchant was the development of negotiable credit instruments, such as promissory notes and bills of exchange. Merchants thus replaced what had been lost with the fall of Rome, namely a reliable currency.[52] Benson notes various features of customary law, of which the Law Merchant was a paradigm case, such as emphasizing individual rights through voluntary cooperation, which was encouraged in order to eliminate recourse to violence; informal sanctions provide incentives for offenders to participate in hearings which could award restitution to victims, with rules evolving in response to changing circumstances (1990, 35–36).[53]

Benson goes on to address the question, if customary law, particularly as developed in the Law Merchant, proved so effective, why it was not continued to the present day. To the extent that such traditions have been abandoned in favour of the king's law, it has to do with the rise of monarchies and the transition from customary to authoritarian law. Even with the eventual transition from absolute monarchies to popular governments of one sort or another, governments have continued to act *in loco regis* as the source of law and social ordering. But, as Benson reminds us, while government institutions and laws have tended to eclipse those of customary law, contrary to Hume, this does not mean that that they are necessary for maintaining social order, to say nothing of the fact that authoritarian law runs counter to the tradition of individual rights and property recognized by customary rules (ibid., 45–46).

On the other hand, royal law in fact had to coerce victims to seek redress at criminal law from the king's courts, since resorting to customary law offered no profit for the monarch; thus, for example, royal law penalized out of court settlements or restitution (ibid., 62). Further, the role of public prosecution and police was greatly enhanced by the inability to absorb into post-war economies large numbers of demobilized veterans who had been overseas fighting the king's wars and found the adjustment to civvy street somewhat onerous (ibid., 64).

---

[52] Nor would this be the last time that merchants produced their own currency: cf. Selgin on privately produced commercial money in late eighteenth century England (2008) and Hayek's view that a government monopoly in money was one way to ensure that we got bad money (2008, 25–26).

[53] Hayek found such characteristics typical of rules which originated in customary practices, which he thought served as a reminder that, if anything, authority derived from law and not the reverse (1973, 85, 95). Leeson also mentions other methods medieval traders used to improve trust and homogeneity, such as intermarriage, religious affiliation and even multiple citizenship, which is often thought to be a more recent phenomenon (2014, 29–31).

Again, Benson emphasizes that the state's expansion of its legal mandate did not occur because this proved a more efficient route to social cohesion. Rather in order to transfer wealth to the politically powerful, you need a coercive apparatus, unlike customary law which relies on cooperation and enforcement by reciprocal incentives. Although defenders of authoritarian law argue that it is essential for maintaining order, Benson responds that the adversarial process of pitting givers against takers undermines order and provides disincentives against cooperation (ibid., 77). Cutler supports the view that it was in the interests of states to juridify what had for centuries been regulated by custom, thus eclipsing private merchant regulation and enforcement (2003, 177).

However, it now appears that independent commercial arbitration never entirely disappeared, and that the Law Merchant has taken on a new lease of life in what some have called the age of globalization, which in fact is not new but has accompanied the Law Merchant since its inception. Cutler cites an observation concerning the Law Merchant to the effect that she is a venerable old lady who has twice disappeared from the face of the earth and twice been resuscitated (ibid., 108). Its first renaissance was in eleventh-century Europe with the rebirth of commerce. Its second reappearance from its moribund condition was in the twentieth century, where functions which the state had assumed have been returned to private organizations (ibid., 190). One area where the return to privatization is noticeable is in dispute resolution, a task which was central to the Law Merchant from its very earliest days (ibid., 225). But if, as Cutler has suggested, the *lex mercatoria* or Law Merchant has taken on a new lease of life, this is apparently not something she particularly relishes, since it has supposedly been brought about by an elite global *mercatocracy* (ibid., 12). The fact that it is an elite association hardly seems troubling, though perhaps the problem is that it is a private one and not a political one which Cutler might think she or others had a greater chance of influencing. Much in this world gets resolved behind closed doors, and government is no exception, but Cutler has apparently chosen the inner sanctums of the law to those of trade, perhaps in the process foregoing greater riches, which Mises reminded us, we are always free to do of course (1972, 10).

But Cutler appears to have in mind what she believes is a more serious objection, namely that, in liberal mythology international trade is conducted privately and somewhat ad hoc, whereas the political domain is that of public orders (ibid., 69). Indeed, liberalism, at least of the classical, or as Cutler would have it, the mythological variety, does claim that to live under a liberal dispensation is to have the right to exchange one's property with anyone willing to do so. As Rothbard explains, if we own something we have the right to alienate it, and the free market rests on the right to property; and, in addition to tangible goods, we may also exchange our labour (1978, 39–40). For Cutler it was also part of the liberal mythology to consider such rights as entirely natural.

Although Cutler does not care to elaborate, doubtless having property in the first place, and then exchanging it for some other property which I value more and someone else values less is natural in the sense that mankind seems to have engaged in trade for so long that it seems a normal and reasonable thing to do. Rothbard would go a step further and say that we have a natural right to own something we have produced or acquired by exchange, beginning with the right to own ourselves, with Narveson agreeing that the latter right further entails a right to property (2006, 3). Moreover, Cutler implies that market relations are not consensual though again she does not make it clear why she thinks that. In Narveson's view, when P and Q agree to exchange x for y, there is no reason to think that such a trade has not been beneficial to both (ibid., 4). If it were true that such exchanges were not consensual, they would not take place since as the old saying goes, it takes two to tango, or as Rothbard observes, although the market appears enormous and complicated, it is made up of endless transactions between the Ps and Qs of the world (ibid., 40). Rothbard's remarks apply just as well to international trade, though Cutler seems troubled by the prospect that the so-called global *mercatocracy* can wield the power she claims it does while refining and extending the global reach of the Law Merchant (ibid., 12).

If indeed merchants are running their own show, that is what you get to do when you own property. It is also something they have been doing since the Middle Ages, since according to Hasnas, in the absence of government, merchants were forced to step up to the plate to secure trade and handle disputes on a case-by-case basis out of which grew a body of law and tribunals to adjudicate matters essential to the free flow of trade (2005, 131). However, now that there is a European government, Cutler thinks that we are into a different ballgame and the merchant hegemonists can't quite carry on as they did before. But, as we pointed out above, the Law Merchant not only was, but is a continuing example of regulation outside of the state, and thus, for Cutler, asserts the paramountcy of the less formal merchant rules and arbitration over their state counterparts (ibid., 191). Not that Cutler welcomes such a development, since it rests on the false liberal assumption that such private mechanisms are more efficient (ibid., 237).

However, Cutler herself reports that the more flexible nature of the Law Merchant allows it to tap into the Chinese *quanxi*, an interconnected system of family and friendship networks facilitating social as well as domestic and foreign economic relations. One would have thought it much to be welcomed in the name of efficiency that there is some overlap between Law Merchant traditions and those of China. On the contrary, Cutler complains that such private negotiations and the governance structures that support them are antithetical to the sort of stakeholder participation essential to democracy (ibid., 235). Schwab echoes similar views when he claims that industry should take the opportunity offered by the Covid disruption to re-affirm what was once called CSR or corporate social responsibility, along with the appropriate dose of ESG or environmental, social and governance measures as prescribed by our self-appointed and would-be rulers at the WEF (2020, 185).

We shall have more to say about the supposed virtues of participation and democratic accountability which Cutler finds lacking in Law Merchant transactions, but which don't appear to any more evident in the WEF's Great Reset or those of its back office, BlackRock.[54] Suffice it to comment that the market offers, not the sort of democracy which, as Narveson puts it, allows everyone to live at others' expense (2006, 4) but one where, for example, one receives one's reward in proportion as one supplies the wants of others, which could mean that the professional sports person is better rewarded than the teacher. Or as Mises further reminds us, for those such as Cutler who claim to be concerned that

[54] Cf Engdahl (2021).

the mercatocratic elite will ride roughshod over the masses, capitalism is the best way yet found for the man in the Clapham omnibus to enjoy a standard of living reserved in earlier times for the very wealthy (1972, 10, 49). Mises further remarks that the supposed concern about unhampered capitalism is nothing but the usual Marxist rhetoric about the inherent tendency of laissez faire to form monopolies, which leads to imperialism and war. In fact, it is government policy in raising the cost of domestic production which creates monopolies, which would disappear with the elimination of protective tariffs (1985, 72–75).[55]

Of course, the capitalist cornucopia can never pour quite enough on everybody, it would seem, or at least not in such a way as to satisfy those such as Cutler who complains of the coercive inequality lurking behind the myth of liberalism (ibid., 69). No doubt to remedy such evils, which for the WEF/Blackrock cartel include the environment and governance, we would have to stop pretending that people freely consent to capitalism.[56] Cutler's view, as well as Schwab's, is like that characterized by Nozick where we have a claim on the goods of others regardless of whether they have contracted with us to supply those goods. For Nozick allowing others to lay claim to what you have produced is tantamount to making them a part-owner of you, and it doesn't matter whether this is achieved by taxes on wages or profits. Regardless of the mechanism, the view that the world's goods should be distributed according to some foreordained principle abandons the doctrine of self-ownership central to classical liberalism for one of at least part ownership of others (ibid., 172).

However, Jasay has, in fact, questioned how much we really need the notion of self-ownership to effectively respond to those, such as Cutler, who think that freedom to engage in capitalist acts should be severely circumscribed. Jasay thinks that we should dispense with the rather inelegant notion of self-ownership and simply emphasize that we are at liberty to do whatever we want with whatever we own or produce, with the onus being on someone else to prove that for some reason, we are not at

[55] The pro-monopoly proclivities of governments can lead them to form cartels, e.g., G7, with other governments to seek the enforcement of high taxes and prevent movement of capital to lower tax regimes. Cf. Zumwalt (2021).

[56] Cf. Nozick (1974, 163).

liberty to do so. Thus, exchanges of property are to be justified similarly to freedom of contract, where a contract is accepted as just until evidence is produced to the effect that it was not (2006, 11, 13).

Cutler, to be sure, has not made any attempt to discharge such a burden of proof other than vague references to supposed elites who make contracts under private rules not subject to democratic oversight. However, with respect to the metaphor of self-ownership which Jasay would be happy to do without, Narveson agrees that many philosophers, and non-philosophers alike, are troubled by the notion that our bodies could be considered our property. Narveson is not sure why this should come as such a surprise, since people have been known to sell themselves to others, as in slavery. Indeed, the libertarian objection to slavery has typically been in terms of self-ownership, namely that we are rightful owners of ourselves and not of other people (1988, 67–68). Jasay, for his part, might simply prefer to say that slavery did not result from the exercise of freedom of contract, though as Hare, who got a personal taste of slavery as a POW on the Burma railway, noted that in ancient Athens one could sell oneself into slavery to redeem debt (1998, 153). While Jasay's reluctance to speak of one's relation to oneself also extended to talk of disposing of parts of oneself, such as one's labour, there are no doubt enough examples of that to go around as well, from those in poorer countries who sell a kidney to strangers, as well as those who donate one, perhaps to a family member, to the man seeking amputation of a transplanted forearm because it doesn't feel like it belongs. Interestingly, G. A. Cohen reports that leftists, who also have qualms about the thesis of self-ownership, at the same time are not overly enthusiastic about being compelled to donate an eye to a blind person, were that technically feasible, despite the fact that their having two good eyes is a matter of luck (1995, 70).

But to paraphrase Nozick, the fact that some lack the normal number of eyes, limbs, parents or other resources, is unfortunate rather than unfair, Cohen's objections notwithstanding. Thus, Jasay asks rightly why fairness requires immunity from luck, or for that matter why justice requires fairness? (2006, 27). The typical response is that most advantages are due to luck and therefore undeserved. But Jasay further points out that it is wrong to assume that if something is not deserved it is therefore undeserved. There are many things neither deserved nor undeserved and most of the advantages and disadvantages of everyday life usually ascribed to luck are in fact neutral with respect to desert (ibid.). Or, as Nozick observes, things do not have to be deserved from top to bottom; Rawls may well earn praise for *A Theory of Justice* regardless of whether he deserved all the assets, natural and otherwise used in its production (1974, 225).[57] On the other hand, at least on his own account, Rawls may well be hoist by his own petard since no one deserves whatever superior qualities he may have possessed. To the extent that one does so, one is to use it to the benefit of the less fortunate. Or if this isn't possible, politically, or otherwise, the better endowed may have to surrender some of their good fortune (1971, 102–103). Though in addition to the problem of deciding whether others have or have not benefited from my excess of arbitrary endowments, Narveson reminds us that it isn't clear how we get from no one deserving more than others to others being entitled to whatever we didn't deserve, which is to say how a principle of non-desert entails one of desert (2002a, 54).

Even if we did allow that, to be fair, or to level the playing fields of Eton where the Battle of Waterloo was supposedly won, we should attempt to correct for chance, Jasay thinks it is still unclear why justice requires fairness, since the latter is a rather obscure notion as we have also had occasion to remark. Not only does fairness dictate that we should control for chance, but it also supposedly involves criteria by which to evaluate all manner of interactions from the personal to the official. Poorly matched prizefighters may lead to an unfair but not unjust outcome, as may stealing a good friend's partner. However, such cases lend little or no support to the view that luck is unjust and the lucky can be coerced as a matter of justice into sharing it with the less fortunate (ibid., 28).

We appealed to the Law Merchant as an important example of rules and conventions which grew up quite independently of the merchants'

[57] Schmidtz sees desert not as a way of comparing people but as a way of commending those who made the best use of whatever advantages they had (2006, 67).

cities or states of residence to facilitate extraterritorial trade.[58] Although Hume thought that the main purpose of government was to establish justice (2003, 20), we believe that we can have the benefit of Hume's magistracy without the great panoply of government from the monarch down to the nomenklatura and petty bureaucracy (2003, 20). Elsewhere, of course, Hume appears to have agreed that while we could live without government, we could not manage without justice, which is to say that conventions about property and contract precede government and were amenable to adjudication long before the advent of the king's courts (1960, 541).

Thus, Jasay is prompted to ask, if indeed government is exogenous to society, that is an effect rather than a cause of justice, if we can reach agreement without the state, we may well wonder why it is thought essential (1997, 14). Hume's short, and somewhat unsatisfactory answer appears to be that government would not have arisen if it served no useful purpose (1975, 205). While Hume thought that government of one sort or another had been evident in Britain since Roman times, he considered the North American Indians to be an example of those who managed to secure peace and order mostly without government as we know it. Such authority as they did have was conferred on an ad hoc basis in war but set aside when peace returned (1960, 540). Holcombe notes, for example, that the Iroquois Confederacy set much store by reaching consensus, with the result that such limited government as there was permitted a greater degree of political freedom than the top-down governments of Europe. (2002, 50–51).

Hume's explanation for the European style of governance was that it was best suited to war and provided a convenient model for post-war civil government to manage its day-to-day crises by reposing decision-making in a single individual (ibid., 541). But not only do we lack the Iroquois consensus mechanism for minimizing the costs government can impose upon its citizens, Higgs contends that crises prove an endless source of government expansion which preclude a return to normalcy

58 Leeson provides a further example of the anarchic production of law in his discussion of the *Leges Marchiarum*, which helped maintain order in the border lands of England and Scotland for several centuries prior to the Union of the Crowns in 1603 (2014, Ch. 3. "The Laws of Lawlessness").

because the crisis allowed government to develop new powers over the lives of its citizens which it could use to address other issues in the hope of expanding its grip on power (1987, 59). The most recent crisis to have caught the attention of many governments is that of Covid which prompted many states to shut down large parts of their societies with the expressed aim of minimizing the spread of disease. Mueller noted early on that by the time politicians take notice, they overreact and rather than improving matters, they tend to make them worse (2020, 2). Some have predicted the arrival of a new normal once governments find something other than Covid to worry about, but for King and Crewe that might simply amount to a never-ending stream of government blunders (2014, 437), about which there is nothing really new.

While we might wish that fiascos on such a grand scale were less likely to be the norm if the state were to wither away as Marx predicted, we would still have to contend with those who commit force and fraud against others.[59] Despite Cutler's worries, it seems that the trend to privatization of law and security, as evident in the centuries-old Law Merchant, continues, with the result, according to Benson, that the private security enforcement industry has overtaken public law enforcement (1990, 201). When Hume spoke of enforcing justice, what he had in mind were the rules of common law and morality, which a later writer such as Narveson finds embodied in the injunction to avoid harming others or their property (2006, 6).[60] Mill reminded us that the state was only entitled to use its coercive power to prevent harm by one individual to another, not to ensure that an individual was acting in his own best interests (1974, 68). Moreover, Sumner has reported that courts themselves defer to Mill's principle when weighing the alleged harm in a publication against that of infringing free speech (2004, 164).

While we are likely to agree with Hume's interdiction against deception and aggression as being a precursor of the harm principle, we do not agree with his view that government or the state is necessary for maintaining moral order since we are more inclined to obey the magistrate

[59] cf. Rothbard (1978, 234).

[60] For a more recent statement of the principle see Matt Kibbe, *Don't Hurt People and Don't Take Their Stuff-A libertarian manifesto* (2014).

than our fellow citizens (ibid., 21).[61] We are of course interested in maintaining order, though we have much less interest than Hume appears to in having it supplied by politics. Just as the Law Merchant was able to bring order to international trade, so it is our contention that more of society could be privately coordinated as well, with policing, for example, being ever more privately provided. As Rothbard commented, the extent to which this has already happened should dissuade us from thinking that public security necessarily falls within the remit of the sovereign state. Those who find the present paramilitary model of policing unsatisfactory could well be persuaded that under Rothbard's model police clients would be better served than they are now as subject taxpayers of the coercive state (ibid., 217–218).

One of the first to advocate market provision of police protection was, in fact, the nineteenth-century French economist, Gustave de Molinari. He held that police interest in society stemmed from a belief that they, as the most visible agents of the coercive monopoly of governments, had the authority to remake it, which is simply Divine Right in the garb of majority rule. As to whether security could be left to the private market, Molinari thought the answer of most writers on government was that a sovereign authority was required whose monopoly on remaking society stemmed directly from God (1977, 10). Hume, on the other hand, writing several years before the American Revolution in 1776, held as a matter of experience that social order is much better maintained by government.[62] But after another couple of centuries, we are much less confident than Hume was that, as Molinari put it, monopolistic governments really possess the higher authority they say they do. On the contrary, as Rothbard argued, it is our job to desanctify and demystify rulers as the American revolutionaries did with the English monarch

[61] While distancing himself from those philosophers who think that government is essential to society (1960, 539), and being surprised how the many readily submit to their few rulers (2003, 16), Hume thinks that to secure justice magistrates will be needed to help mankind overcome a tendency to satisfy their immediate rather than long-term interests (2003, 20–21).

[62] Emsley reminds us that in Hume's time, order was not the responsibility of the state so much as local bodies such as the parish vestries, who often selected soldiers returning from England's various wars to serve as watchmen and constables, which was one way of providing employment for men whose martial skills might otherwise find less civically beneficial outlets (2010, 15–16).

(2007a, 6). Moreover, according to Albert Jay Nock, the early colonists shared the same realistic view of the State as their forebears, who were beneficiaries of the merchant-state in England, or of the ancient feudal state, where, as Voltaire is supposed to have remarked, the state is a device for taking money out of one set of pockets and putting it into another (1994, 51).

While Hume seems prepared to consider the possibility that just as we can have good and bad citizens, we could also have a magistrate who was lazy or corrupt, he lacks the scepticism of his colonial contemporaries. Hume seems to think that merely by dint of taking office, the magistrate will be impartial and respected by the citizens. Moreover, there is no shortage of those ready and willing to obey the dictates of government, just as there is a ready supply of those willing to meet the apparent demand for those in charge. Most often would be administrators supposedly find they can rise above their own interests to meet the demands of justice, helped no doubt by the customary emoluments and perquisites of office (ibid., 21).

But, as Molinari pointed out, holding that some are fit to rule, while others must be ruled, is just an example of the divine right fiction, namely that rulers are appointed by the Almighty. Molinari thought that the prestige of leadership was a function of the belief that the magistrates took orders from on high, which led theoreticians to take great pains to establish the superiority of the ruling class (ibid., 10). Hume seemed to believe that the governors were superior to ordinary mortals, something another couple of centuries of democracy might have disabused him of (ibid.). And for those who find themselves less persuaded of the official's merit, the latter can always resort to the use of supposedly legitimate force, on which he has a monopoly.

Towards the end of his essay "Of the Origin of Government", Hume concedes that government is characterized by a perpetual struggle between authority and liberty, and although the former stops short of being absolute, it tends to cast a shadow over the latter (ibid., 22). Of course, we have been arguing throughout this discussion that there appears to be no basis for political authority as such, or, as Narveson has written, even though mankind has subscribed for millennia to the omnicompetence of the state, it is an intolerable fiction (1988, 214). Hume is right that government requires considerable loss of liberty, and we have discussed various examples which illustrate just that. As to the supposed struggle between authority and liberty, while this might be true as a matter of *Realpolitik*, from the point of view of this discussion authority is a non-starter. In the case of liberty, on the other hand, it is something we all have a right to.

However, as noted above, Hume thought it unreasonable to believe that a peaceful society could be founded on freedom. He appeals to the longstanding notion of omnipotent government to justify his claim that it is entitled to limit our liberty since we cannot guarantee that its exercise will invariably produce social benefit (1975, 205). Of course, if Hume means simply doing as we please, without regard to others, then it is unlikely that acting that way will be harmless and of benefit to others. But those, who contend that there is a general right to liberty, and that it is in fact the only basic right there is, add the important proviso that, as Narveson suggests, our actions do not interfere with a similar right of others. Those that do so interfere act wrongfully and are liable to sanction (2002b, 40).

As we have suggested, something much closer to a libertarian society than we now have would not put an end to the use of force and coercion. Again, according to Narveson, libertarianism, perhaps contrary to first impressions, is a doctrine about the rightful use of coercion (1988, 50). Or as Freeman observes, libertarians think it right to use coercion to defend person, property and contracts (2001, 124). Indeed, they do, but in doing so they are merely enforcing rights that have been long held to exist at common law. We should also not lose sight of the fact that most people have been brought up to respect those rights and generally manage to avoid harming others. Thus, as Rothbard remarks, even in a large city like New York, one does not depend on police protection but on the fact that most people have been brought up to respect the right of others to live in peace (1978, 201). If that has changed in recent years, Sowell thinks it has to do with the belief that so-called social justice calls for greater leniency towards those who interfere with that right (2011, 478).

In reply to Hume's question as to why we should abridge our native freedom, we might reply with Narveson that we do so to protect the liberty of everybody else, since there is no such thing as an unlimited right to liberty (ibid.). However, ensuring observance of something like Mill's no harm principle is not the same as issuing a blank cheque for government, as Hume seems to think. We have suggested that most of the work can readily be accomplished by ourselves, developing spontaneous conventions over time, without the troops who are rarely there when needed anyway. One such example is queuing, where most people observe the first come first served rule. While the uncommon ignoramus who tries to butt in may fly below the radar of official peacekeepers, who are doubtless busy attending to more important matters, he may well have various forms of opprobrium heaped upon his head for his failure to conform.

So, Hume is wrong to think that the only thing keeping us from the evils of anarchy is government. Moreover, the same private arrangements by which two farmers may agree to drain the field they share may also permit of projects on a much larger scale which nowadays are mostly built by private contractors. However, Hume continues to believe that government management of such endeavours involving casts of thousands are somehow exempted from the usual human frailties. Perhaps if he could have witnessed the endless record of government failure noted earlier, such as poor flood control and subsequent response in the wake of Hurricane Katrina, he might have realized that government was far from omnipotent (1960, 539). On the contrary, Hume seems convinced that politics can solve the problem of coordinating large numbers of people on a solution and prevent free riding; the magistrates can push the project which they claim favoured by a majority and, unlike most of us, only need convince themselves of a project's merits (ibid., 539). But as Jasay has argued, if we can contract into Pareto-superior solutions to a cooperative game, it is not clear how adding a state and its coercive apparatus can reduce transaction costs (1997, 13).

Hume's claim that bridges or harbours might not be built has continued to be a popular argument for the political provision of so-called public or collective goods. However, as Rothbard has observed, even if there are collective goods, they do not have to be supplied by one agent, typically government, nor should all be coerced into paying for them. Indeed, he considers the notion of collective goods very suspect, since only individuals exist and have preferences. In the case of so-called public defence, for example, not all inhabitants of a particular area require either protection, or the same level of it (2001, 883–884). In fact, there is a complex variety of levels of protection, determined by factors such as available manpower (1978, 215–216). According to Rothbard, the main question raised by putative collective goods is whether everybody can be forced to pay for a good which he may not even want; the pacifist, for example, may have as little use for police protection as a Jehovah's Witness for the Canadian Blood Service. As Seldon remarks, governments fail to understand that collective charging for individual benefits is resented by non-beneficiaries (2002, 30).

For Rothbard, the collective goods argument turns out, on analysis, to reduce to the external benefit argument (2001, 884). While individuals may be left to their own devices to benefit one another, positive or negative externalities which spill over onto others are often held to constitute grounds for government intervention. Rothbard claims that criticisms levelled against externalities are typically of two varieties: first that A is not doing enough for B, and second that B is free riding on A. Such cases may be used to warrant a coercive state response, either to get A to do more for B, or to get B to pay for what A does (ibid., 886–887). However, Rothbard rightly rejects the view that the state is in any position to remedy such transactions, which are optimal in the sense that any free-market transactions are, namely that they are freely expressed consumer preferences, which means that state intervention will of necessity be less than optimal (ibid., 887). When government does interfere and compel public provision of goods to remedy such supposed market failures, as Rothbard noted, for example, with respect to the mix of services offered by publicly supported police, government spending will be subject to all the usual political inefficiencies with little regard to satisfying consumer preferences (1978, 216).

Similarly, Jasay has argued that it is often simply assumed that non-excludability or the inability to prevent free riders is sufficient justification for a good to be supplied by government. Hayek thought that the only question to be asked about the government's undertaking to supply such goods was whether the benefits exceeded the cost (1978, 222). If indeed this is the only question, as Jasay comments, it is a large one and it is far from clear how to answer it; it is certainly problematical whether we should take the outcomes of politics as revealing society's true preferences (2002, 23). Part of the answer to Hayek's question as to whether a good is a benefit will depend on which side of the winning political coalition an individual is on. The winning side will skew the bag of goods in its own favour and against the losing side, with the result that the redistributive mix is likely to be seen as beneficial by the winners and not worth the candle by the losers. Jasay further notes the tendency to over-provide public goods, with users having no incentive to economize, as one typically finds in what are thought to be public goods *par excellence*, namely healthcare and education (ibid., 24).

With respect to overconsumption of health care, Gratzer reports that under state provided systems patients see doctors more often and demand more tests and specialized services (1999, 131). Not that overconsumption is entirely the fault of the consumer. High demand ensures that doctors do not have to compete and face the prospect of lower earnings (ibid., 133). Although greater accessibility is often advanced as one of the justifications for supposed public goods, with respect to publicly provided health care, such as the National Health Service, Seldon comments that they are often under-provided as well, with the result that for the poorest care has often not been readily available when needed, as it would have been had it remained a private service (2002, 71).

In Canada, the failure of central health care planning results in rationing in the form of resource shortages and lengthy queuing for treatment, with politicians grandstanding about their refusal to seek readily available private solutions. The Canadian Institute for Health Information reports the average waiting time for knee replacements in Ontario to be around 9 months from decision to treat to surgery. CIHI reports further that this post-decision waiting time only accounts for about 60% of the total; the other 40% will be taken up with the wait from initial referral to decision to treat (2006, 19). More recently Barua et al. have estimated the median wait for this procedure to be 7 months, with 50% of cases being treated by then and the remaining 50% still awaiting treatment. Depending on different methodologies this may or may not represent any improvement over the past dozen years. It is still twice as long as physicians would recommend and much longer again than most patients would prefer (2018, 16). As for other waiting times, of 5 countries surveyed, Canada had the highest percentage of adults who had to wait longer than 2 hours for treatment in an emergency department, and in both Canada and the UK respondents were more likely to have experienced longer waits for specialists than in other countries surveyed. In general, CIHI concludes that the main problem seems to be the wait for an appointment in the first place (ibid., 16–17).[63]

With respect to public education, at least in Britain, Seldon holds that the only solution to poor-quality public schools would be to allow parents to send their children to schools of their own choice (ibid., 73). The Montreal Economic Institute has observed similar problems in various advanced countries involving waste, bureaucracy, slow reaction to changing labour demands and hostility to efficiency assessment. They believe that competition and decentralization are essential to improving service (2007, 4). For Rothbard the basic fault of public education is that, like much else under the aegis of the state, it is compulsory, a fact which West found especially striking in the case of democratic governments (1994, 334). Rothbard thought that forcing children into classrooms was unjust, both to the dull as well as to the bright, believing that parents should have the responsibility for educating their own children, especially in the early years. The Prussian model of compulsory education was quite influential in the US, and Rothbard considers it much to the discredit of mandatory state education that the Nazi regime seized upon the institutional structures laid down by Imperial Germany to further its own totalitarian objectives (1999, 34–35).

In addition to Rothbard's worry about teachers as civil servants being part of the long arm of government (ibid., 48–49), they also typically belong to powerful unions, as Lieberman points out, which employ all the tactics of the closed shop to restrict their membership, drive up wages

---

[63] The Canadian system is typically contrasted with that in the US, which is often mistakenly thought to be a free market system: cf. Gratzer (2002, 193). But despite their differences, US shortcomings seem little different from those of Canada, namely too much top-down control and red tape: cf. Sally Pipes (2004, 137). With respect to the US system Salerno agrees that similar problems affect the supply of resources and costs (Postscript to Mises 1990, 69).

and limit competition (2000, 30).[64] Not surprisingly, Lieberman finds that such powerful producer unions with large funds at their disposal will continue to stand in the way of parents seeking something better for their children (ibid., 282). Indeed, Rothbard argued that compulsory public education was on a par with compelling everyone to read newspapers put out by a national chain supported by the state (ibid., 17–18). Moreover, he is a vigorous critic of the Rousseau–Pestalozzi–Dewey doctrine which has held sway during the past century in American education, the net effect of which he believes is to destroy any independent thinking in children. In the name of equality, grading is often made relative to the child's supposed abilities, which Rothbard argues does justice to none. Such dumbing-down of schooling might have been avoided if the so-called progressives had drawn the appropriate conclusion and abandoned compulsory education for all. However, the belief that children should be prepared for democracy is the source of yet another hazard, namely the suppression of individuality in the interests of group solidarity (ibid., 54).

Milton Friedman, who favoured some minimum of education for all, but thought there were no grounds for the nationalization of the education industry, famously proposed his voucher system as a step towards providing greater freedom of choice in schooling, with government being restricted to monitoring minimum standards (1982, 89). Lieberman notes that for various reasons vouchers never caught on, among them no doubt the fact that the bureaucracy and teacher unions saw them as a threat (ibid., 267). Sowell has more recently discussed an educational venture which has not yet succumbed to such threats, if only because of its academic successes, namely the charter schools of New York City, which operate semi-privately within the public system. This parallel arrangement facilitates comparisons of educational results, showing that charter students, who mostly consist of minorities, perform better than their public counterparts. Those with a vested interest in the status quo of public schools from politicians to unionized teachers generally view the more independent charter operation as a fifth column and take no

[64] In so doing they were likely following the example of the medical profession: cf. Hamowy (1984, 262).

comfort from its doing better by disadvantaged students (2020). Similarly, Sowell notes that despite the outstanding achievements of graduates of the Dunbar High School in DC, the fact that it was for reserved for blacks, meant that the Court a few blocks away would come to find that the school's record on behalf of its underprivileged clientele could not withstand the attractions of desegregation (2005, 204–214).

With respect to producer monopolies, it is also worth noting that Friedman proposed an interesting remedy which appears to have received even less attention than that of vouchers. He argued that the medieval guild system was still with us in the form of occupational licensure and that it was time we rediscovered the spirit of nineteenth-century liberalism according to which people could follow their vocational interest without needing a government seal of approval (ibid., 137). Professions and trades have claimed that licensure is in the public interest, a notion to which the state has typically appealed to expand its writ by approving licensing authorities. While this may sound innocuous enough, Friedman observes that the awarding of licences may often be based on considerations having little to do with professional competence, but rather with the fashionable political correctness of the day (ibid., 141).

One might be inclined to think that there is something of concern to the public interest, when say in the case of barbers, most jurisdictions have passed licensing regulations of one sort or another. In fact, according to Friedman, it has little to do with supposed public interest but rather, as has been already noted, with the fact that producers have a greater interest in matters affecting their trade and will devote more time and energy lobbying on behalf of it than their consumers will (ibid., 143). The social cost produced by such producer interest is that it becomes a mechanism for that group to develop a monopoly, one which is in fact aided and abetted by the state. Friedman's observations about barbers also apply to the barber-surgeons, or latterly the medical profession, where the effect of licensing has been to run a closed shop with the features noted above in the case of teacher unions such as undersupply of those willing and able to deliver the required service to the public at the price they are willing to pay (ibid., 155). As to whether licensure even in the case of medicine has been of any benefit, other than adding to the monopoly powers of the profession and the licensing state, Friedman concludes that it has simply been an obstacle to the beneficial practice of medicine and should henceforth be abandoned (ibid., 158).[65]

However, despite serious medical manpower shortages, which according to CIHI, result in Canada's reporting the highest use of emergency departments, as well as the longest wait times for such treatment (2006, 16), Friedman's solution is likely to remain politically unpalatable,[66] as is Rothbard's concerning compulsory public education. Although Friedman thought that governments might be responsible for setting minimum standards in schools and schooling, we have argued that their authority to do so is very much in question, and even if that matter could be settled, schools themselves could monitor their own standards. Nor, as Rothbard remarked, is it any help to have the state inspect private schools since this removes their independence and makes them creatures of the state (ibid., 16). It is therefore not surprising, that in the two areas where public provision has tended to predominate, and, according to some, necessarily so, Seldon predicts that improving incomes will enable increasing numbers of dissatisfied parents and patients escape to private schooling and medicine (2002, 85).

With respect to the standard criteria which are thought to determine whether a good is publicly, or politically, supplied, Jasay argues that they are not as straightforward as often assumed. In the case of exclusion costs, for example, or the costs of protecting full property rights, these may range from the fairly objective to the quite subjective: in the case of the former we talking about a good which could not be delivered profitably, and in the latter where political costs might militate against its production (2002, 25). In the case of the two principal public goods we have been discussing, the main barriers to having them supplied privately to a much greater extent would appear to be subjective costs, such as electoral defeat, especially in the case of Canadian health care. Jasay also

[65] Lest Friedman's findings, confirmed around the same time by Arrow, be thought somewhat dated, a study by Svorny reaches similar conclusions, namely that states should eliminate licensing because it adds nothing to safeguards provided by courts and markets, but if anything reduces access to care and gives consumers a false sense of security (2008, 12).

[66] Svorny is also aware that her recommendations might run into political difficulties, so she suggests more gradual improvements in workforce flexibility by wider recognition of licenses and attention to qualifications and scope of practice of non-MDs (ibid.).

notes that politicians cannot be counted on to properly assess exclusion costs, thus tilting the balance in favour of public provision (ibid., 26). One of the most famous examples of underestimating the case for private provision was that of the lighthouse, which had long been seen as the paradigmatic non-excludable good. However, Mill and Sidgwick notwithstanding, Coase famously reported that lighthouses in England and Wales were successfully privately owned and operated, financed by tolls collected by port agents (1988, 212–213).

Jasay observes further that it has often been assumed that the provision of public goods is best seen as a prisoners' dilemma, where the best strategy is noncontribution. But if the benefits of a particular good are high enough the benefits to be gained by contributing, regardless of what others do, may well exceed the cost. If this is the case, we are no longer dealing with a prisoners' dilemma where default or noncontribution is the dominant strategy. While contributing may risk providing a free ride to noncontributors, not contributing also involves the risk that others will do likewise and a valuable good will not be provided. People will no doubt differ as to their assessment of the greater risk of the two, with the result that we cannot rule out the private production of public goods, as in the case of Trinity House, the private lighthouse agency, nor can we necessarily appeal to the prisoners' dilemma as our reason for doing so. As Jasay concludes, public goods may well be produced by voluntary cooperation, with the decision to adopt sucker or free-rider roles being spontaneously assigned by individual risk assessment, rather than by the government (ibid., 29).

### 3.4.2 The Authoritative Solution to Prisoners' Dilemmas

Having questioned whether the provision of public goods is best interpreted as some sort of prisoners' dilemma from which we need to be rescued by authoritative fiat, Jasay examines the extent to which the authority of the state can be thought to rest upon the existence of prisoners' dilemmas of one sort or another. In general, he contends that strong consent to the state rests on the belief that it is seen as indispensable to overcoming the cooperative failure inherent in the prisoners' dilemma (2002, 31). We might resort to virtue to produce the necessary commitments but, as the tale goes, virtue cannot be relied upon since it may be in short supply in large anonymous social groups. Thus, Heath reminds us that while trade depends on a promise to pay, it is in our interest to promise, but rarely to pay (2001, 52). Since according to the traditional story virtue cannot be uniformly counted upon to deliver the goods, prudence dictates a state to deliver us from the inexorable logic of the prisoners' dilemma.

Jasay considers two sorts of challenges. With respect to the logic of the dilemma we can ask whether it does mean what it seems and is widely thought to mean. Secondly, we can ask what the dilemma is relevant to, that is, whether it models any actual interactions between people. The first sort of challenge involves denying that the PD, hooked up to a maximization assumption, does in fact imply a dominant default strategy. Gauthier, for example, proposes that the interest of both players requires that we adopt constrained rather than straightforward maximization, which will improve the game sum as well as individual payoffs. This supposedly has the result, *pace* Heath, that performance by one player will result in performance by the other, because the costs of non-cooperation are borne by both (1987, 179).

In Jasay's view such an attempt to avoid the inexorable logic of the PD is subject to the objection that constrained maximization appears to require us to ignore the dictates of rationality which itself is irrational (2002, 35). Constrained maximization, he argues, would only make sense if we could assume each player had access to the other's thoughts; only thus could we transform PP into an equilibrium and break the dominance of DD. However, to assume that both players could read one another's minds well enough to make PP dominant is simply to change it from a prisoners' dilemma to a cooperative game by making commitments credible. Even if we are stuck with the strict logic of the one-shot PD where mutual default is the Nash equilibrium, one may legitimately ask whether that really matters and how often we are likely to get one-shot PDs in a social setting. Indeed, Jasay responds that they are the exception rather than the rule (ibid., 36).

Such an exceptional case might arise if at least two conditions are met, namely independence and irrelevance. If independence obtains, then whatever the player plays in the present game will have no effect on how a future partner might play. On the other hand, Jasay argues that one may run the risk of a sanction in the form of banishment from future games, which will make the defaulter aware of his foregone gains—something even below the security payoff of DD—thus switching on the so-called Folk Theorem, by which the mutual performance strategy or PP is an equilibrium, as is any other mutual solution which is an improvement on DD (2002, 37–38).

If we transfer this theorem to the social situation where there are many potential players, resource constraints of one sort or another will send us in search of the best games, namely those which offer payoffs above the security level. This in turn amounts to finding the best partners to play with, such as employers, customers, and spouses, and to accomplish that goal we need to build a reputation as a reliable player. According to the independence condition, in the transition from *Gemeinschaft* to *Gesellschaft* the Folk Theorem does not get switched on, with the result that one can free ride without it having any effect on being able to find willing partners in future games (ibid., 40).

Whereas the independence condition claims that the present casts no shadow over the future, under the irrelevance condition, absent much of a future there is nothing to affect present strategies. One such case would be where a player knows this is the last game and will therefore play it as a one-shot game. Similarly situated are the fly by night operators, transient tourists, and the proverbial *Mann ohne Eigenschaften,* who tends to have so little to offer that the most he can get from other players is poorly paid casual employment. Although there are such irrelevance-of-the-future cases, Jasay does not consider them a likely source for underwriting the state enforcement of agreements (2002, 41).

As to whether independence-of-the-future offers greater promise as grounds for strong consent to the enforcer state depends on the strength of what Jasay calls the anonymity argument where because anonymous players cannot be linked to their game strategies, they have nothing to lose by defaulting (ibid.). However, the anonymity argument is, as it turns out, false, and this has to do with the fact that a PD performance can only be met by default if either the players' strategies are hidden from each other, or the game is sequential. Simultaneous performance, coupled with at least partial transparency will produce either of two symmetrical solutions, that is, PP or DD, for while I might be happy to have you perform and me default, you will not perform if I don't do likewise (ibid.). Simultaneous performance in fact turns it from a PD into an assurance game, whose real-life analogue is the spot exchange or cash transaction. While it does admit to anonymity, there is no free-ride option, nor will it offer grounds for a contract enforcer, since the game is cooperative and the contract self-enforcing (ibid., 42).

On the other hand, sequential, non-simultaneous play does not support anonymous social interaction. As in a credit transaction the performance of the first player precedes that of the second. But the first is unlikely to advance goods on credit to an anonymous individual. Thus, for Jasay, while the spot transaction can take place anonymously, it will not work for the non-simultaneous one, where default tends to lose its appeal (ibid.). Hobbes's Foole discovers that even if there is no such thing as justice to enforce the keeping of covenants, there are still considerations of prudence or expediency. If he breaches his covenant, the only person likely to play with him is another fool, but as Jasay again reminds us, stupidity doesn't sound like much of a foundation for an enforcer of contracts (2002, 43).

However, Heath is convinced that without the enforcer we will end up with outcome 3 in his schema, or DD, where he fails to deliver, and you fail to pay. That is, our natural propensity to truck and barter, of which Adam Smith so fondly spoke, will be undermined by our tendency to free ride. In reply of course we can simply remind Heath that truck and barter long preceded the state, as noted earlier in this chapter, and continues under private dispensation even today, much to the chagrin of people like Cutler. Indeed, it was noted in the aftermath of 9/11 that following the money trail was made difficult by similar private customary arrangements in Islamic countries. Heath's predictions notwithstanding, we are not confined to simultaneous exchange and much-touted globalization would not have occurred if we were.

Heath claims further that trade must be backed up by something more than self-interest, such as moral or legal sanctions. No doubt it must, in the sense that some such constraint is in our interest. After all Gauthier thought that it was in our interest to constrain our maximizing tendencies, and Jasay thought the Foole might at least be prudent, if not moral. Besides, as Foot reminds us, prudence has its place under the tent of practical rationality (2001, 13). If legal constraint is also necessary, we suggested that we do not need Hume's machinery of the state to produce it, but that firmer rules may evolve as did the common law or the Law Merchant. As Hasnas notes, for most people law is co-extensive with the state, whereas in fact there are many examples of law which the state has not produced such as bargaining and mediation, or institutional management. The common phrase *law and order* implies that the two necessarily go together. However, as Hasnas further explains, law is one method of producing the order we need for a harmonious existence, though in its present incarnation it tends to be rules generated by the state (2007, 184; 186).

However, Heath maintains that the only way of getting ourselves out of the prisoners' dilemmas into which our self-interest has led us is by handing over some of our freedom to the state and living under its rules, since freedom is only good when it leads to good things, and if it doesn't we are better off doing with less. He assumes of course that the state will somehow know what has escaped the rest of us, that is, which of the consequences of freedom are good, and which bits of freedom we are better off without. Again, there is little need to stand in line at some state bureaucracy in the hope of getting an answer which is readily at hand, namely Pareto's idea that something constitutes an improvement if it makes at least one person better off than she was, and no one worse off than he was.

Heath claims that following Hobbes society has laws and institutions designed to ward off the effects of our exercising our natural liberty, including the free riding which erodes any attempt to cooperate socially or economically (2001, 53). But as we have argued, the rules and institutions of society are many and varied and extend well beyond those produced by the magistrates. To the extent that free riding is a problem, it tends to be a self-limiting ailment and one largely managed without the ministrations of the state. The Pareto principle or Mill's no harm principle would certainly qualify as examples of the rules of society, and as moral principles most people are quite capable of putting them into practice to produce the order without which life would be even more nasty, brutish and short than it is. Though as Jasay noted, there is something peculiar about saying that one prefers the state to the state of nature in much the same way as one might prefer familiar objects such as tea or coffee, since most of us have only lived under states which by definition preclude any direct experience of the state of nature (1998, 19). Binmore makes the further point that the social contract theorist not only needs to show how the social game differs from the state of nature game, but why the players would feel committed to the rules of the new game (1995, 118).

As we saw, considerations of prudence would dictate that even the Foole should keep his agreements, lest he be confined to playing with fools like himself in future games. While this lesson may have been lost on the Volk, according to Jasay, some version of the proverbial War of All Against All does seem to have remained in the public consciousness, with the result that the doctrine of the authority of the state has come to rely rather heavily on a prisoners' dilemma, the supposed importance of which doesn't appear to bear close examination. Though Heath is one of those who leverages his theory of the state on the dubious significance of the prisoner's dilemma, he admits that in his view a prisoner's dilemma is a one-shot game. However, for Jasay it is on the contrary one of a longer series of games which will produce future payoffs as the result of present strategies chosen by the player in question (2002, 43).

Heath however is not consoled by the thought that there might be a series of games, since this might just mean that people get stuck in one prisoners' dilemma after another (2001, 55). However, Binmore, like Jasay, believes that the prisoners' dilemma does not correctly map the way societies produce cooperative solutions and is thus not troubled by the fact that cooperation is impossible in a one-shot game. Moreover, he holds that repeated games are strategically quite different because time permits players to take into consideration opponents' past behaviour (1995, 114, 115). Heath insists that once people get stuck in repeated prisoners' dilemmas, they typically go from bad to worse, the so-called race to the bottom. But although it sounds rather dramatic, it simply isn't clear in what sense the outcome supposedly gets worse and worse. The

Nash equilibrium of a prisoners' dilemma is DD, or as Binmore prefers to call it (hawk, hawk), which is not to say that there is no solution which would be a Pareto improvement, such as PP, (dove, dove) which has a higher payoff than DD. If a series of Pareto inefficient outcomes strikes Heath as somewhat worrisome, Binmore does not find it problematic that rational individuals can make choices which produce such outcomes, since a prisoners' dilemma is generally hostile to cooperative solutions (ibid., 103).

It appears that Heath has committed what Binmore regards as the mistake of arguing that because rational individuals sometimes fail to keep their promises, they can never be counted on to do so. Moreover, he thinks that the fact that we find the prisoners' dilemma somewhat bleak is indicative of the importance we attach to developing a reputation for keeping promises, and only dealing with those who do (ibid., 112). Jasay also emphasizes the importance of reputation in becoming a desirable partner and enlarging the pool of future partners. Reputation is not just one of mechanical reliability, but that B knows that A knows that honesty pays (2002, 38–39). In fact, Heath should heed Binmore's admonition that he is backing the wrong game with the prisoners' dilemma and should direct his attention elsewhere (ibid., 114). Indeed, as Binmore reminds us in a later work, for the repeated games most of us participate in, the folk theorem suggests that given a reasonable amount of self-interest, we will likely find no shortage of like-minded cooperators in the future (2002, 293).

### 3.4.3 The Principal-Agent Problem

Having shown that the supposed existence of prisoners' dilemmas does not provide support for the authority of the state that Heath and others are inclined to think, let us advert to a related issue, which Jasay argues contractarian statists must contend with, namely the principal-agent problem. Under such a view the principals or parties to the social contract set up an agent-state to manage the collective choice mechanism provided for in the contract, as well as in some versions of the theory, a sub-contract with the agent spelling out his fiduciary duties. However, as

Jasay notes, the fact that there is an agent to enforce collective decisions provides incentives to free ride on public enforcement. Various special interest groups manage to get deals enforced from the public purse if for no other reason than that the mere existence of the agent-state gives rise to a game in which some principals will collude with the agent at the expense of other principals (ibid., 50–51).

Not only is the agent-state the cause, rather than the cure of the most incorrigible free-rider problems, the prisoners' dilemma, for which it was the much-heralded silver bullet, as Jasay observes, now returns with a vengeance directed towards those who have not managed to form an alliance with the agent and lose out in the great redistribution game. Although the typical contract is largely self-enforcing, the social contract is not. Enforcement might in turn be contracted for, but that contract will itself need enforcing, and so on into the afternoon, no doubt leading Juvenal to famously ask: *Quis custodiet ipsos custodes?* Thus, the only way out of the infinite regress of enforcement dependence is to set up a cooperative game where the contract is self-enforcing. What we are not entitled to claim, according to Jasay, is that although contracts or promises are incurably infected by the prisoners' dilemma, the social contract itself manages to avoid contamination (ibid., 52).

## 3.5 Summary

Throughout this chapter we question the supposed need for authoritative solutions to problems such as coordination, enforcement and prisoners' dilemmas of one sort or another. As Edmundson agrees, the class of *malum prohibitum* laws, which comprise the bulk of modern legislation, are a good test of the authority of the state, which we contend is non-existent. While consent is now widely thought to offer little hope for justifying the state's authority, we also discuss other proposals such as estoppel, fairness and associative obligations, which we find similarly wanting. Although Raz thinks we should have no more difficulty accepting the authority of the state than that of a doctor, we see no relevant similarities. Over the past century the state has vastly increased the scope of problems thought to require an authoritative solution, for which it imposes ever-increasing taxes, supported by coercive measures dressed up in the trappings of sovereignty. As for the public goods which, it has been widely believed, can only be provided by the state, the two classic cases of medical care and education exhibit all the disadvantages inherent in central provision, such as both under and over-supply of a poor-quality product. Similarly, prisoners' dilemmas, which have been thought to depend for their solution on the heavy hand of the state, turn out on closer inspection to be iterated games, where, to paraphrase Jasay, the future casts some solution over the present.

## Works Cited


Ackerman, Kenneth D. *Boss Tweed*. New York: Carroll & Graf, 2006.

Anderson, Terry L, and Peter J. Hill. *The Not so Wild, Wild West.* Stanford, CA: Stanford, 2004.

Aquinas, Thomas. *The Political Ideas*. New York: Hafner, 1953.

Arthur, Terry. *Crap: A Guide to Politics*. London: Continuum, 2007.

Barclay, Harold. *The State*. London: Freedom Press, 2003.

Barnett, Randy E. *The Structure of Liberty.* New York: Oxford, 1998.

Barua, Bacchus et al. *Waiting Your Turn: Wait Times for Healthcare in Canada, 2018 Report.* Vancouver: Fraser Institute, 2018.

Bastiat, Frederic. *The Law.* London: IEA, 2001.

Bennett, James T., and Thomas J. DiLorenzo. *Underground Government: The Off-Budget Public Sector*. Washington: Cato Institute, 1983.

Benson, Bruce L. *The Enterprise of Law*. San Francisco: Pacific Research Institute, 1990.

———. *To Serve and Protect*. New York: New York University Press, 1998.

Bentham, Jeremy. *A Fragment on Government*. Cambridge: Cambridge University Press, 1994.

Brennan, Geoffrey. "The Myth of Ownership" Liam Murphy and Thomas Nagel: A Review Essay. *Constitutional Political Economy* 16 (2005): 207–219.

Bergland, David. *Libertarianism in One Lesson.* Cartersville: The Advocates for Self Government, 2005.

Binmore, Ken. *Game Theory and the Social Contract: Playing Fair*. Boston: MIT Press, 1995.

———. *Just Playing*. Boston: MIT Press, 2002.
Blainey, Geoffrey. *The Tyranny of Distance*. Melbourne: Sun Books, 1966.
Block, Walter. Cut the Murder Rate in New Orleans, 2007. http://www.lewrockwell.com/2007/01/walter-e-block/cut-the-murder-rate-in-new-orleans/
Blundell, John, and Colin Robinson. *Regulation Without the State*. London: IEA, 2000.
Bolick, Clint. *Leviathan: The Growth of Local Government and the Erosion of Liberty*. Stanford: Hoover Institution, 2004.
Bovard, James. *Freedom in Chains: The Rise of the State and the Demise of the Citizen*. New York: St Martin's Press, 1999.
Browne, Harry. *Why Government Doesn't Work*. New York: St Martin's Press, 1995.
———. *The Great Libertarian Offer*. Great Falls: Liam Works, 2000.
Canadian Institute for Health Information. *Waiting for Health Care in Canada*. Ottawa: CIHI, 2006.
Canadian Taxpayers Federation, *On the Dole: Businesses, Lobbyists, and Industry Canada's Subsidy Programs*. Toronto: CTF, 2007.
Carter, April. *Authority and Democracy*. London: Routledge, 1979.
Coase, R.H. *The Firm, the Market, and the Law*. Chicago: Chicago U. Press, 1988.
Cohen, G.A. *Self-Ownership, Freedom and Equality*. Cambridge: Cambridge U. Press, 1995.
Creveld, Martin van. *The Rise and Decline of the State*. Cambridge: Cambridge U. Press, 1999.
Cutler, A. Claire. *Private Power and Global Authority*. Cambridge: Cambridge U Press, 2003.
Denning, Lord. *The Discipline of Law*. London: Butterworths, 1979.
Denson, John V. *A Century of War: Lincoln, Wilson, and Roosevelt*. Auburn: Mises Institute, 2006.
DeSoto, Hernando. *The Mystery of Capital*. New York: Basic Books, 2000.
DiLorenzo, Thomas J. *How Capitalism Saved America*. New York: Three Rivers Press, 2004.
Dworkin, Ronald. *Taking Rights Seriously*. London: Duckworth, 1977.
———. *Law's Empire*. Harvard U. Press, 1986.
Dunn, John. *Democracy: A History*. Toronto: Penguin, 2005.
———. *The Cunning of Unreason*. New York: Basic Books, 2000.
Edmundson, William A. *Three Anarchical Fallacies*. Cambridge: Cambridge U. Press, 1998.

Ellickson, Robert C. *Order Without Law: How Neighbors Settle Disputes.* Cambridge: Harvard U. Press, 1991.
Emsley, Clive. *The Great British Bobby: A History of British Policing from the 18th Century to the Present*. London: Quercus, 2010.
Engdahl, F. William. "There Is More to Blackrock Than You Might Imagine. WilliameEngdahl.com, June18, 2021.
Epstein, Richard. *Forbidden Grounds*. Cambridge: Harvard U. Press, 1995.
———. *Principles for a Free Society.* Reading: Perseus, 1998.
———. *Scepticism and Freedom.* Chicago: Chicago U. Press, 2003.
———. *Free Markets under Siege*. Stanford: Hoover Institution, 2005.
Essex, Christopher, and Ross McKittrick, Ross. *Taken by Storm: The Troubled Science, Policy and Politics of Global Warming.* Toronto: Key Porter, 2002.
Faust, Drew Gilpin. *This Republic of Suffering: Death and the American Civil War*. New York: Vintage, 2008.
Fitzgerald, Randall. *Mugged by the State*. Washington: Regnery, 2003.
Foot, Philippa. *Natural Goodness*. Oxford: Oxford U. Press, 2001.
Foster, Peter. *Self Serve*. Toronto: Macfarlane Walter & Ross, 1992.
Freeman, Samuel. "Illiberal Libertarians: Why Libertarianism Is Not a Liberal View." *Philosophy & Public Affairs* 30, no. 2 (Spring, 2001): 105–151.
Friedman, David. *The Machinery of Freedom.* La Salle: Open Court, 1989.
Friedman, Milton. *Capitalism and Freedom.* Chicago: Chicago U. Press, 1982.
Gauthier, David. *Morals by Agreement*. Oxford: Oxford U. Press, 1987.
Gilbert, Martin. *The Will of the People*. Toronto: Vintage Canada, 2006.
Godwin, William. *Enquiry Concerning Political Justice*. London: Penguin, 1976.
Graetz, Michael J., and Ian Shapiro. *Death by a Thousand Cuts: The Fight Over Taxing Inherited Wealth*. Princeton: Princeton U. Press, 2005.
Gratzer, David. *Code Blue*. Toronto: ECW Press, 1999.
———. ed. *Better Medicine.* ECW Press, 2002.
Grazia, Alfred De. *Political Organization.* New York: Free Press, 1952.
Green, Leslie. *The Authority of the State.* Oxford U. Press, 1988.
———. "Associative Obligations and the State." In *Dworkin and His Critics,* ed. J. Burley, 267–284. Oxford: Blackwell, 2004.
Greenhut, Steven. *Abuse of Power: How the Government Misuses Eminent Domain.* Santa Ana: Seven Locks Press, 2004.
Hamowy, Ronald. *Canadian Medicine: A Study in Restricted Entry.* Vancouver: Fraser Institute, 1984.
Hardin, Russell. *One for All: The Logic of Group Conflict*. Princeton: Princeton U. Press, 1995.

———. *Liberalism, Constitutionalism and Democracy*. Oxford: Oxford U. Press, 2003.
Hare, R.M. *Essays on Political Morality*. Oxford: Oxford U. Press, 1998.
Hart, H.L.A. *The Concept of Law*. Oxford: Oxford U. Press, 1961.
———. "Are There Any Natural Rights?" In *Theories of Rights*, ed. J. Waldron, 77–90. Oxford: Oxford U. Press, 1984.
Hasnas, John. "Toward a Theory of Empirical Natural Rights." *Social Philosophy & Policy* 22, no. 1 (Winter 2005): 111–147.
———. "Unethical Compliance and the Non-sequitur of Academic Business Ethics." *Journal of Private Enterprise*, 21, no. 2 (Spring, 2006): 87–105.
———. "The Myth of the Rule of Law." In *Anarchy and the Law*, ed. Edward P. Stringham, 163–192. New Brunswick: Transaction Publishers, 2007.
Hayek, F.A. *Law, Legislation and Liberty*, vol. I. Chicago: Chicago U. Press, 1973.
———. *The Constitution of Liberty.* Chicago: Chicago U. Press, 1978.
———. *A Free Market Monetary System.* Auburn: Mises Institute, 2008
Hazlitt, Henry. *Is Politics Insoluble?* Irvington-on-Hudson: Foundation for Economic Education, 1997.
Heath, Joseph. *The Efficient Society*. Toronto: Penguin, 2001.
Hebert, Philip C. *Doing Right*. Toronto: Oxford U. Press, 1996.
Higgs, Robert. *Crisis and Leviathan.* New York: Oxford U. Press, 1987.
———. *Against Leviathan.* Oakland: The Independent Institute, 2004.
———. *Resurgence of the Warfare State*. Oakland: The Independent Institute, 2005.
Hobbes, Thomas. *Leviathan.* Oxford: Oxford U. Press, 1909.
Hogue, Arthur R. *Origins of the Common Law*. Bloomington: Indiana U. Press, 1966.
Holcombe, Randall G. *From Liberty to Democracy*. Ann Arbor: Michigan U. Press, 2002.
Holmes, Stephen, and Cass R. Sunstein. *The Cost of Rights*. New York: Norton, 1999.
Hospers, John. *Libertarianism*. Santa Barbara: Reason Press, 1971.
Hume, David, *A Treatise of Human Nature*. Ed. Selby-Bigge. Oxford: Oxford U. Press, 1960.
———. *Enquiries Concerning Human Understanding and Concerning the Principles of Morals*. 3rd ed. ed. Nidditch. Oxford: Oxford U. Press, 1975.
———. *Political Essays*. Ed. Haakonssen. Cambridge U. Press, 2003.
Hurd, Heidi. *Moral Combat.* Cambridge U. Press, 1999.
Ignatieff, Michael. *The Lesser Evil*. Toronto: Penguin Canada, 2004.

Jacobs, Jane. *The Death and Life of Great American Cities*. New York: Vintage, 1992.
Jasay, Anthony De. *Choice Contract and Consent*. London: Institute of Economic Affairs, 1991.
———. *Against Politics*. London: Routledge, 1997.
———. *The State*. Indianapolis: Liberty Fund, 1998.
———. *Justice and its Surroundings*. Indianapolis: Liberty Fund, 2002.
———. "Justice, Luck, Liberty." In *Liberty and Justice*, ed. Tibor Machan. Stanford: Hoover Institution, 2006.
Kibbe, Matt. *Don't Hurt People and Don't Take Their Stuff: A Libertarian Manifesto*. New York: HarperCollins, 2014.
King, Anthony and Crewe, Ivor. *The Blunders of Our Governments*. London: One World, 2014.
Laski, Harold. *The State in Theory and Practice*. New York: Viking, 1935.
Leeson, Peter T. *Anarchy Unbound*. New York: Cambridge University Press, 2014.
Lemieux, Pierre. *In Defense of Bribery*. Auburn: Mises Institute, August 8, 2005.
Leoni, Bruno. *Freedom and the Law*. Indianapolis: Liberty Fund, 1991.
Leroy, Sylvia. "How Giving Are Canadians? The 2004 Generosity Index." *Fraser Forum*, December 2004–January 2005, 9–13.
Lester, Jan. *Escape from Leviathan*. London: St Martin's Press, 2000.
Lieberman, Myron. *The Teacher Unions*. New York: Encounter, 2000.
Lucas, John. "Against Equality." In *Justice and Equality*, ed. Bedau, 138–151. Englewood Cliffs: Prentice-Hall, 1971.
Macey, Jonathan. "On the Failure of Libertarianism to Capture the Popular Imagination." In *Problems of Market Liberalism*, ed. Ellen Frankel Paul. Cambridge: Cambridge U. Press, 1998.
Machan, Tibor R., and James E. Chesher. *A Primer on Business Ethics*. Lanham: Rowman and Littlefield, 2002.
Machiavelli, Nicolo. *The Prince*. New York: Norton, 1992.
McChesney, Fred S. "Government Prohibitions on Volunteer Firefighting in 19th Century America: A Property Rights Perspective." *The Journal of Legal Studies* 15, no. 1 (January 1986): 69–92.
———. *Money for Nothing: Politicians, Rent Extraction and Political Extortion*. Boston: Harvard U. Press, 1997.
Martin, J.C. *Martin's Annual Criminal Code*. Toronto: Canada Law Book, 1971.
Mavor, James. *Niagara in Politics*. New York: Dutton, 1925.

Mencken, H.L. *Prejudices: A Selection*. Ed. James T. Farrell. New York: Vintage, 1958.
Milke, Mark, *Tax Me I'm Canadian*. Calgary: Thomas & Black, 2002.
Mill, J.S. *On Liberty*. London: Penguin Classics, 1988 [1974].
Mises, Ludwig von. *The Anti-Capitalistic Mentality*. Spring Mills: Libertarian Press, 1972.
———. *Omnipotent Government*. Grove City: Libertarian Press, 1985 [New Haven: Yale U. Press, 1944].
———. *Economic Calculation in the Socialist Commonwealth*. Auburn: Mises Institute, 1990.
Molinari, Gustave De. "The Production of Security", Translated by J. Huston McCulloch, *Occasional Papers*, Series 2. ed. R. Ebeling. New York: The Center for Libertarian Studies, May 1977.
Montreal Economic Institute. *Economic Note*, February 2007.
Mueller, Antony, "Coronavirus Crisis Management—What Really Happened and Why It Failed." Medium: May 15, 2020.
Murphy, Liam, and Thomas Nagel. *The Myth of Ownership*. New York: Oxford U. Press, 2002.
Narveson, Jan, *The Libertarian Idea*. Philadelphia: Temple U. Press, 1988.
———. *Ethics in the Business and Professional Life*. U. Waterloo, 1998.
Narveson, Jan. *Moral Matters*, 2nd ed. Peterborough: Broadview, 1999.
———. *Classics of Political and Social Philosophy*. U. Waterloo Dept of Philosophy, 2000a.
———. *Lectures on Political Philosophy*. Waterloo: U. Waterloo Dept of Philosophy, 2000b.
———. *Respecting Persons in Theory and Practice*. Lanham: Rowman &, Littlefield, 2002a.
———. "Liberty and Equality: A Question of Balance". in *Liberty and Equality*, ed. Tibor Machan, 35–59. Stanford: Hoover Institution Press, 2002b.
———. "The Free Market: How to and How Not to Defend It." [unpubl. 2006].
———. *A Fairly Short Introduction to Political Philosophy*. Lanham: Rowman & Littlefield, 2008a.
National Commission on Terrorist Attacks on the US. *The 9/11 Report*. New York: St Martin's Press, 2004.
Nock, Albert Jay. *Our Enemy the State*. San Francisco: Fox & Wilkes, 1994.
Nozick, Robert. *Anarchy, State and Utopia*. New York: Basic Books, 1974.
OECD. "Economic Survey of Canada, 2006." *Policy Brief*, June 2006.

Otteson, James R. *Actual Ethics*. New York: Cambridge U. Press, 2006.
Pipes, Richard. *Property and Freedom*. New York: Random House, 1999.
Pipes, Sally C. *Miracle Cure: How to Solve America's Health Care Crisis and Why Canada Isn't the Answer*. San Francisco: Pacific Research Institute/Vancouver: Fraser Institute, 2004.
Plamenatz, J.P. *Consent, Freedom and Political Obligation*. Oxford: Oxford U. Press, 1968.
Plimer, Ian. *Not for Greens*. Ballarat: Connor Court, 2014.
Plato. *The Republic*. Ed. Cornford. Oxford: Oxford U. Press, 1941 [1970].
Popper, Karl R. *The Poverty of Historicism*. New York: Harper and Row, 1961.
Porter, Bruce. *War and the Rise of the State*. New York: Free Press, 1994.
Rand, Ayn. *Capitalism: The Unknown Idea*. New York: New American Library, 1967.
Rawls, J. "Justice as Fairness." In *Philosophy Politics and Society*, 2nd Series, ed. Peter Laslett and W.G. Runciman, 132–157. Oxford: Blackwell, 1962.
———. *A Theory of Justice*. Cambridge: Harvard U. Press, 1971.
———. *Political Liberalism*. New York: Columbia U. Press, 1993.
Raz, J. *The Authority of Law*. Oxford: Oxford U. Press, 1979.
———. *Morality of Freedom*. Oxford: Oxford U. Press, 1988.
———. *Authority*. New York: New York U. Press, 1990b.
Robb, Graham. *The Discovery of France*. New York: Norton, 2007.
Rockwell, Lew. "The Right to Bribe." *The Free Market* 15, no. 8 (August 1997).
Rothbard, Murray. *Power and Market*. Kansas City: Sheed Andrews & McMeel, 1977b.
———. *For a New Liberty*. New York: Collier, 1978.
———. *The Logic of Action Two*. London: Edward Elgar, 1997.
———. *Education: Free and Compulsory*. Auburn: Mises Institute, 1999.
———. *Man, Economy and State*. Auburn: Mises Institute, 2001.
———. *The Ethics of Liberty*. New York: New York U. Press, 2002.
———. "Libertarians of Will, Intellect and Action." article@mises.org [February9, 2007a].
Sandefur, Timothy. *Property Rights in 21st Century America*. Washington, DC: Cato Institute, 2006.
Schmidtz, David. "Justifying the State." In *For and Against the State*, ed. John T. Sanders and Jan Narveson, 81–97. Lanham: Rowman & Littlefield, 1996.
———. *Elements of Justice*. New York: Cambridge U. Press, 2006.
Schwab, Klaus, and Malleret, Thierry. *Covid 19-The Great Reset*. Geneva: World Economic Forum, 2020.

Schweizer, Peter. *Secret Empires*. New York: Harper, 2019.
Seldon, Arthur. *Capitalism*. Oxford: Blackwell, 1990.
———. *The Dilemma of Democracy*. London: Inst. Econ. Affairs, 2002a.
Selgin, George. *Good Money*. Ann Arbor: U.Michigan Press for the Independent Institute, 2008.
Skoble, Aeon. "Liberty, Policy and Natural Disasters." In *Liberty and Hard Cases*, ed. Tibor Machan, 83–102. Stanford: Hoover Institution, 2002.
Simmons, A. John. *Moral Principles and Political Obligations*. Princeton: Princeton U. Press, 1979.
———. *On the Edge of Anarchy*. Princeton: Princeton U. Press, 1993.
Singer, Peter. *Democracy and Disobedience*. Oxford: Oxford U. Press, 1974.
Smith, Adam. *The Wealth of Nations*, vol. 2. Oxford U: Press, 1976.
Sowell, Thomas. *Affirmative Action Around the World: An Empirical Study*. New Haven: Yale U. Press, 2004.
———. *Black Rednecks and White Liberals*. New York: Encounter Books, 2005.
———. *Intellectuals and Society*. New York: Basic Books, 2011.
———. *Discrimination and Disparities*. New York: Basic Books. 2018.
———. *Charter Schools and Their Enemies*. New York: Basic Books, 2020.
Spooner, Lysander. *The Lysander Spooner Reader*. San Francisco: Fox & Wilkes, 1992.
Stone, Julius. "Justice in the Slough of Equality." *Hastings Law Journal* 29 (May 1978): 995.
Stossel, John. *Give Me a Break*. New York: HarperCollins, 2004.
Sumner, L.W. *The Hateful and the Obscene*. Toronto: U. Toronto Press, 2004.
Sunstein, Cass R. *The Cost Benefit State*. Chicago: American Bar Assoc, 2002.
Svorny, Shirley. "Medical Licensing: An Obstacle to Affordable Quality Care." *Policy Analysis* No. 621. Washington: Cato Institute, 2008.
Symonds, Richard. *Oxford and Empire*. Oxford: Clarendon Press, 1991.
Tamanaha, Brian Z. *Law as a Means to an End*. Cambridge: Cambridge U. Press, 2006.
Taylor, Michael. *The Possibility of Cooperation*. Cambridge: Cambridge U. Press, 1987.
Treitschke, Heinrich von. *Politics*. ed. Hans Kohn, New York: Harcourt Brace and World, 1963.
Tullock, Gordon. *Government Failure: A Primer in Public Choice*. Washington, DC: Cato Institute, 2002.
Veldhuis, Nick and Palacios, Milagros. "Canadians Celebrate Tax Freedom Day on June 19." *Fraser Forum*, July–August, 2006.
Waldron, Jeremy. *Liberal Rights*. Cambridge: Cambridge U. Press, 1993.

West, E.G. "The Political Economy of American Public-School Legislation." *10 Journal of Law and Economics* 10: 101–128, 1967.

———. *Education and the State.* Indianapolis: Liberty Fund, 1994.

Wolff, R.P. *In Defense of Anarchism.* New York. Harper & Row, 1970.

Zakaria, Fareed. *The Future of Freedom.* New York: Norton, 2003.

Zumwalt, Robert. "The Global Minimum Corporate Tax Exposes the G7's Hypocrisy." https.mises.org, July 1, 2021.

# 4
# Democracy

We have thus weighed in the balance several of the more influential recent apologies for the authority of the state and so far, found them wanting. In this chapter we shall address the question as to how democracy might or might not be a source of the state's authority, which is to ask with Dworkin, what it is that entitles the rulers to rule, and why it is that a majority gives them the power to rule over those who didn't vote for them (1986, 191). I have already answered the first of Dworkin's questions, namely nothing, and the short answer to the second is that it doesn't, an answer I shall attempt to argue for in the course of this chapter.

## 4.1 Singer on Democracy

In *Democracy and Disobedience* (1974), Peter Singer explores the question as to whether the fact that a government is more democratic would lend greater moral weight to claims that its decisions ought to be obeyed. While we shall refer to several points that Singer makes in developing his view, we shall be less interested in the sorts of obligations we might

© The Author(s), under exclusive license to Springer Nature Switzerland AG 2022

G. Booker, *Coercion, Authority and Democracy*, Palgrave Studies in Classical Liberalism, https://doi.org/10.1007/978-3-031-16883-3_4

or might not have towards a putatively democratic order, even though Dworkin thought that his questions raised the problem of the legitimacy of coercive power which in turn piggybacks on another, namely political obligation (ibid.). Our concern will be rather, given what Singer has to say about democracy, why anyone would think it had enough going for it as a way of deciding anything to even consider putting a new spin on the old question about political obligation. On the latter issue I would agree with Pateman that arguments for political obligation have ceased to be of much interest (1979, 194), or with Simmons, who supports Baier's view that the main question about political obligation is whether there is any such thing (1979, 3).

The Byzantine workings of governing bodies at Oxford seem to have inspired several interesting reflections on democratic decision-making. For example, Black devotes the last chapter of his *Theory of Committees and Elections* to the earlier work on elections of the famous nineteenth-century Student of Christ Church, the Rev. Charles Dodgson (aka. Lewis Carroll). In a similar vein, Singer asks us to contrast different ways of governing an institution within a college, in this case a common room association. Of course, he is not concerned with any such association, many of which have doubtless existed, as it were, *ab universitate condita*, and been governed more by tradition than written codes. As well as having, like most governing bodies, considerably predated the advent of the present generation of college members, they do have the virtue of being a much simpler model of government to examine.

Singer thus asks us to consider three models of such associations. The first apparently exemplifies the *Fuehrerprinzip*, ruled as it is by a self-appointed leader who according to oral history was installed in his present post by some sort of coup. The leader avoided serious challenges to his authority by not only having powerful allies within the association, but also by supposedly making good on his promise to rule in the interests of all. Under the second model, decisions are made in the interests of the members by that member, who according to tradition and rule is most senior, and who apparently rules without any of the intimidation which accompanied the accession to power of the first. Finally, in the third governance model, decisions are taken along democratic lines, that is, by majority vote.

Singer then asks that we consider the case of a dissenting member who disagrees with the decision of the common room to subscribe to a newspaper which he considers racist. When the dissenter sees that neither the leaders under the first two models, nor the majority who carry the vote under the third are inclined to change their views, he decides to take the law into his own hands and remove the newspaper from the common room. The purpose of Singer's thought experiment is to explore the question as to whether there is something about the democratic way in which decisions are taken under the third model which makes it harder to justify the dissenter's disobedience than in the first two models, where decisions are taken by one man on behalf of the members. As Singer puts it, although the dissenter flouts the customary decision procedure in each case, we should be able to discover whether the fact that a decision was taken democratically under the third model confers upon it a special privilege not available to the other procedures (1974, 17).

One of the common responses from *The Crito* onwards to such acts of disobedience is to say that it is wrong to disobey, because even the dissenter has benefited in some way from the organization he disobeys. As Socrates points out, the state has nurtured us from before the time we arrived on this earth by regulating the marriage of our parents and our subsequent education and upbringing (Plato 1953, 380). However, Singer responds that just about any sort of state could make a similar claim on our allegiance. In the case of the governing body of the common room, all three versions could claim to govern in the best interests of their members, a claim which Singer thinks reasonable to take at face value. The question is whether a democratic government of the sort envisaged by Singer's third model, as opposed to the Athenian democracy which prevailed in Socrates's time, is somehow more deserving of our allegiance.

Singer outlines the views of other commentators since Plato who have sought to ground our allegiance to the state on some supposedly relevant property of democracy such as popular sovereignty or equality. Common to many of these views is the claim that the legitimacy of popular government and of any obligations allegedly incumbent upon its citizens is derived from some form of consent on the part of the governed. The doctrine of consent as such goes back at least to *The Crito*, where Socrates argues that if you do not agree with the way "the laws" order your society, you may take your business elsewhere. But if you stay, you can be considered to have accepted the deal offered by the state and are not entitled to ignore your obligations owed to it, even if doing so should result in your death, as was the case with Socrates who claimed that to live under the state order implies that you have agreed to obey when so ordered (ibid., 381).

As to the merits of Socrates's take it or leave it principle, Nozick asks why it is you may opt out of the state by emigrating, but not out of its coercive social arrangements (1974, 173). With respect to his third model, where members of the common room form a governing committee with each member having an equal vote, Singer holds that its most salient feature is that of fairness. By that he seems to mean that power is equally divided with each person having only one vote. Such a franchise is supposed to be fairer than, say, that proposed by Mill, who argued against extending the vote to the illiterate or those on welfare rolls. On the other hand, those demonstrating a superior education or station in life might have more than one vote to avoid having the great unwashed pass legislation unfavourable to the elite (1958, 135, 139). Of course, Mill was speaking of the national electorate, rather than an Oxford common room, which constitutes some sort of meritocracy.

We might still ask, however, in what respect the third model association is fairer than the other two where one individual makes decisions on behalf of the other members. While there may be grounds for questioning the method by which the leader of the first association acceded to his position, it is not immediately clear what is unfair about a rule which says that government of the association is in the hands of the senior member, provided, one may imagine, that there is general agreement about such a rule including the determination of seniority. Singer in fact seems to admit that we may well be hard put to demonstrate by argument and may simply have to assume that the more democratic model of governance is fairer, and that it therefore has a greater claim on our allegiance.

The question of fairness seems connected to that of legitimacy, though with respect to the view that only popular governments can possess legitimate authority, Singer observed that legitimacy can be notoriously difficult to agree upon. This may have to do with Hare's view that acknowledging a government as lawful is not to state any facts about it (1967, 172), though Singer responds that even if we agreed we should obey governments which are legitimate, we would still need to show what it is for a government to be legitimate, as opposed to those that aren't (ibid., 23), implying that this might be a rather tall order. Hare himself suggests that to ascribe lawfulness to a government is simply to express one's allegiance to that government, which one does for moral, prudential, or political reasons, rather than legal ones. In declaring such allegiance, I agree to treat its laws as binding, and like Socrates, will not complain if I end up in prison (ibid., 168–169).

Singer does attempt to clarify the sense in which the third model association is fairer. It no doubt stops short of being fair in any absolute sense, if indeed there is one to be had. Rather it is fair in the sense that a compromise is fair, given the circumstances, as when we are forced to draw lots to decide some outcome. A particular compromise might be less than fair, because it results in someone doing more than her fair share, as in Singer's example of the woman tending her baby every weeknight, while the husband only does so on the weekends. Of course, it may be that even this case is not as unfair as first appears. Perhaps there are any number of reasons why in any given situation domestic chores are divided the way they are, having possibly to do with work, domestic and otherwise, performed by each spouse according to their respective aptitudes. Indeed, it could turn out to be an instance of that famous principle of fairness where more will be demanded from the capable to distribute to those less so.

Again, Singer emphasizes that the feature of the third association, which supposedly makes it harder to justify disobedience is that it is founded on a fair compromise. Moreover, he argues, the democratic alternative, where each member has an equal say in decisions, is preferable, for example, to Malatesta's anarchism, whose solution to the impossibility of ever getting any agreement as to who is going to run the show is not to bother having one to run in the first place. Further, with respect to Mill's meritocracy, Singer believes that it is not so much a question of its being unfair, but rather imprudent, because it could prove to be a hard sell, especially to the uneducated. For there is a sense in which attempting to fine-tune voting along Mill's lines amounts to pursuing an unattainable level of fairness, the net result of which will be much political unhappiness. In that case the compromise represented by one man, one vote would be preferable (ibid., 35).

Another reason why the third association is held to represent something of a fair compromise is because it doesn't favour any one party to a disagreement which prevents it from becoming irreconcilable (ibid.). Again, it is not clear why this is necessarily superior to the second association, where the decisions are made by the senior member, and where the basis for his right to decide, which may pass on to others who in their turn qualify for election by seniority, is understood and accepted as appropriate. Political differences will arise, and the decision procedure may have little to do with heading off an all-out brawl. During a difficult period before World War I, Gilbert reports that Churchill apparently did not think that one man one vote would be sufficient to bridge the great political differences of the day and set up a regular dinner club where members of the government and opposition could meet and settle their differences more amicably (2006, 48).

In fact, as many have pointed out, there is often little satisfaction to be had from being able to cast a vote, which led Churchill, for example, to seek other ways of exploring political differences. For example, voting is known to generate paradoxes, such as explained by Narveson, where three different voters assign different ranks to three alternatives with the result that no clear majority results (2008, 123). One solution to this sort of problem is to hold some sort of backroom gathering, no doubt reminiscent of Churchill's Other Club where perhaps, as Narveson adds, those having more influence than the one man one vote principle might suggest will cajole or bully a solution out of those with less influence (ibid.).

Another mechanism for managing democracy, as Mr. Putin would no doubt call it, is vote trading or logrolling which is often thought to be morally wrong because it distorts the legislator's true preferences. But as Tullock observes, most people know it is what goes on in the backrooms that counts, since legislation is inseparable from deals and horse-trading (2002, 30). Nor, as Tullock reminds us, is logrolling confined to the US; some of Churchill's political heirs under Mrs. Thatcher had to support policies they didn't like to receive party support for those they did.

Indeed, according to Tullock, logrolling is as widely used as it is morally condemned by the public (ibid., 79).

Thus, when one considers the wide array of human institutions with which one has dealings, not only does it seem that one rarely negotiates on equal terms in the way that Singer's fair compromise recommends, but it is also unclear why that would necessarily be a desirable state of affairs. An airline captain could be bound to follow the democratic wishes of his passengers, or for that matter draw lots, which Singer thinks is the fairest decision method, but it is far from obvious that to do so would be either practicable or sensible. If members of the second association become dissatisfied with some aspect of rule by the senior member, perhaps because it had led to a declining quality of decisions by people who had stayed on past their prime, then they might be motivated to explore alternative models of governance, one of which might be Singer's one man one vote. But it still isn't clear why any such alternative is fairer than its predecessor, or why it is easier to justify disobeying the rulings of the senior member, as opposed to the majority of members in a democratic body.

Nor is it apparently sufficient for Singer that a voting structure such as that of the third association represents what he considers a fair compromise. Not only must we have fair or equal opportunity for participation, but we must guarantee fair outcomes as well. Minority groups within the association must not feel that they get the short end of the stick. For example, Singer asks us to consider the case of a common room consisting mostly of white members and a handful of non-whites. Because a majority carries the day, we have at least in theory the possibility of a vote splitting along racial lines, with little that the non whites could do about it since they are in a minority. Thus, in addition to the decision procedure being a fair compromise, minorities of whatever sort should not feel they have been unfairly dealt with (ibid., 43).

Perhaps it is worth recalling at this point that the dissenter, whose grounds for expressing his dissent in the way he did are supposedly diminished under a democratic dispensation, was a minority of one, who disagreed with the common room's decision to subscribe to a newspaper, which he claimed was prejudiced against the black minority (ibid., 15).

If neither the dissenter, nor those who voted against him on the newspaper issue, were to change their minds, then it is conceivable that he would continue to be a minority of one every time this or some related matter came to a vote, in which case he might well feel unfairly treated because of repeatedly losing.

Thus, even if we could make any sense of what a fair compromise amounts to in the first place, it is far from clear what is involved in adjudicating the fairness or otherwise of a pattern of decisions, as Singer thinks we need to do to ensure that what began as fair remains so. Voter paradoxes and logrolling seem to be part and parcel of various democratic arrangements, but does that mean they are to count as fair compromises, even though one of them has often been considered immoral? Who is to decide whether there is, as so often claimed, some systemic unfairness, such as voter paradoxes, or discrimination? What would it be like for a particular claim of unfairness on the part of the dissenter or some other minority to be thought to have merit, or not, as the case may be? If that too is decided by majority vote, then the dissenter could lose again, and for all we know, deservedly so.

Singer admits that in any large society, there will be groups who allege unfair treatment, a matter which will need to be adjudicated in each case. But this in turn raises the question as to whose judgement will count, that of the minority complainant or the majority. The reason we cannot leave it to the majority, supposedly, is that this would make the majority judge in its own cause (ibid., 44), so the cards must be stacked in favour of the complainant, and we may just have to hope there aren't too many wrong decisions. Of course, it is far from obvious why this solution doesn't just as easily fall afoul of the same principle of natural justice: *nemo iudex in causa sua*, especially when we take account of Dahl's observation that minorities more often threaten majorities than the reverse (1985, 27). Thus, on the one hand Singer thinks there is no solution to claims about overall unfairness, yet any there are ought to be resolved in favour of the complainant, if for no other reason that we might face endless disobedience on the part of those who consider themselves wronged. This again reminds us of Mill's prudential worries about a restricted franchise, or Binmore, who is one of those who favours conservative reforms because they are less likely to destabilize society, though we need to be on our guard, since our present standard of living depends on a system of rather fragile customs (1995, 4–5). However, Mises reminds us that from the social instability of the eighteenth century, for example, resulting from a surplus of people on the land, modern capitalism arose. Thus, from the efforts of some of the social outcasts of the day to provide work for themselves, industries arose to produce goods for the masses rather than luxuries for the few (2000, 3).

As for Singer's view that considerations of prudence might suggest we favour minorities, adjudicators specializing in complaints from those who claim to have been dealt poor hands in the great crap game of life have been known on occasion to find against a minority complainant. The Ontario Human Rights Commission once dismissed the complaints of a physics professor at the University of Toronto that he had been unfairly passed over for a permanent post, though it took some 6 years to reach that finding. Fairness seems never to have quite recovered from the popular wisdom that it largely exists in the eye of the beholder. Perhaps it is not a robust enough notion to carry the increased load which Singer places upon it. Although we might be able to get a rough idea of the sense in which one man one vote might be said to be fair, for example in the sense, as Narveson puts it, of an equal sharing of political power (2008a, 115), it is not clear why the dissenter can claim that the outcomes of supposedly fair voting must meet evermore stringent tests of fairness.

### 4.1.1 Voting as Quasi Consent

Assuming for the present that Singer's enthusiasm for fairness has not got the better of him, and that we can coherently talk of some sort of fair decision procedure as being characteristic of his third model, let us then see how Singer thinks participation might be relevant to the justification of disobedience. If we participate in the decision-making of something like the third model association, we cannot when it suits us pretend we haven't done so, ignoring votes that may go against us, as the dissenter claims to do. Following Socrates, obedience is seen to be required in exchange for the benefits conferred by the Laws. Moreover, Singer proposes fine-tuning the doctrine of consent, the traditional source of duties of obedience, along the lines of *quasi* rather than the *tacit* consent which Locke thought we could be presumed to have given to the government of that dominion where we enjoyed life or property (1960, 347–348).

With respect to the theory of tacit or unexpressed consent, there seems little reason to think that it may be any more promising as a ground of obligation than express consent, about which Simmons noted that there seemed to be a glaring absence of people who had expressly consented. As for tacit consent, Simmons concludes that very few of us appear to have consented tacitly either (1979, 79, 93). The question is whether Singer's notion of quasi consent is different enough from its predecessors to escape a similar fate. As an example of this quasi, or *as if* consent, Singer asks us to consider the case where we participate in a drinking party, with each round being bought by one of the participants in turn. When it is your turn, you would be rightly thought to have acted badly, if you simply got up and walked away. You are not bound by any consent, acknowledged to the group or yourself, yet by participating in the ritual you may incur an obligation, which you cannot reject on the grounds that you never consented (ibid., 49).

Similarly, the dissenter by participating in the decision process incurs a quasi obligation to abide by the majority decision, and one cannot after the fact walk away from the process and pretend never to have participated. Indeed, the only way one can act as if one had no obligation is to declare at the outset that one has no intention of reciprocating (ibid.). Similarly in the political context, one can be presumed to have consented if one participates in the voting ritual and doesn't declare that this does not signal consent (ibid., 51). Further, Singer believes that the legal doctrine of estoppel can help clarify the way in which quasi consent can give rise to obligations. Estoppel is akin to a promise, and thus one is estopped from denying that one consented once one voluntarily agreed to participate (ibid.).

With respect to the notion of estoppel, Green agrees that it could explain the way in which, for example, by my sitting in a restaurant and ordering a meal, I can reasonably be held to have consented to pay the price shown on the menu, although I have not explicitly promised to do so, and may have no intention of doing so. Or for Jasay this amounts to a non-simultaneous credit (2002, 42). While Green agrees that estoppel might help explain obligations under this sort of forward contract, thus providing an account of one type of consent, he is less sure that it is available to justify a duty to obey the state (1988, 164). Singer cites Lord Birkenhead's opinion, to the effect that estoppel addresses the harm that B may suffer as the result of his believing that a certain state of affairs existed as the result of A's words and conduct.

However, according to Green, democratic theory assumes that the state is not there to serve its own interests but rather those of its citizens (ibid.). Or, as Jasay claims, the state is not a party to the contract, but rather an agent of the principals who contracted with it to serve their interests; though as we saw above, the state seems to have enormous discretion for an agent under contract, acting more often like one of the parties, and the dominant party at that (ibid., 50–51). Green thus rightly denies Singer's appeal to estoppel, since, unlike the restaurant situation, people vote without relying on the compliance of others, so there is no reason to think that voting should be taken as a sign of consent to or acceptance of the state's authority (ibid., 172).

On the other hand, Plamenatz has also upheld the view that voting is tantamount to consenting where one hands over authority to those elected (1968, 170). Simmons, however, does not think it reasonable to see voting as an act of consent to the authority of the successful candidate. Rather he thinks that most people are unaware of what voting supposedly commits them to. Indeed, Simmons goes on to argue that to the extent that voting is seen as a duty, so much so that some states make it compulsory, the duties of citizenship must be on a different footing from any consent involved in voting (1993, 224). This divorce of political obligation from voting is further underscored by the fact that the state does not consider our political obligations to be contingent upon whether we have voted or not. Simmons concludes that election rules and the rationale given for them do not underwrite any obligation to those in power (ibid.). Thus, *pace* Singer, voting is not an *as if* or quasi consent, and if others act on the assumption that we have so consented, that is their problem, or as Simmons puts it, if we later deny having consented, others have not suffered the harm Birkenhead thought estoppel could address.

But as Simmons points out, it is a rather odd feature of Singer's view that our obligations from voting are a function of the beliefs which others form based on our participation, suggesting that our obligations may be restricted to those who happen to have those beliefs (ibid., n. 13). Nelson adds the further point that we do not need the notion of consent to explain the point of voting, if it has one, as Singer seems to suggest. Given the highly structured and coercive context of the state, people may vote because they might as well try and influence whatever result they will be stuck with (1980, 44). Of course, as Narveson has reminded us, it isn't just a matter of whether your preferred candidate wins, but also how much her winning will depend on your vote, which is very little (2008a, 124–125).

As we saw earlier, Singer thought that we could avoid our obligations by clearly announcing our non-participation at the outset. Others of course could do likewise, in which case the prospects for voting also look rather bleak with a majority vote leading to nothing (ibid., 55). Unfortunately, Singer does not go on to explain why we should shrink from a democratic meltdown if that in fact was a likely outcome. After all, on his own account we have two other reasonably efficient governance models to fall back on. Rather than telling us why we have reason to fear the breakdown of democracy, Singer repeats his charge that the dissenter is free riding on the majority, regardless of whether he has declared his non-participation, since if everyone did that, there would be no democracy.

### 4.1.2 Fair Play as a Solution to Consent

Again, it doesn't seem entirely clear what is or is not unfair about the dissenter's actions. Much of Singer's argument is restatement of Hart's principle of fair play discussed earlier, namely that those who have submitted to rules governing a joint enterprise have a right to a similar submission from other beneficiaries. We already saw that the attempt to clothe this principle in the mantle of estoppel added nothing of significance; as Green points out, if voters feel obliged because of possible effects on others, consent should not be confused with anything that may or may not follow from it (ibid., 171–172).

However, as Simmons reminds us, Hart's principle of fair play, also endorsed by Singer, is designed to get around the difficulties posed by the consent doctrine, which was embarrassed by a lack of subjects who had in fact consented. Fair play promises to provide such a general account, for simply by participating one incurs obligations (1979, 117). Thus, Singer at this point in his argument emphasizes participation rather than consent. The fact that we participate in the decision-making process, and receive benefits thereby, makes it harder to justify non-compliance, much harder than under the first two common room associations where decisions are left up to a leader. To refuse to be obliged by the deliverances of a fair democratic compromise is to take advantage of those who accepted them.

We earlier discussed Nozick's response to the fair play principle, where he argued that we were not bound to cooperate with such schemes as a neighbourhood entertainment system. Nozick's PA system was put in place by only some of the neighbours which might suggest from Singer's point of view that it was less entitled to call upon contributions from everyone. But if the consent doctrine faces a paucity of consenters, then the fair play principle is going to have to explain what sorts of things constitute cooperative schemes, and what it is to accept a benefit and be beholden in return. In the case of public goods such as a PA system, Nozick is right that the principle should be rejected (1974, 93). Or, in Simmons's more measured assessment, even at the level of the neighbourhood association, *pace* Hart and Rawls, setting up a public venture does not necessarily confer any right to cooperation from the non-excludable beneficiaries (ibid., 136).

As we saw earlier, when we attempt to ramp up from what might or might not be true at the level of the neighbourhood association to the larger polity, Simmons rightly concludes that it is unreasonable to hold that actual political communities function on anything like this basis, which is to say that whatever lessons could possibly be drawn from the association have little bearing on the political state, which for most of us is not a cooperative enterprise in the relevant sense. Indeed, as Simmons observes, people who see themselves as fellow cooperators in a large state enterprise are few and far between (ibid., 140).

So far then, neither consent nor fair play seems to have offered much promise as a way of explaining what Singer has in mind by participation. Yet he would doubtless reply that participating in voting in and of itself meant that we could not pretend we had not done so, and therefore ignore the outcome. But as Green pointed out with respect to the failure of Singer's estoppel argument, it is difficult to say anything about the significance of voting, Plamenatz's conviction to the contrary notwithstanding (1968, 171). According to Simmons, voting is better seen as a matter of expressing preferences rather than consenting. Voters are presented with options, rather like condemned prisoners who may be offered a choice as to how they are to die. Just as the prisoners could not be said to consent to either option, since they despise both, the voter chooses the least unappealing of those on offer. But this is only a matter of preference, not one of agreeing to hand over authority to the candidate (1993, 223). Moreover, if participation amounts to consent, Nelson is not so sure that participation is a good thing, because having handed over the keys of the kingdom participants have little say thereafter (1980, 45).

## 4.2 Democratic Rules

As well as any question of unfairness to individuals who may have gone along with the majority vote, Singer claimed that some of the unfairness resulted from violating some rule essential to democracy. Singer's next task then is to explain which rules are supposedly essential to democracy, and which not, to determine the proper role for disobedience within a democratic organization. We noted above that that Singer had already observed that majority rule in and of itself was no guarantee that a democratic compromise was as fair as it should be. Now he proposes to clarify what sort of rights an individual has against a majority decision, such that if those rights are infringed, there may well be grounds for disobeying the will of the majority. In his view there are some rights which are essential to the democratic decision procedure, such as freedom of speech, voting and assembly, which if prejudiced by the association, could undermine its authority, and make acts of disobedience justifiable.

But even if we assume with Singer that the decision procedure is as sure a foundation for fair government as we can hope to find, and superior to the other models because of the degree to which it permits participation, it is not clear how we are going to separate the rights essential to democracy from those that are not. Apparently it requires judgement to discern the difference (ibid., 69), but not the judgement of the decision procedure, it seems, since as Singer ruled in the case of aggrieved minorities, the decision procedure cannot be the source of its own justification (ibid., 68). Since he doesn't think that a higher tribunal such as a supreme court is a workable solution, it will simply be up to the judgement of the individual to decide whether a right is fundamental to democracy and whether it has been infringed.

If indeed it is up to the individual, there seems to be nothing to prevent someone from deciding that some of the rights Singer is inclined to treat as non-essential, such as freedom of religion or gay rights, are in their judgement essential. Indeed, it looks as though Singer is prepared to countenance a situation where a perceived infringement of these supposedly less important rights would constitute grounds for disobedience (ibid., 69), something again which will be up to the individual to decide. The individual can decide, according to Singer, whether she has got a fair hearing, and short of coercion, may attempt to persuade the majority of that fact. It is a matter for individual judgement again as to whether one has gotten a fair hearing, since there seems to be no independent way of deciding the issue (ibid., 80). If we think we have not, we are apparently entitled to such disobedience as will allow us to fairly present our case.

Of course, how much disobedience is enough to do the job will presumably also be an individual judgement call, though Singer thinks that as famous a dissenter as Bertrand Russell can confuse acceptance of his views with getting a proper hearing (ibid., 76). As an example of disobedience which goes further than necessary to protest lack of a fair hearing, Singer mentions filing false registration papers for military service. Even though such disobedience is non-violent, it is coercive rather than persuasive (ibid., 83). If others attempted to mess with the system in this way, it could supposedly lead to a democratic failure, something we were earlier enjoined to avoid at all costs.

However, it seems odd to worry about not doing the bidding of the state, which we consider the paradigm case of a coercive institution, as being coercive, and prima facie wrong. It is the state which threatens various and sundry unpleasantries to those who fail to carry out its orders, even if they are not persuaded that it has any authority to make those orders in the first place. Edmundson, for example, thought we had a duty not to interfere with the state's administrative directives, or as Singer might have put it, not to screw up the system, but Edmundson does not appear to suggest that the reason we should refrain is that doing so would be coercive. Perhaps the source of some of Singer's difficulty here is that he has slipped from talking about a small association to talking about the state, although he has yet to show that anything instructive about the latter can be derived from the former.

Indeed, if we are talking about the state, we have already argued that Edmundson has not shown that we owe the state even as much as cooperating in its administration, which is to say we are under no obligation to correctly register for the draft or supply information required by the census, or whatever else the state believes it needs to fulfil its supposed mandate. Singer is right that this sort of interference with the functioning of the state goes beyond the persuasion he thinks we should be engaged in. Of course, he readily forgets that the state is not remotely like the debating society model of the common room association, and while we could attempt to persuade our local MP that we ought not to have to comply with some directive, most of us have better things to do.[1] No doubt Singer thinks we should make the effort because if other groups in the community did likewise, we would face the implosion of democracy which is tantamount to solving our disputes by force rather than reason (ibid., 83).

Again, Singer seems a good deal more troubled about the possibility of a democratic meltdown than I am. There is no reason to consider

[1] I did in fact e-mail many articles to local provincial and federal representatives critical of many aspects of government policy on Covid but never received any acknowledgement. Perhaps they didn't wish to suffer defenestration from the caucus, unlike some of their more courageous colleagues.

not complying with the state's directives as either coercive or verging on the violent, which is to say it is not on the same footing as burning down the *Reichstag*. Nor do I think that there is much hope of separating democracy from the interventionist or *dirigiste* state, as Mises did, which is to say that the only way to get rid of the latter may well be to get rid of the former.[2] If the left could bring democracy into disrepute by burning their draft cards, Singer thinks that widespread disobedience might also encourage those towards the other end of the political spectrum to dismantle the welfare state (ibid.). Well, I suppose it might, though if he has in mind inundating the bureaucracy with illegitimate welfare claims, I'm not sure why such a strategy would be peculiar to the right. Libertarians, on the other hand, can be hard to categorize as either right or left, but are likely to engage in the sort of persuasion Singer approves of, in this case, to persuade their audiences that welfare legislation is but another example of state interventionism, which is to say, as Mises put it, any measure by government attempting to override consumer preferences in the market (2000, 40). Inspired by Voltaire, Bastiat also described the state as the great fiction enabling all to live at the expense of others (1995, 144). More recently Hazlitt has written in the same vein that, since the government has nothing to give which it hasn't taken from somebody else, welfare is simply a matter of stealing from Peter to pay Paul (1969, 209).

Thus, it is not clear what one would have to do to make welfare legislation unworkable, since in the libertarian view it already is. As to what the government can do to help the poor, according to Rothbard, it simply needs to get out of the way to release the productive energies of rich and poor alike, with a resulting enormous benefit for all (1978, 162). Rothbard lists various ways government could increase the welfare of the poorest, namely by removing its own regulatory roadblocks from finding their own solutions, such as minimum wage laws, trade union and licensing regulations. He mentions the case of Dr Thomas Matthew who set up a multiracial hospital in the black section of Jamaica, Queens, arranging his own bus transportation because the city system was inadequate for patients and staff. The City of New York put his buses out of

[2] cp. Mises (2000, 99).

business because they did not have a license, as they did another low cost hospital Matthew set up in Harlem, citing fire violations.[3] One can only assume that Singer sees merit in such obstacles because they are the result of a democratic decision procedure, and any attempt to by-pass them, as people like Dr Matthew did, will no doubt strike Singer as misguided and coercive.

If Singer is concerned about coercion, supposedly bordering on the violent, he need look no further than one of the above roadblocks, especially favoured by the left, namely trade unions, whose privileges vouchsafed by government, according to Rothbard, prevent poorer workers from improving their lot (ibid.). As Mises also remarked, a union is granted the right to resort to violence and disruption against entrepreneurs and those of their own members who do not go along with a strike (2000, 67, 87), which leads Henderson to recommend removing their legal privileges, and defend those wanting to work against those who would stand in their way (2002a, 111). While, according to Hazlitt, such violence is tolerated in the name of supposed justice for workers (1973, 142), in Mises's view, what will raise the standard of living is not union activity, but increased investment (ibid., 87–88).

As we saw, Singer thinks that we need to uphold the principle of democratic decision-making and not simply ignore it when it results in unwarranted restrictions on individual freedom. This is not to say that it does not have some shortcomings as a principle. According to Singer, one of the characteristic weaknesses of democracy is that because it simply counts votes, it is unable to take account of the intensity with which some views are held. It might be considered a much fairer compromise if the degree of dissent could be more accurately registered. We noted earlier that Mill thought it a good idea that democratic voting reflects levels of education or political intelligence, a view not favoured by Singer because he thought it might have trouble garnering popular support. Perhaps the proposal to take into account voter intensity would run into similar problems, to say nothing of the fact that it seems to have even

[3] University of Waterloo students, who once tried to set up a low-cost bus service, found out that government stumbling blocks remain much as they were in 1960s New York; such enterprises are a privilege reserved by the state, as Dr Matthew no doubt could have told them, to inefficient but protected monopolies.

less to recommend it than Mill's meritocracy, since political intensity, as well as perhaps being hard to measure, may not be worth measuring in the first place.

Singer also defends his view of democracy against Russell, who claims it is essential to civil disobedience to flout the law which one believes unjust, and to suffer the consequences, than to take the legal way out, for example, in the case of the draft dodger, to apply for exemption as a conscientious objector. For Singer, Russell's position betrays a misunderstanding of democracy, in particular the democratic decision procedure. Accepting the majority decision does not mean simply acquiescing in the law passed by the majority, as Russell thinks, but rather that one respects the process. One may make one's opposition to war as widely known as possible, using all legitimate means available to change the law in question, but breaking the law undermines the democratic process.

### 4.2.1 Wollheim and the Paradox of Democracy

Curiously enough, in a footnote to his claim that Russell has misunderstood the democratic decision procedure, Singer levels a similar charge against Wollheim with respect to the democratic paradox referred to in the latter's well-known paper. Although Wollheim does think there is something paradoxical about the fact that when we vote for option A, the democratic machine may deliver option B as the one favoured by the majority of voters, he spends the rest of his paper explaining the supposed paradox away. If anything, Singer may in turn have misunderstood Wollheim, who seems to agree with Singer on the need for maintaining the democratic decision procedure, or democratic machine, as Wollheim calls it. Wollheim arrives at his formulation of the paradox of democracy, after having rejected the solution that in voting for option A, the individual voter was merely expressing his want, as opposed to recommending the best course of action. A voter is indeed faced with the odd situation that he is committed both by choice to A and by democratic result to B (1962, 78–79). If Wollheim had simply left us with this paradox, as one might perhaps have expected, given the somewhat sceptical tone of his opening remarks about democracy, Singer's hasty dismissal might have been in order, but Wollheim does attempt to resolve the paradox in a manner not incompatible with Singer's position.

Again, Wollheim canvasses a couple of possibilities, first that one's support for A is hypothetical and contingent upon the majority read-out provided by the machine. Wollheim rejects this explanation on the grounds that a majority vote would only mean something if it aggregated unconditional choices, as opposed to hypothetical ones, which could be more easily set aside in the face of an opposing majority choice. The second possible solution is to consider the individual who supports A as making an unequivocal moral recommendation, whereas the machine in supporting B is simply offering a counsel of prudence, which A can then agree to without appearing to give up on the moral convictions which led him to vote for A in the first place.

Despite its initial plausibility, Wollheim similarly rejects the second solution to the paradox, since for him belief in democracy amounts to more than a readiness dictated by prudence to fall into line behind the democratic machine, should the majority vote differently; he is in fact a born-again democrat (ibid., 84). Given that neither of the proposed solutions, which involve discounting the force of voting for either A or B, prove satisfactory, Wollheim trots out his *deus ex machina*: we can avoid a head-on clash between A and B, if we distinguish direct from indirect moral principles. To say that murder is wrong is a direct moral principle, whereas the belief that it is right for the state to command what it does is indirect or oblique. The citizen who votes that A ought to be enacted and is later outvoted by the majority which favours B, derives his support of B from an oblique principle, namely the principle of democracy.

However, it is not surprising that Wollheim finds this distinction rather unsatisfactory (ibid., 85). Even if the voter can comfortably support both A and B because of what Wollheim claims is an important difference in their respective derivations, whatever B is seems always guaranteed to carry the day, since it is underwritten not only by an oblique principle, but also one that has some prior claim on obedience, such as the principle of democracy. To those who are not persuaded, and who are inclined to the view that there is no way around the incompatibility of holding that both A and B ought to be the case, Wollheim asks us, for example, to consider the claim that Jews ought to be given privileged treatment. Such a claim can be uttered directly, perhaps as an expression of Jewish chauvinism, or obliquely, where it follows from some facts about Nazi Germany together with a principle that the persecuted merit special attention.

Wollheim is right of course that one proposition can lend itself to rather varied interpretations, depending on context and supporting data. But even in the case of a direct principle we have to supply a context within which it is to be understood. The chauvinistic interpretation of the claim for special treatment of the Jews, for example, could just as easily be the result of a majority vote, and thus result from an institutional action, perhaps that of a Zionist group. Coupled with the relevant facts of Jewish history, and the principle of democracy, the less favoured or chauvinist interpretation could also be said to have an oblique derivation, if that is what Wollheim thinks is important. In response to a second objection that one could not coherently opt for the implementation of both A and B, knowing that simultaneous implementation of both is impossible, Wollheim replies that voting for A does not commit one personally to implementing A. If I am committed to A, then I am committed to strongly advocating on A's behalf, but once votes are cast, I am also committed to swinging my support behind the majority vote for B, so that for Wollheim it does make sense to say that one is committed to two different outcomes (ibid., 87).

If there really isn't a paradox in the theory of democracy after all, as Wollheim claims to have shown, it isn't clear why Singer thought that Wollheim's discussion was another example of Russell's mistake of failing to understand the nature of democracy. While Singer may have had cause to disagree with the first part of Wollheim's paper where he presents what he takes to be the findings of social choice theory about democratic voting procedures, he has little reason to be concerned with Wollheim's proposed resolution of the paradox, which would only lend further support to Singer's own position. Of course, Singer may well have thought that Wollheim was wrong to suggest that there was a paradox about democracy in the first place. In the absence of a fuller discussion by Singer, the question about whether Wollheim was more friend than foe need not detain us, nor would it in our view particularly redound to Wollheim's credit, should he turn out to be the former rather than the latter. With respect to his formulation of the paradox, as one way to characterize what is wrong with democracy it has something to recommend it, though his proposed solution is unconvincing.

Wollheim's view that one's enthusiasm for one's own vote is always under tight control seems to be at odds with his earlier position that there would be no point in aggregating votes that were based on less than unconditional support. Similarly, with respect to majority vote B, Wollheim had earlier claimed that there was a commitment on the part of the genuine democrat to the deliverances of the democratic machine. But when he presents his resolution of the paradox, support for B is also qualified to narrow the gap between A's vote and that of the majority. A need not believe that any obligation to enact the wishes of the majority is incumbent upon him personally, but rather his obligation may amount to no more than simply not impeding the majority vote being translated into action. As we saw earlier, Edmundson argued in similar fashion that instead of a general obligation to obey the law, we were subject only to a duty not to interfere in the administration of laws duly passed by the majority.

### 4.2.2 The Relevance of Singer's Models to Large-Scale Democracies

In the latter part of his essay, Singer turns from a discussion of the ideal form of democracy as represented by the third or democratic model, to explore in more detail whether anything that might be true of that model would also hold in something closer to real-world democracies, though as we noted, some of his discussion thus far seems to have assumed that such a transition is possible. In any case Singer now proposes to ask whether any of the countries commonly thought to be democracies meet the criteria characteristic of the third model, such as an equal vote of all members, impartial procedural rules, as well as some concern that justice not only be done to minorities, but also be seen to be done by them. Only thus, according to Singer, could a governance association be considered to represent the sort of fair compromise of power and participation, such that one could reasonably expect the membership to support the outcomes of the association's deliberations.

However, such democracies as actually do exist present significant departures from the ideal sort of direct democracy envisaged by the third model, which according to Singer hearkens back to the Athenian democracy where the citizens met in an assembly to debate and resolve matters of concern to everyone (1974, 106). With respect to the origin of democracy in Greek antiquity, Wollheim further notes that the government of the demos contrasted with a modern democracy by being the government of a particular segment of the population, namely the populace or poor. The names of other parallel structures referred to the section of the population which wielded power within that sphere, such as aristocracy, or government by the best, or oligarchy, government by the few.

Moreover, Wollheim observes that it is a feature peculiar to modern democracies that the governing body is drawn from the citizens as a whole (ibid.72), a fact which has led to democracy being no longer direct, but representative. Although the view that democracy meant some sort of direct rule by the people seems to have persisted until at least the eighteenth century, by the middle of the nineteenth Mill remarked that because of practical considerations direct participation was likely to be restricted to relatively small organizations (1958, 55). According to Dahl recent scholars have estimated the average Greek city state to have numbered between 2000 and 10,000 full citizens, which in their view was about the right size for the ideal *polis*. However, those of us who have sat on much smaller governing bodies, say of 20, have long since realized that if every member is to talk on average for no more than 10 min, we need to set aside at least 4 h, which is already beyond what most of us want to spend in a meeting. If we crank up the numbers to a small town of 5000, a town hall meeting where each tried to speak for 10 min would take over 100 working days for all to be heard, leading Dahl to remark that for the supposed ideal *polis* of 10,000 full citizens, the time required would be completely impossible (1998, 107).

Curiously enough, Singer dismisses a view such as Dahl's to the effect that direct democracy is only workable in very small units as a common, but false platitude of political theory. Singer thinks that although representative systems came into existence at a time when it was not practical for citizens to come together, given our modern methods of communication, we are now within easy reach of government, and it is only fashion which dictates otherwise. While Dahl would agree that electronic meetings are possible, it is another matter for large numbers to engage in productive electronic discussion (ibid., 105–106), as those who have attended recent Zoom meetings may be inclined to attest. On the other hand, Schwab as the self-appointed world planner-in-chief is pleased to note that Zoom's market capitalization reached $70 billion as at June 2020, a sure sign that we were well on the way to the weightless digital economy (2020, 178).[4]

Goodin is nevertheless proof that the ingenuity of democratic enthusiasts is not to be underestimated, with deliberative democracy being touted as one of the more interesting developments to have appeared in recent years.[5] However, as innovative, and valuable as deliberative democracy supposedly is, Goodin suggests that because of some of the practical difficulties already alluded to, we shift the focus from group to individual reflection. Deliberating with oneself does put things on a more manageable scale, but Goodin suspects that this modality cannot quite replace group discussions. By setting more store by internal reflection than others have done, Goodin hopes to improve the quality of the face-to-face encounters which remain indispensable in most accounts of deliberative democracy (2003, 170–171, 179).

No matter how fruitful the deliberation, we will eventually have to call the question, and Goodin considers the final vote to be the criterion of legitimacy (ibid., 192). However, one may still wonder what the show of hands really signifies, other than the end of deliberation at least for the time being. As we saw, Singer thought that the final decision was not

[4] Schwab can also barely contain his excitement at the fact that whereas telemedicine was virtually non-existent in Britain pre-Covid, it reached 100% under lockdown (ibid., 179). I am much more inclined to see the refusal to meet patients in person as symptomatic of the larger failure of primary medicine to provide timely treatment and prevent hospitalization, thus aggravating the appalling social consequences of lockdowns, which like other non pharmaceutical interventions do not appear to have even lived up to the first principle of medical ethics, *primum non nocere*.

[5] cf Gibson (2003, 229).

enough to confer democratic legitimacy, because a clear majority vote could still raise questions about the fair treatment of the losers or the minority. Narveson also acknowledges that some think it unfair that a sector of the Canadian voting public, such as Quebec, is persistently relegated to minority status, something which separatist parties have often hoped to remedy (2008a, 127).

Singer proposed various corrective measures to cure the perceived unfairness of being in a permanent minority, as does Goodin, who recommended an internal accounting of the various ways in which other parties may be treated unfairly in the democratic process. Internal deliberation is also supposed to make up for some of the practical difficulties which Dahl thought inevitably attended large-scale assemblies, and according to Goodin, the more democratic our internal deliberations are, the less significant the logistical problems of obtaining large-scale collective decisions will be (ibid., 193). However, even if we could decide what it would be for our imaginary deliberations to be more democratic and why that would be a good thing, it seems that could only increase the cost of doing democracy's business rather than reduce it.

So instead of recognizing with Narveson that democracy is by definition the rule of the majority and not just a contingent feature (ibid.), Singer and Goodin in their own different ways offer us more of the same. But, as Harper once observed, deciding by majority rule is equivalent to the old principle of might makes right (1949, 60). Thus, it should come as no surprise, widespread beliefs to the contrary, that it is inimical to individual liberty. More recently, Narveson has also argued that it is often just assumed that democracy is morally right, rather than just perhaps the least reprehensible; if so, we need to ask how it is we find in favour of the former, rather than the latter (2002a, 176).

As both Harper and Narveson point out, democracy possesses moral authority to the extent that it promotes liberty and not otherwise. Indeed, as Harper reminds us the conflation of democracy with liberty is wholly mistaken. While the right to vote is a liberty some think worth preserving, so much so that it is seen as one which cannot itself be abridged by voting, there is no guarantee that the outcome of any vote will in turn preserve liberty (ibid., 56–57). Moreover, to the extent that democracies have been successful, as Narveson observes, this is because their support of liberty has not simply been confined to that of voting, but has been written into their constitutions, perhaps in the form of some of the standard liberal freedoms, such as those mentioned above by Singer, and as a result influenced community practice.

### 4.2.3 Representation and Authority

Given that various attempts to improve democracy appear to involve our getting more of what we don't need, assuming of course that those who currently avoid the ballot box like the plague will show any interest in doing the mental homework Goodin has in mind for them, we seem to be left with some version of the sort of representative democracy with which we are now reluctantly familiar. Singer thus canvases some of the standard theories of representation to see in what sense the criteria he is interested in, such as fair compromise and participation, are preserved under different versions of representative democracy. If representation is taken rather literally, it means the representative sees himself in some straightforward sense as representing those who for various reasons couldn't be there, as well as taking some pains to represent the views of his electors. Although Singer thinks that there might be circumstances where the voters would feel betrayed by a representative who was greatly imbued with Burke's doctrine of independence, in general he concludes that if there is a case for obeying the decisions of a direct democracy there is no reason to think that wouldn't also be true for representative democracy (ibid., 111).

Of course, as we have been suggesting, if there are any reasons for obedience, they are of an independent moral sort, and have nothing to do with whether a position was arrived at democratically, either directly or indirectly via representatives. Further, while thus at least *prima facie* there is no reason to think that representative democracy would in and of itself give rise to grounds for disobedience which would not exist under the hypothetical model association, it also remains to be seen how closely actual representative democracies conform to any theoretical account of them. In fact, Singer concedes that most theories of representative democracy do not describe real political systems since representation does not really represent anything or anyone (ibid., 112). According to Singer, if we have been able to revise the traditional myth of representative democracy, it is because of the work of commentators such as Schumpeter, or Dahl, who echoed Schumpeter's criticisms.

Indeed, Schumpeter disposes of the classical doctrine of democracy according to which there is a mechanism for translating the will of the people into political determinations of the collective good (1954, 250). Schumpeter holds that there is no such thing as a common good which might be arrived at by rational discussion, if for no other reason than that in political matters rationality is in short supply. Even if people were capable on more than the odd occasion of forming consistent rational desires there would be no reason to think that the political process managed to track anything remotely resembling the supposed general will (ibid., 254).

Moreover, given the opposing preferences surrounding most political decisions it is unlikely that the result will conform in any way to what people really want, nor *pace* Singer, is it a foregone conclusion that what they come away with is some sort of fair compromise. Schumpeter thinks that something resembling a compromise might be possible when dealing with quantitative issues, e.g., when there is general support for a particular expenditure, but where the actual amount may need to be decided via compromise. However, when the question turns on qualitative or value issues, such as in Singer's example, whether the common room should subscribe to a particular newspaper, there is much less chance of reaching what the dissenter and maybe others would consider a fair compromise. In fact, Schumpeter contends that decisions produced under governance models more closely resembling Singer's non-democratic ones, at least when dealing with the more problematic qualitative decisions, might well be received more favourably, a point which Schumpeter illustrates by an example drawn from Napoleon's First Consulship, a governance structure similar in some respects to Singer's first model association.

According to Schumpeter, the ordinary citizen has trouble generating the mental energy to understand more complex domestic and foreign policy issues, or as Narveson writes, given the vast scope of government, acquiring the relevant information is beyond most of us, and given how little our vote counts, it is not worth our while (2008a, 125). However, ignorance has never been known to stand in the way of citizens responding with enthusiasm to politicians' assurances that the day of the free lunch is not yet over, which is not quite what the classical theory had in mind when it spoke of the voter seeking to promote his rational interests. As Schumpeter observes, political rationales and plans are typically of a short-term nature, with the average citizen voting by feeling rather than reasoning (ibid. 261–262). This means that the non-existent will of the people has to be manufactured by the politician, who appeals to those subconscious thinking patterns by borrowing from the techniques of advertising.

It is not surprising then, as Narveson has reminded us, that governments communicate via sound-byte how they plan to set the world aright, or for a different audience, to have it rain beer, with the help of funds which the taxpayer has apparently been only too happy to donate to the cause. Of course, the sound-byte is wholly inadequate to properly treating just about any issue of importance, such as global warming, a subject of considerable political enthusiasm of late, which only serves to illustrate Schumpeter's comment to the effect that most of what government communicates is utterly uninformative sloganeering (ibid.). Or, as Narveson again suggests, democracy is synonymous with poor-quality government and information.[6]

Having shown the classical theory of democracy to be largely a myth, Schumpeter states that the role of voting in a democracy is simply to produce a government. Those who would rule must compete for the favour of the electorate, ably assisted by an assortment of image makers and political operatives, to say nothing of the media and more importantly of what Rectenwald has called *The Google Archipelago* (2019). In case we thought that we had some control over those we elect to office, Schumpeter reminds us that the best we can hope to do is to turf them out, if they prove incompetent, as they generally do.[7] So on Schumpeter's view it sounds as though Wollheim, for example, has got the modern

[6] "Government by sound-byte," 5.

[7] Narveson also speaks of democracy as a mechanism for throwing the rascals out ( "Liberalism and Democracy," 5b). Another reason for doing so, as Schweizer reminds us, is that politics has proved a sure path to riches for many (2011).

version of democracy wrong as well, since for him democracy implies that the people rule, not by writing legislation, but by overseeing the process (ibid., 73).

According to Schumpeter, while we choose the legislators in some sense or other, we don't control either them or their legislation, even though the number of those, who think we do, including Wollheim, is legion. Dworkin, for example, claims as one of his background assumptions that everyone participates equally in monitoring the work of legislators (1986, 178). Shapiro speaks of democratic justice, which is not simply procedural but ensures that those on the receiving end of political decisions exercise some control over their impact (1999, 89–90). This is achieved by improving participation, perhaps by reflection prior to voting, as suggested by Goodin, even though he himself admitted at the outset that one individual's vote is unlikely to make much difference (2003, 5). Shapiro's fine-tuning of democracy, like Goodin's, is inspired by the view, which we have already called into question, namely that democracy is correct in principle, and something to be encouraged (ibid., 90).

As we also saw above, Singer placed Dahl in the same camp as Schumpeter who was intent upon revising traditional democratic theory to make it less of a normative account and more descriptive of actual practice. Thus, Dahl states that if we expect elections to reveal the will of the majority on various questions, we are mistaken since that rarely happens (1956, 131). However, Dahl thinks that elections not only install leaders along with their governments, but also provide some sort of control over the leaders, if not over policies. While, unlike Schumpeter, Dahl stops short of saying that political activity both at elections and in between is of no importance for determining policy, he does hold that there is no guarantee that policy will match majority preferences. In fact, for him democracy is wrongly described as majority rule. Nor is it rule by one minority, which is what constitutes a dictatorship. It is in fact government by competing minorities, with the majority simply along for the ride (ibid., 133).

Thus, if Singer was hoping to find some reassurance from influential commentators such as Schumpeter or Dahl that there is anything corresponding to his third model association in the real world, he can only have been somewhat disappointed. Dahl thinks that polyarchal democracy, or government by minorities, is preferable to dictatorship, because he believes more people at least get in on the act under the former regime than under the latter and have some chance to influence leaders and policy. While in his view no real-world governments are true democracies, polyarchies offer a wide range of public participation (1971, 8). Perhaps one obvious sense in which we get government by minorities is where governments are elected by at most 40% of voters, in exchange for 100% of government power, as typically happens in Canada.[8] As for the benefit of elector contestation conferred by polyarchy, for most of the voters, who even bother to vote, it means nothing more than going to the polls every four years or so. On the question of whether polyarchy offers us any greater influence over government than a dictatorship or monarchy might have done Gibson et al. claim that rather than being democracies, Canadian governments constitute a dictatorship from one election to the next (2003, 248).

Canadian democratic enthusiasts need not immediately rend their garments, however, since the *Economist Democracy Index* lists the country in 5th place among the 23 which qualify as *full democracies*, the top category which apparently tolerates the odd bit of dictatorship, as well as enough corruption to warrant its being excluded from the top 10 least corrupt countries (2021, 46). Canada's overall score at 9.24 out of 10 perhaps reflects the fact that it still has some way to go in achieving that likely forever elusive control of governments by the governed. Small European countries such as Norway, Iceland and Sweden are apparently closer to the holy grail of democracy, if *The Economist* has managed to measure anything of significance, while the US is in 25th place, and the UK, home of the mother of all parliaments, is in 16th place. In the 2nd tier of *flawed* democracies are two European countries, France, and Portugal, along with the US. Despite its supposed role as a beacon of democracy, the US has been awarded this somewhat tarnished accolade since 2016 because of what the *Democracy Index* sees as a great distrust of state institutions which brought Trump to power, as well as profound political divisions which continue to impede what the *Economist* believes

[8] Cf. Gibson (2003, 255).

are the necessary functions of government (2021, 43–45). It is also worth noting that the 23 full democracies only account for 14% of the world's countries and 8.4% of its population, suggesting that the golden age of democracy may be a long time in coming (2021).

The *Democracy Index* carries on the Schumpeter/Dahl tradition of looking democratic practice squarely in the face, something which strikes Singer as making a virtue out of a necessity, as Churchill perhaps also did with his famous remark in the Commons in 1947 that although far from perfect, democracy is perhaps the best of a bad lot.[9] Even if we think that democracy, such as it is, is about as good as it gets, Singer would still want to ask of this revised view, whether it could meet the criteria which he thought sufficient to dissuade the dissenter from disobeying the wishes of the majority, such as that of being a fair compromise. For Singer, fairness seemed to be bound up with the traditional model where members allot their votes to the candidate, they believe will do the best job overall (1974, 116).

Singer was no doubt inspired by Plamenatz, who also thought that we might be able to clarify the notion of a fair compromise, provided we keep to small groups of half a dozen members, thus perhaps even smaller than Singer's common room association. Even within such small groups there may be on any given issue as many opinions as there are members. One way such a group could attempt to reach a compromise is by appointing an outside arbiter whose judgement they all trust. They may on the other hand attempt to reach a compromise among themselves after due consideration. Plamenatz suggests we also consider the worst-case scenarios for each modality, namely where the arbiter is less professional, or in the do-it-yourself version, where a couple of members feel their views have received a less than sympathetic hearing. While Plamenatz notes that Schumpeter is in good company in believing that democracy has nothing to do with giving expression to the supposed will of the people (1973, 104), Plamenatz wants to show that there are at least some cases, such as the two less problematic small group instances, where we might say the decision reflected the will of the group. In both cases the six members may all agree that the final proposal constitutes

[9] For full text see Gilbert (2006, 124).

a fair compromise, whereas in the two worst versions, there is less than unanimous agreement that either the arbiter acted fairly, or that all views received a fair hearing.

Within the fair compromise subgroup, one arrived at via an arbiter and the other via group discussion, a decision may be reached because some members sided with the majority after due deliberation. Others may stick to their original proposals, while agreeing that the overall decision represented a fair compromise. Plamenatz argues that two different senses of *the will of the group* are needed to distinguish the first case where all agree with the decision arrived at, from the second where they agree that the decision was fair, even though their views did not coincide with the majority. While Plamenatz thinks the first will primarily be of interest to theoreticians, the second will more likely occur in practice, or if it doesn't, is something democrats think they should aim at (ibid., 106).

Plamenatz also thinks that the collective will may manifest itself even in cases which some believe rest on an unfair compromise, such as where the arbiter was less than impartial, or where they feel that their views were not given a proper hearing. In that case he responds that if you have agreed to submit to an arbiter, or to majority rule, that agreement is binding and to be considered a fair compromise, regardless of how biased the arbitration was, or how unsatisfactory the deliberation, since all were aware of the ground rules for a decision. However, in the case of the former, it does sound a little like insisting that those who complained about the notorious partiality of Nazi judges really had nothing to complain about. In the latter, you might have good reason for complaint, if for some reason or other you were unable to state your case, perhaps because of time constraints.

Thus, despite Plamenatz's intention of clarifying the notion of a fair compromise, we don't seem to be any further ahead than we were with Singer, who doesn't even pretend to explain it. What is really driving Plamenatz's account is the notion of a *collective will* which he thinks has more going for it than Schumpeter does, and which is revealed in the sort of small group cases already mentioned, including those supposedly involving unfair compromises, since those involved had a chance to make their views known (ibid.). Of course, it may be that those who complained of not getting a fair hearing, did not in fact get a chance to express their preferences.

However, in the case of macro-level decisions such as that of Napoleon's religious settlement, Plamenatz argues that the Concordat could not be seen as giving effect to the will of the people, unless those affected had a chance to say what they thought and were satisfied that any decision was fair (ibid., 107). Plamenatz incorrectly assumes that Schumpeter was simply putting the Concordat forward as an illustration of the will of the people, whereas he is more interested in pointing out that democracy could almost never be counted on to deliver any such thing (1954, 254).

Indeed, it may well be that in complex qualitative issues, a dictatorship, such as that of Napoleon, to say nothing of the Holy See, could take decisions which proved acceptable to the people in the long run. This was the case with the Concordat, a decision which Schumpeter claims could not have been reached democratically, and yet if it was ever true that the people could have been said to favour something this was it (ibid., 255). The fact that such a non-democratic decision came as close to being a paradigm case as anything could of such an improbable notion as the will of the people leads Schumpeter to conclude that if an outcome acceptable to most is the criterion of good government, then democracy as classically conceived would often fail to live up to it (ibid., 256).

If Schumpeter is right, democracy does not have a monopoly on fair compromise since the Concordat seems to fit that bill too if anything does. In any case Singer thinks that the notion of a fair compromise, although it could in principle survive the transition from direct to representative democracy, is unlikely to survive in practice, at least as that has been characterized by the revisionists. In fact, any hope that Singer might have had that any actual large-scale democracy could replicate the equal division of power envisaged by his model association should be finally laid to rest by Dahl's observation that power has never been shared equally throughout history, and democracies, at least in their latter-day polyarchic manifestation, are no exception (1989, 271). In fact, he thinks that full political equality is probably beyond the reach of humanity (2006, 119).

Of course, if we agree with Narveson that under democracy everyone gets the same amount of basic power (2008a, 115), then what you see is what you get. Expecting democracy to deliver something more than one person one vote, as presumably implied by Dahl's goal of full political equality, may be even more futile than the hope that one vote will really make a difference. On the other hand, the politically astute have decided that it is equally futile to await the golden age of democracy and have decided to make the best of the existing version, or what Dahl calls polyarchy. While it hardly pays the individual *qua* individual to vote, being part of a minority or pressure group, if the political timing is right, can make it worth one's while when it comes to feeding at the political trough, where notably some animals are more equal than others. Indeed, there are endless opportunities for political enthusiasts to generate rents as full-time politicians or government bureaucrats, both of whom can wield disproportionate influence in their own favour. As Seldon reminds us, government rewards go to the organized at the expense of those who lack the skills of political organization, and thus to equate majority rule with that of the people is a wanton misuse of language (2002a, 44).

### 4.2.4 Political Parties

Another important feature of contemporary parliamentary democracy is the political party, which has no real counterpart in a direct democracy such as the third model association and which probably developed after the traditional theory of democracy had already taken hold. Perhaps because of this it seems difficult to account for something like party discipline along the lines of the traditional model, or for other features of parties which have struck some commentators as rather undemocratic. Michels famously observed a universal tendency of organizations such as parties and unions to morph into oligarchies. As for any control over the leader, which the revisionists thought was still to some extent a feature of democratic practice, Michels concludes that this is largely fictitious, since the leader soon acquires the habit of making his own decisions without consulting the rank and file (1959, 32, 34).

While Michels's belief that hierarchy was essential to the functioning of a political party might strike some as dated, having been first enunciated almost a century ago, Simpson reminds us, with reference to the Canadian parliamentary machine, that little has changed. Although the title of prime minister suggests a first among equals, the cabinet and party, to say nothing of the parliament itself, exercise very little control (2001, 62). With respect to public support for what some have called the imperial prime-ministership, Ibbitson points out that of the 15 majority governments Canada has enjoyed since World War I, in only 4 of those cases did the government receive 50% of the vote. Voter turnout has also been on the decline in recent years, with the one of the lowest ever in the 2004 Federal election of 62%, and since there is no guarantee that the list of voters contains all those eligible, less than 50% may end up voting. Indeed, Ibbitson concludes that younger people are staying away from the polls in droves which can only make one wonder in what sense a modern democracy is democratic (2005, 214, 215). If this is right, perhaps it just confirms the prognostications of Plato and Tocqueville that democracy would degenerate into despotism.

On the other hand, there is much to suggest that democracy is just despotism dressed up as the mythical will of the people, that Hart's Rex never really departed, but just exchanged the orb and scepter for a business suit. In that case we can only hope that the alleged disengagement from politics is indeed on the increase, and rather than something to be deplored, as journalists with an appetite for politics are fond of claiming, it is to be welcomed as an important step in the decline of the state. As Chodorov asked himself, why bother attempting to clean up the den of thieves when every vote for good government gives more of the same? He recommends we all do as he did many years ago and ignore election day (1980, 205).[10]

Michels's view that political parties are undemocratic and ruled by oligarchies appears to be shared by Dahl, who observes, for example, that both major US political parties are better described as oligarchic cartels (1967, 245). However, in later writing, Dahl held that Michels was somewhat hasty in extending his iron law of oligarchy from political

[10] Thus, the title of O'Rourke, *Don't Vote: it just encourages the bastards* (2010).

parties to the government as a whole. Dahl thinks that while it is not impossible that dominant elites or minorities should rule, if not directly then by indirect manipulation, competition between parties, as well as Dahl's theory of polyarchy, where a variety of minority groups have some influence, reduce the chances of government by oligarchy. As much as anything else, Dahl believes that theories of minority domination will fail for want of empirical evidence in support of any such tendency. In fact, he argues that because of the vast range of government interests a ruling elite or inner circle will be forced by circumstance to focus on what it considers to be key issues, which means that other minorities can have considerable influence in areas important to them and perhaps less important to the central committee, for example farmers on agricultural policy, or seniors on pensions and health care. In general Dahl believes that theories like the iron law of oligarchy are an obstacle to an accurate assessment of what democracy can and cannot achieve (1989, 279).

As to the true account of democracy, our discussion thus far has not proved very encouraging for those who see it as the obvious source of the authority of the state. We may look forward with Marx to the eventual withering away of the state, as a prelude to establishing a liberal rather than a state-sponsored order, coming somewhat closer to Dahl's longed for land of liberty, though we are realistic enough in his sense to believe that this will more likely be accomplished by increments than earth shattering change. What isn't clear is what democracy supposedly has to do with that, since, as Narveson has observed, liberal freedoms, such as those of contract, or speech, to the extent they have anything at all to do with democracy, are likely to be threatened by it (2002a,172).

With respect to Dahl's worry that we might be distracted from the grand vision where we govern ourselves democratically as free and equal citizens, one would have thought that, as a card-carrying revisionist, he would have long since consigned that collection of confusions to the rubbish tip. Mueller contends, for example, that rather than promoting equality, democracy is much more likely to result in political inequality (1999, 137); while Mill famously reminded us that to speak of self government is not to speak about governing oneself but being governed by everyone else (1974, 62). And if it is the latter that we are really talking about, then, as Narveson has remarked, this becomes a rather difficult exercise, if rule is in the interests of the ruled and not the rulers, which is to say we decide whether a supposed rule is in our interests, not the rulers (ibid., 172).[11]

Moreover, with respect to Dahl's criticism of Michels, it doesn't seem too much of an oversimplification to suggest that as the party goes, so does the government, if only because under the Westminster system, the leader of the party that wins the election is called upon to form the government. The leader continues to lead the party as well as heading the government as prime minister. As for evidence of a tendency to oligarchy at all levels, there is no shortage of at least anecdotal evidence of one sort or another attesting to dictatorial behaviour of prime ministers, ministers, caucus members, party whips, to say nothing of the vast bureaucracies who claim to deliver the government's policies. Simpson compares the prime minister to Louis XIV and who like the famous monarch holds court at the centre of government (ibid., 4). The fact that most of us are not privy to discussions held in the corridors of power is noteworthy in and of itself, as well as making such events hard to document.

Further, Dahl argues that even if we agree with Michels that political parties tend to oligarchy, one of the guarantees against oligarchic government is competition between political parties. To support this contention, Dahl offers us an analogy with business, where although an individual firm may internally be an oligarchy, competing firms set limits to its ability to control the external environment and become a monopoly. However, in the case of Canada, the Liberal Party governed for almost 70 years of the past century, suggesting that genuine political competition was largely absent and that they can with some justification be considered the natural governing party.

More recently Shapiro has noted that with the small number of major parties in countries such as Canada and the US such competition as we get is that of oligopolies where the attention parties pay to their members is much less than that of competing businesses. While

[11] O'Rourke reminds us of Cincinnatus, often held up as a model politician when he twice returned from the dictatorship to farming once the Roman crisis passed. However, as an aristocrat he opposed legislation which would have applied to everyone, plebeians, and patricians alike (2010, 261).

governments have not hesitated to prosecute firms such as Microsoft for supposedly breaching antitrust laws, in the face of a constrained political market, Shapiro thinks it surprising that similar actions have not been brought against political duopolies. While it is often thought to be a good thing that individuals and parties engage in deliberation to overcome their differences and reach consensus, Shapiro holds that such behaviour should be met with an antitrust suit as being in restraint of democratic competition (2003, 204).

### 4.2.5 The Supposed Virtues of Polyarchy

As for the claim that what we are really dealing with is not democracy as traditionally understood, but rather polyarchy, or competing minorities, while this may describe an important feature of contemporary democracy, more recent critics of democracy have correctly found this to be one of its more harmful characteristics, including, as Seldon points out, the producer lobbies which are spawned in staple industries such as manufacturing, transport and education (2002a, 45). The alleged strength of polyarchy is that everybody can get on the minority bandwagon at some point and that all minorities or lobbies have roughly equal clout and can in some sense or other keep one another in check. The view of Seldon and more recent critics is that democracy does not come anywhere near the fair compromise Singer talked about, but that its deliverances are distinctly unequal, favouring as it does the politically skilled and organized over the unskilled and unorganized (1990, 115).

No doubt the classical view of democracy would have us believe that a representative acting in the interests of all his electors might help overcome some of these inequities. Indeed, it might, but chances are it won't because political considerations will likely dictate otherwise. Though, you might be in luck, according to Tullock, if your preference on some issue is around the middle, since parties wanting to be elected gravitate towards the position of the median voter (2006, 53). But regardless of your preferences, shopping at the one-size-fits-all government store, in Seldon's view, is never a sure thing, since much can be lost in passing the message up the complex chain of government command and back (1990,

115). Although escape to other suppliers is often blocked by government regulation, Seldon lists several escapes which are becoming increasingly popular, such as affluence, which enables people to use the schools or medical services of their choosing, the parallel economy or black market, the internet, and finally the world, via emigration (2002a, Ch. 3). Schwab and the globalist elites doubtless hope that such workarounds would neither be necessary nor permitted as we enter the New Normal following the Covid crisis they trust will usher in the Great Reset (2020, 249).

The various escapes from over-government are doubtless prompted by the lack of any choice between parties, which, as Tullock pointed out, are falling over themselves to govern from the centre, a centre which continually shifts, it seems, in a statist direction, despite the pretence of some of the rulers to be interested in doing otherwise. Indeed, this tendency for there to be little difference in the actual performance of the two governing parties is further evidence of Shapiro's anti-competitive collusion in restraint of democracy. Rothbard reminds us that, at least in the case of the US, bipartisanship is not only typical of foreign policy, promoting global intervention in the name of democracy, foreign aid and trade mercantilism, but is equally pervasive on the domestic front, where the collectivism which might have been advanced by Democrats has if anything been ratcheted up by Republicans (1994, 4).[12]

On the question of any real competition between parties and their leaders for the people's vote, Schumpeter thought it was only one of potential competition. Although elections generally preclude military coups, he also thought that they do so at the price of actions which in the economic arena might be called unfair or restrictive trade practices. However, being the political realist that he is, Schumpeter thought this preferable to some unattainable ideal since there is great variation along a continuum from the ideally democratic to the autocratic, where the leader brooks no opposition (ibid., 271). As for parties and party discipline, Schumpeter contends that if we want to understand how things work, rather than philosophize how they might, then in a similar spirit

[12] And the situation appears no different in Canada. According to Kheiriddin and Daifallah, the Mulroney Conservatives proved no better than the Trudeau Liberals when it came to government expenditure, and if anything, they were more profligate (2005, 21).

to Michels we will realize that the party boss and his machine are not just a sideshow but the soul of politics, whose aim is to get one up on the competition just like a trade association (ibid., 283).

In any case it looks as though the realities of democratic politics as described by seasoned observers such as Schumpeter and Dahl require much more by way of compromise than Singer bargained for when he talked about his third model association representing some sort of fair compromise, with the result that he is forced to concede that there may not be much carry-over from his model democratic community to those with which we are familiar (ibid., 128). The latter may well be polyarchic, but that is no guarantee that they are fair. Moreover, as he concludes, some groups are more equal than others and many voters belong to no group at all (ibid., 134). To be sure, those same theorists would think that Singer's fair and equal compromise is nowhere to be found, and the best we can hope for is a system open to more influence, such as Dahl's polyarchy, rather than a hegemonic, or autocratic one, though as Dahl remarks some will balk at the idea that polyarchy is about as close as we can hope to come to the ideal of democracy (1971, n.4, 9).

Indeed, such institutional arrangements often appear to be far from any ideal, despite having been the source of largesse to many and sundry supplicants. Tammany Hall, which began life as a patriotic social club, eventually became synonymous with political influence, graft and vote-rigging, as well as providing a helping hand to Irish immigrants in return for political support. Perhaps Schumpeter had Tweed of Tammany Hall in mind when he noted the importance of the political boss and his machine, which Ackerman sees as a way of operationalizing democratic theory (2006, 359). Thus, confronted with the rough and tumble of everyday democratic life, Singer, whose worry is that some will fail to be adequately represented in decision-making, so much so, that he is less than convinced at the end of his essay that a democratic society produces stronger reasons to obey than a non-democratic one. If this were ever true, and Singer never really showed that it was, it did not survive the transition from his model society to the one in which most of us live.

Moreover, in the years since Singer wrote his essay, not only have the electors continued to vote with their feet, but more theorists are now prepared to doubt that democracy can be the source of authority, as Singer initially hypothesized. Even if democracy is better described as polyarchy, as Dahl thinks, Singer remains unconvinced, and as Narveson has pointed out, to the extent that democracy has retained any appeal, it is because it is regularly identified with certain liberal rights which flow from the basic right of all to liberty compatible with a similar liberty for others, and not from democracy. On the contrary, as he has also written, democracy hardly merits the exalted position where many have placed it, but should rather be seen for what it is, everlasting interference in individual liberty on behalf of special interests (2008a, 133). As already noted, one of the main problems of democracy is that it is majoritarian, which means, according to Hardin, that at most elections most of us lose more than we gain most of the time (2003a, 309). Indeed, as Tocqueville famously argued, life under a reasonably benevolent monarch might be preferable to a democratic ochlocracy which confines its despotic acts to those in the minority on any issue (2003, 298–299).

In fact, Dahl responds to Tocqueville on this very issue, namely the supposed threat to liberty posed by majoritarian democracy with its predilection for equality. Dahl attempts to clarify in what sense Tocqueville claimed that democracy was likely to lapse into tyranny, that is, whether the tyranny consisted in some sort of injustice perpetrated by the majority, or whether majority tyranny per se constituted the injustice in question. Since he doesn't think that Tocqueville has been sufficiently clear about what democratic tyranny amounted to, Dahl proposes that we look first at primary political rights, such as the right to vote or freedom of speech as ways of bench-marking democratic performance. In the 150 years or so since Tocqueville penned these observations, Dahl claims there is empirical evidence to suggest that such primary rights have expanded rather than contracted but agrees that what we make of such data will perhaps depend on theoretical questions about the nature of these rights and their relation to democracy. Some favour a doctrine of prior rights according to which such primary rights are both anterior and superior to democracy or rights against democracy (1985, 25).

However, rather than construe these primary rights as independent of democracy and therefore as yardsticks against which democracy might be measured, Dahl prefers to think of them in a manner more inspired by democratic thinking. He recommends that we settle upon one basic right, namely the right to self government, from which other primary rights can be derived. One of the main advantages of this approach from Dahl's point of view is that it heads off a direct challenge between liberty and democracy which was at the centre of Tocqueville's analysis. Moreover, such rights are inalienable in the sense that any attempt to abridge them would be tantamount to destroying democracy, in much the same way that Singer thought that violation of essential democratic rights could undermine democracy and provoke disobedience. Thus, in response to a concern that, if it suited them, a majority might be able to override the rights of a minority, Dahl claims that they could not rightfully do so and would not be acting democratically if they did. Nor can a majority decide to quit the whole programme since such a decision would be incoherent (ibid., 29). To the extent that Tocqueville saw tyranny of the majority as implying riding roughshod over the rights of minorities, or selling the democratic farm, Dahl thinks that he failed to appreciate the significance of primary political rights within a democracy.

### 4.2.6 *Rex Nunquam Moritur*

However, Tocqueville thought that the transition from monarchy to democracy does not remove the centralizing tendency of the state but rather that it will in fact tend to reinforce the same sovereign authority. If anything, authoritarianism is even more easily practised under a democracy, and requires one single principle, namely equality (ibid., 789). So, it is not surprising that in the two centuries since the revolution eventually handed off command from a monarch to his democratic successors, Hardin would claim that democracy has had a limited profile in most places, and was often largely a sideshow (2003a, 290). Indeed, as the Romans noted quite some revolutions ago, *rex nunquam moritur*, the king never dies. Or as Hobbes wrote, there is one sovereign, who at different times assumes the various guises of monarch, aristocracy or democracy, with little to choose between them where one form already dominates, since all three possess the absolute sovereignty that belongs to the monarch (1909, 428).

While we are more interested in general questions as to the possible basis for sovereign authority, there is a narrower legal sense in which the monarch is never entirely absent even in a parliamentary democracy, such as Canada, where Parliament includes the Queen and both Houses, while the Executive Government is vested in the monarch, with many of her powers delegated to the Governor General.[13] With respect to the latter powers, Evatt thought that perhaps the most important question was whether the sovereign or his representative could override the advice of his elected ministers, and at least with respect to legislation, it appears that the sovereign may indeed withhold assent, a view shared by more recent writers.[14] While such constitutional oddities can serve as a reminder that the sovereign has only disappeared behind a democratic facade, exercises of the royal prerogative are in fact fairly rare. More recently attention has been given to the right of the Upper House or Senate, consisting of appointed rather than elected members, to withhold assent to bills originating in the elected Commons.

Tocqueville of course does not believe that the tendency to arbitrary rule is confined to such lapses in democracy which are a throwback to earlier days of absolute monarchy. It is rather to be found in the regular use of sovereign authority by democratic governments to advance the cause of what Mises calls *etatism*, which holds its citizens in tutelage and substitutes state initiative for that of the individual (1985, 46). Or Tocqueville a century or so earlier, having premised that democracy was likely to bring in its wake forms of tyranny unknown in earlier centuries, spoke of an immense paternal authority whose aim was to be the monopoly provider of its citizens' needs, acting forever *in loco parentis*. While democracy appears to be some sort of compromise between the sovereignty of the state and that of the citizens, the latter are wrong to think that their freedoms remain secure once they have been turned over to the state (2003, 805, 807).

Of course, with the benefit of another 150 years since Tocqueville wrote, it now seems quite clear that democracy, which traditionally has claimed to embody the sovereignty of the people, has indeed proved the

[13] Cf. Forcese and Freeman (2005, 10).

[14] Cf. Evatt (1967, 2, 286) and McWhinney (2005, 27).

source of enslavement that he predicted. However, Dahl responds, no doubt in the true spirit of democracy that when we review the historical record to see whether any actual democracies had succumbed to the despotism predicted by Tocqueville, relatively few have done so, if we are talking about countries which began life as democracies, but later fell off the wagon and ended up as dictatorships. Dahl concludes that except for Uruguay, in countries such as Argentina, Germany or Spain, the decline into despotism had mostly to do with the fact that democracy was not as firmly rooted as in other countries which did not suffer a similar fate.

As we saw earlier, Dahl claimed that Tocqueville had not made it clear in speaking of democracy resulting in majority tyranny whether he was referring to specific injustices brought about by majority rule, or to the fact that democracy per se could be every bit as tyrannical as the hegemonies it replaced. Tocqueville, it seems, inclines to the latter, pointing out that whether rulers are anointed by divine right or by election, they believe that it is natural that some rule while others obey, and better they than others less fit. Tocqueville's concerns about the rule of the majority were not new when he raised them half a century or so after the American republic had thrown off the tyranny of George III. Plato had raised similar issues, when Thrasymachus argued in *The Republic* that might was right, and that the rulers make laws in their own interest, not in the interest of those they rule.[15]

Several years after Tocqueville, and within weeks of the 1848 Revolution in Paris, Proudhon expressed little faith in the democratic dogma about the right of people to govern themselves much celebrated by Dahl, since there is no such thing as just representation while elections prove a loss for most.[16] And as Mill famously remarked a decade later, self government is actually a misnomer, since what we really mean is not the individual governing himself, but everybody else governing the individual; thus the need to guard against the tendency of the rest to tyrannize the minority (1988, 62). Indeed, with respect to governments, democratic or otherwise, it is by their power to coerce that we shall know them. Plamenatz thus shared Tocqueville's sentiment that there was no

[15] Cf. Narveson (2000, 17).

[16] In Hoffman (1970, 60).

guarantee that government by consent would be any less coercive than the absolutism it had replaced, but rather that present-day governments acting in the name of the people have proved to be just as tyrannical, if not more so (1968, 175, 181).

In the case of the suppression of minority opinion Mill thinks that government can all too readily convince itself that in doing so it speaks with the voice of the people, whereas Mill considers the right of the government to coerce to be illegitimate, whether the majority supports it or not (1974, 76). Similarly, Bovard rejects the view that coercion becomes acceptable because democracy permits us to elect our coercers (2005, 225). Indeed, the error that democracy amounts to nothing more than the right to govern ourselves, a notion which Dahl thought we should receive with enthusiasm, implying that in obeying the edicts of government we are only obeying ourselves, can be traced back at least to Hobbes, who held that in accusing the sovereign of wrong was tantamount to accusing oneself (1909, 136).

It is interesting to note that Singer characterizes Dahl and Schumpeter as revisionists or realists in political theory, who are largely responsible for his concluding that any actual democratic government is but a poor reflection of his ideal common room association. However, both Singer and his mentors stop short of the more thoroughgoing scepticism of some of the writers we have mentioned. The former seem to have assumed that government, like the poor, is with us always, as well as the fact that democracy is quite high on the evolutionary chain of government, with the odd banana republic that relapses into an earlier stage being the exception that proves the rule.

As we saw, Dahl seemed anxious to avoid putting democracy on trial and to avoid any suggestion from people such as Tocqueville that there might be better ways to preserve liberty than to hitch it up to the democracy bandwagon. According to Dahl, democracy contains all things necessary to salvation, and instead of addressing the question as to whether democracy is compatible with a right to liberty, he offers us the right to govern ourselves, a right which Proudhon decided long ago was largely empty. Provided we stick with the programme, and refrain from heading off into the jungle like Colonel Kurtz in "Apocalypse Now" to try our hand at a little despotism, then all our needs will be ministered unto by Tocqueville's guardian angel. Indeed, in one of his more recent essays, Dahl responds to sceptics that rumours as to the demise of democracy have been greatly exaggerated; although the institution is not in the best of health it has proved remarkably resilient (1998, 188). To such a resounding affirmation of the faith one can only ask with Schumpeter how such a doctrine whose falsity is known to all can have persisted to this day (ibid., 264–265).

Dahl is right that there has been no shortage of commentary to the effect that democracy is in some sort of crisis. Harold Laski wrote years ago that legislatures needed much reform; as for minority governments of the sort seen in Canada of late, he found that they tended to pursue policies which they hoped would keep them in office rather than those they believed in. Majorities on the other hand condemn the opposition to years in the wilderness (1933, 77, 78), and lead to complaints about the country degenerating into a one-party state. The fact that governments have often been elected by less than a majority of the voters leads Gibson to suggest that in fact it is the majority, which is being oppressed by the minority, particularly when parliamentary rules create a virtual dictatorship between elections (2003, 8, 13).

As for Dahl's claim that democratic institutions once established have tended to prove very resilient, it would appear to follow from what Hardin sees as the minimal effects of democracy that so-called democratic institutions are simply window-dressing for the more important order we have managed to coordinate on (2003, 280, 281). In fact, Hardin finds that there are such serious problems with rule by majority that Dahl's talk of the resilience of democratic institutions simply appears to Hardin to amount to making do with such a flawed institution (1993, 157). We have already referred to the difficulties in deriving a collective preference from diverse individual preferences, first formulated by Arrow, for example, where among the three possible choices x, y and z, we end up with the odd result that x will be preferred over y by a majority, y over z by a majority and z over x by yet another majority (1967, 227). Lest we think that such a paradox might be merely a theoretical curiosity or perhaps peculiar to some fault in majority voting, Arrow reminds us that its implications are so general as to render impossible any rule for deriving social choices from a set of individual preference orderings.

Thus, Hardin concludes that the belief that social choice procedures occasionally work is not based on any very clear understanding of how they do, while plausible instances of such choices often prove to be as undemocratic as they are coercive and fraudulent (ibid., 164). However, as we saw in the previous chapter, Hume thought that the magistrates never let such quibbles stand in the way of getting things done with the result that all manner of public works from harbours to armed forces get done (1960, 539). Though, Hardin rightly thinks that Hume's somewhat naïve account of a government which miraculously escapes the manifold frailties of the individuals who comprise it, only to shower blessings upon its subjects, is not quite sufficient to justify overriding the wishes of those who did not necessarily seek the largesse in the first place, or who might have benefited, had it come their way instead. While government might overcome a collective action problem, there is always a question as to whether it overcame the right one, and whether it is justified in coercing those who thought that if any collective solution was needed, this certainly wasn't the one (ibid., 165).

Of course the reason we end up with q and s rather than p and t may be due to any one of a number of maladies, such as those suggested, for example, by Seldon, and to which we have already had occasion to refer, such as a voting system which tends to frustrate voter preferences, while promoting rent seeking, log-rolling, bureaucratic interests and the taxes necessary to pay for them (2002b, 134). Hardin comments that even assuming knowledgeable voters, there is no reason to believe that their preferences are tracked by voting outcomes (ibid., 166), with the result that Hardin is not reassured by Churchill's oft quoted bromide. As a priori claim it is of little use if, as he suspects, the doctrine of majority rule is conceptually incoherent. Considered as an empirical claim there is the problem of a lack of coherent principles by which to support the supposed superiority of certain forms of government over others (ibid., 170).

On the question of basic political rights which Dahl vouchsafed us, on the ground that to do so would not upset the democratic apple cart, Jasay rightly notes the emptiness of any such justification, since if a proposed action confers much on the many and less on the few, many will favour it, and talk of democratic rights is otiose (1998, 134). No doubt we could also add that such a move, rather than giving more, only must appear to give more to many and less to a few.

As to democratic rules, which either refer to the sorts of rights Dahl claimed were implied by the basic right to self government, or to ways of operationalizing such rights, in the context of whether democracy is to be seen as a process or result, Jasay remarks that mere application of such rules would not necessarily lead all to conclude that what resulted was democracy. He notes further that the term *democratic* has become largely devoid of meaning, having been equated in recent political discourse with the good life, which could be seen to justify a change in the democratic rules to achieve a better and more democratic outcome (ibid., 139). Someone who loses an election might claim, for example that the rules as presently constituted should be overridden because they were not conducive to a democratic result, having manifestly failed to preclude unfairness, caused perhaps by an unsympathetic press, or other ways in which the playing fields of Eton are thought to have become notoriously uneven of late.

Samantha Power, for example, was concerned about Russian interference in the US 2016 Presidential Election which she saw as an attempt to undermine the expected presidency of Hillary Clinton (2018, 88). When Clinton lost, Democrats continued the narrative of Russia collusion to explain how upstart Trump could possibly have defeated the pretender, with Jarrett concluding that there was never any evidence that Trump's campaign colluded with Russia (2018, 286). When Trump lost 4 years later, many Republicans were convinced that it was not so much outsiders this time but internal voter fraud which caused the election upset, a view supported by Lott's report to the Dept of Justice (2020) and Navarro's independent assessment (2020).[17] Molly Ball agreed that there was indeed a conspiracy which however saved democracy from the machinations of the tyrant Trump (2021), who never conceded defeat, with election audits in some states continuing at this writing.

With respect to the concern that a majority might decide to do away with democracy, Dahl, we may recall, offered the rather unconvincing

---

[17] One is reminded of the Nast cartoon which has Boss Tweed saying in effect that it's not who votes that counts, but who counts the votes.

response that though a majority might empirically do so, logically they could not, or at least not justly. Jasay, on the other hand, thinks the worry is a genuine one, which does not admit of any pat answer. Indeed we would consider any such decision in the light of feasible alternatives rather than resorting to simplistic pronouncements such as it must be democratic because we took a vote (ibid., 138). Indeed, Narveson thinks that there is nothing whatever preventing a majority from doing whatever it pleases, including throwing away the democratic scaffold by which it ascended to power, and in this respect a majoritarian democracy is no more trustworthy than any other form of government. Contrary to Dahl, Narveson argues that there is at least one right logically prior and morally superior to democracy or the right to self government, namely liberty. Like Tocqueville, there is for Narveson a question as to whether democracy preserves liberty, and generally it doesn't since it has it in common with any form of government that it is in the business of coercion. It therefore hardly seems to place much of a constraint on democracy to insist that it act democratically, if for no other reason than, as Jasay pointed out, it is by no means clear what it is to make such a demand. Thus, Narveson responds that Dahl is wrong in assuming that democracy is simply to be desired for its own sake; if we want democracy at all, it is because ends we seek are better attained democratically than by some other means.[18]

## 4.3 Liberalism v. Democracy; Recent Trends

While earlier classical liberals such as Hayek and Mises would probably not have disagreed with much of our criticism of democracy, they generally felt that democracy represented something of an improvement over absolute rule, though, as Hayek warned us, the supposed antidote to arbitrary power, if not itself constrained by liberal principles, might well become yet another arbitrary power (1978, 106). Mises for his part rejected as nonsense the view that only monarchs are evil and capricious, while the people are pure and uncorrupted; nevertheless, he

[18] Cf. "Liberalism v. Democracy," 6.

thought that democracy provided a mechanism for orderly and non-violent changes of government (1996, 42). On the other hand, we have been suggesting that it is no longer clear that democracy is as compatible with liberalism as Mises and Hayek may have thought. As Narveson puts it, liberalism is finally incompatible with democracy, since if we have a choice between acting on our own preferences, provided we do no harm, or being coerced to obey the wishes of others, it isn't obvious why we would choose the second (2002a, 175).

Hoppe also holds that democracy has little to be said for it, and if we are going to have a state at all, a real monarchy without the democratic posturing is likely to offer both economic and moral advantages (2002, xx). With monarchy come the benefits of privatizing government, since the monarch is less likely to squander the resources of the realm he owns. Similarly, Hoppe contends, he is likely to be more moderate in the expropriation of his subjects, since to do otherwise would kill the goose that laid the golden egg, that is, cause a decline in the productivity of his subjects and therefore in his monopoly on extracting tribute (ibid., 19). A democratic ruler, on the other hand, while he can and typically does use the government to his personal advantage, does not own it, unlike the monarch. The democratic leader is under no pressure to preserve the capital of the realm, and even if he wished to do otherwise, since the property is public and lacks a market price, it would not be possible. The democratic steward has no incentive to moderate his expropriation, because unlike an hereditary monarch, he is not in the business for the long haul (ibid., 24). But short of selling the country there is nothing to stop the politician from restoring his sagging fortunes with projects financed by Chinese debt with various strings attached that may not be in the country's long-run interest, as Gelpern et al. have reported (2021).

To be sure, one might respond that the possibility of being turfed out at the next election should act as a brake on the profligacy of democratic rulers. On the other hand, as Hoppe suggests, elections may simply spur them on to seek rents while the sun shines; or they can always appeal to the need to provide what Juvenal considered particularly close to the heart of every Roman, *panem et circenses*. About the latter Narveson comments that democratic perks are typically at someone else's expense, a fact which political grandstanding mostly obscures (2002a, 175). Then again, providing bread and circuses, or their even more costly contemporary analogues, requires the raising of vast amounts, which governments typically do via taxes or debt instruments of one sort or another.[19] We saw in the previous chapter that direct taxes on income, for example, were a relatively recent phenomenon, for which there appeared to be no satisfactory justification.

But given that modern governments have also granted themselves a licence to print money, they regularly resort to this more recondite method of financing their pet projects. As Mises has noted, this inevitably causes inflation, since more money for the same basket of commodities increases demand and therefore prices. This is not to say that there aren't some beneficiaries whenever it rains dollar bills. Those directly involved in the project for which the new money was printed stand to gain, e.g., materiel manufacturers during wartime, whereas those much lower down the feeding chain, such as teachers and clergy during World War 2, were at a disadvantage because their salaries took much longer to catch up (2000, 58, 61). Mises emphasizes that although some do better than others under inflation, they can hardly be reproached for profiteering, since it was the government which decided on a policy of inflation, not that it would ever call it by its real name (ibid., 63).[20] While Mises also thought that governments would be eventually forced to abandon inflationary policies or face catastrophic currency failure, as in Germany in 1923, or Zimbabwe in 2007, Rothbard is less sanguine, believing that the only alternative is to replace the fiat currency of the politicians with something they cannot so easily manipulate, such as the gold standard (1990, 111).

In the light of Hoppe's earlier remarks, we should inquire as to whether a democracy is more likely to debase the coin of the realm than a monarchy. He in fact admits that monarchs did tend to enrich themselves

---

[19] Buchanan notes that while politicians may find it hard not to shower gifts on the populace, unlike a private citizen who bears the costs of his impulsive actions, the whole country may suffer from the politicians' lack of restraint (2000, 191).

[20] Despite the government's complicity in the 2008 financial crisis (Norberg 2009; Woods 2009), they kept a watchful eye on what they considered business profiteering. Buchanan reminds us that it is typical of government to blame business for the effects of inflation on ordinary citizens (2000, 148–149).

by monopolizing the mint and coin clipping, beginning with the foundation of the Bank of England in 1694. Indeed, it seems that relatively few empires, except for the Byzantine from about 500–1000 AD, were able to resist the attempt, at least from time to time, to corrupt gold or silver with base metals. However, in general not even kings managed to establish monopoly fiat currencies (ibid., 57), which we have had since the US finally abandoned the gold standard in 1971. Since then, the US debt has risen from $370 billion to around $30 trillion at this writing, which for Hoppe is a result of the time horizons epitomizing the democratic ethos (ibid., 59, n.25) and which Buchanan observed were characteristically short (2000, 166). Kant, for his part, thought that the ability to rack up vast amounts of offshore debt in the service of war, as opposed to national infrastructure, was an important stumbling block to peace, and should be subject to international interdiction (2007, 9–10).

### 4.3.1 The Democratic Peace

Having raised the subject of war, let us address another issue, which for many has been considered at least since Kant and Tocqueville as an important article of the democratic faith, namely that unlike war-mongering monarchs down through the ages, democracies are slow to wage war, and typically avoid wars with other democracies. Although Kant has been thought to favour such a view, his position is a little more complicated, since he sharply distinguishes republican from democratic constitutions, with the former being characterized by the separation of the executive power from the legislative (ibid., 15). The republican constitution, Kant claims, is more conducive to perpetual peace because consent of the populace is needed to wage war, which will allow them to fully consider the costs, including post-war reparations. However, under a non-republican constitution it is much easier to resort to war, since the prince is the nation's owner rather than a citizen and is as likely to give as much thought to opening hostilities as he might to going on a hunt (ibid., 9–351). Of course, with respect to the people acting as a check on their leaders, as Radnitzky points out, this requires voters to be much better informed about the justification and costs than they typically are (2003, 178).

Interestingly, since it supports what we have argued above, Kant considers democracy to be a form of despotism, being necessarily majoritarian and relying upon the incoherent notion of the general will (ibid., 15). While Kant thought it reasonable to conduct citizen military training, he contended that standing armies were likely to cause wars and should be demobilized (ibid., 9), not that Prussia seems to have heeded his message, since it continued to supply the backbone of the general staff.[21] Writing some 40 years later, Tocqueville believed all countries, including democracies, could find themselves at war, and therefore would require an army. However, while the officers' corps of old Europe had been reserved for the aristocracy, whose social status was more important than an army career, the forces of democracies exemplify Napoleon's claim that every French soldier carries a field marshal's baton in his cartridge pouch. While the nobleman was motivated by *noblesse oblige*, the possibility of attaining high rank, aided by a belief in meritocracy was what drove the soldiers of democracies. Peace of course is not conducive to promotion since there is nothing like a war to clear the market for officers. Thus, Tocqueville reaches what he considers the rather paradoxical conclusion that the enthusiasm for equality which undergirds democracy's love of peace, also inspires its soldiers to be the most eager (ibid., 753).

Hoppe agrees with Tocqueville that democratic armies may be even more bellicose than those commanded by a monarch, while drawing different conclusions from Kant about the royal owner of the nation. In Hoppe's view a king desirous of expanding his realm, unlike a president, does not have war as his only option. The former may unite kingdoms through marriage, an option not available to the non-state owner president, whose treaties or contracts with other governments may be revoked by his successors, if not by him when politically expedient. Moreover, the king's wars are much less likely to be ideologically motivated than to be over expanding his real estate holdings (ibid., 34). But as Howard observes the more popular war became, it also became more violent,

[21] See Goerlitz (1965).

whereas those, for example, of the *ancien regime* tended to be limited at the very least by cost (2002, 33). Hoppe argues that the democratic-republican temper of the French Revolution found a champion during World War I in Woodrow Wilson, who sought to use war to make the world safe for democracy (ibid., 41). The Wilson doctrine has been reiterated by later presidents, including for example, Bill Clinton who claimed in his State of the Union Address in 1994 that the US should support the advance of democracy throughout the world because democracies refrain from attacking one another, a view which Radnitzky claims has become a shibboleth of American foreign policy (ibid., 185). Eland finds that paradoxically this could lead to continual war in search of peace (2004, 42), while Kant thought that mutual interest and the spirit of trade would lead us to promote the former and avoid war (ibid., 39).

Rothbard writes, however, that we are still labouring under the Wilsonian delusion that, unlike dictatorships, democracies do not start wars. While citizens of a democracy are unlikely to find much about the domestic policy of a dictatorship very appealing, Rothbard claims that it is wrong to assume that a dictatorship's foreign policy will necessarily include war, for some despots have largely kept to themselves while many democracies have been belligerent (2007b, 2). Because the Wilsonian myth is seen to be politically correct,[22] a president may have a more difficult task than a dictator and therefore need to resort to greater manipulation and subterfuge. This will typically involve the characterization of the enemy as non-democratic, a charge which will generally not be that hard to make out, given the small number of states that are paid-up members of the democratic club.[23]

Moreover, a president may have to devote considerable effort to selling a war, and in the case of the Iraq war, we never seem to have gotten beyond the sales propaganda. As Creveld comments, we are still left guessing as to the reasons for the Iraq War (2006, 246). Pena claims that the war on terrorism was subject to mission creep where the Bush administration was able to sidestep the original congressional mandate largely by ratcheting up rhetoric from WMD to the axis of evil, whereas the

[22] Cf. Radnitzky (ibid., 184).

[23] Cf. The Economist (2021).

actual threat from either appeared to be minimal (2006, 10). According to Radnitzky, one of the ways that a democratic president can circumvent constitutional oversight and assume personal control of foreign policy, much as monarchs of the *ancien regime* were wont to do, is to claim that the enemy fired the first shot (ibid., 181). In the case of Iraq, one might believe that Sadam was involved with those that did, or that a pre-emptive strike was necessary to prevent his firing first. In fact, such a rationale for the attack on Iraq was propounded by the US administration and has come to be known as the Bush Doctrine, despite the fact that Clinton had authorized at least three such actions.[24]

Indeed, in some of the discussion prior to the Iraq war one commentator offered yet another version of the *pax democratica*, namely that democracies, in particular the US, do not fight preventive wars.[25] Dershowitz responds that pre-emption is somewhat of a paradox, since if used we cannot be sure what it achieved, or if not, what it might have achieved (ibid., 159). However, at least in the case of Nazi Germany he is inclined to say that in hindsight the democracies should have taken preventive action against Germany. While rejecting analogies between Hitler's Germany and Sadam's Iraq as flawed, Dershowitz does not wish to rule out cases where preventive action by a democracy could be justifiable (ibid., 160). Again, Radnitzky emphasizes that while it may not be the case that democracies are more reluctant to go to war, preventive or otherwise, a democratic president has more legal and political hurdles to overcome than a dictator (ibid., 181). No doubt launching a war against Sadam when he could not have posed much of a threat following his rout in 1991[26] required considerable political shrewdness on the part of the Bush administration. Sometimes duplicity is used to provoke others, such as allies or enemies, into action. Thus, according to Raico, it now appears likely that Churchill engineered the sinking of the Lusitania in 1915 to bring the US into World War I.[27] Similarly, Denson accuses Roosevelt of provoking the Japanese attack on Pearl Harbor and

[24] Cf. Dershowitz (2006, 157).

[25] Cf. Dershowitz (ibid., 159).

[26] Cf. Creveld (ibid., 246).

[27] "Rethinking Churchill," in Denson (2003, 332).

withholding information which might have prevented it (2006, 102). Raico also observes that by contrast with leaders intent on occupying the supposed high moral ground of democracy, Frederick the Great happily confessed to launching the Seven Years War to increase Prussian prestige (2020, 1). Moreover, as Cavallar suggests, Frederick's ruthless foreign policy may have eventually influenced Kant, who apparently never quite shared Voltaire's enthusiasm for the philosopher of Sans Souci, to favour republican democracy over enlightened absolutism (1993, 129ff).[28]

As for Clinton's version of the *pax democratica* that democracies do not go to war with one another, according to Radnitzky, it is falsified by the American civil war itself, a war of secession between two democracies with the same currency (ibid., 191). Nor is there any reason to think that Wilhelmine Germany was any less of a democracy than the UK, and indeed as welfare states go, Germany was far ahead of Britain. Indeed, President Wilson demonstrated a democratic totalitarianism which the Kaiser could only wish to have emulated, instituting a system of neighbourhood watchers who would report suspicious individuals.[29] In fact much like Tocqueville, Radnitzky sees totalitarianism as being at the very core of democracy and particularly evident in its ability to concentrate power during a supposed crisis. German industries under Albert Speer were for example less tightly regulated than those in the US, with consequent reduction in US output (ibid., 182). According to Radnitzky such totalitarianism is supported by the quasi-religious democratic ethos which treats the results of an election as an oracular pronouncement from the mouth of the people (ibid., 188).

Thus, war is undertaken as a democratic jihad which often results in prolonging hostilities until the infidels have been wiped out or made to see the error of their ways. Taylor informs us that those who entered World War I to make the world safe for democracy were in no great hurry for an armistice but were willing to fight on until Germany offered an unconditional surrender (1964, 45). Radnitzky again contends that since wars waged by democracies are more ideological, they also tend to be

[28] Kant considered Frederick to have possibly nodded in the direction of representative government when he described himself as merely its first servant (2007, 16).

[29] Cf. Nisbet (1989, 44–46).

harsher and more difficult to finish than those of autocrats. Roosevelt's enthusiasm for democracy apparently did not get in the way of friendship with Stalin, though like his predecessors, it probably prevented his being in a hurry to end the war (ibid., 181, 192).

As for cruelty, democracies could more than hold their own when it came to the bombing of civilians. American insistence on unconditional surrender prolonged the Pacific War and resulted in the nuclear bombing of Japan. Terror-bombing of German cities authorized by Churchill killed about 600,000 and injured another 800,000, compared to about 70,000 killed in raids on Britain. Nevertheless, according to Gilbert, Churchill thought there were a couple of important differences between parliament and a dictatorship, namely that the former avoided open brawls and provided for orderly regime changes (2006, 134). Throughout his long career Churchill appears to have relished the many opportunities for wielding power, from First Lord of the Admiralty to Prime Minister, which according to Raico, allowed him to pursue a dramatic life of perpetual bellicosity. Indeed, Raico's final assessment of the great champion of parliamentary democracy is that he was totally devoid of principle and hardly deserving of the historical pedestal on which he has been placed.[30]

Talmon once claimed that there were two types of democracy, the liberal and the totalitarian. The former is called liberal because of its emphasis on freedom, characterized by spontaneous and non-coercive order. Totalitarian democracy, on the other hand, undertakes a messianic mission in search of universal order.[31] While liberal democracy holds that we will gradually succeed to a more harmonious state with little coercion, totalitarian democracy has a sharper vision of that ideal state, and has much less hesitation in using coercion to reach it, since it finds no conflict between coercion and the democratic principle (1970, 1–3). Indeed, it is the second, or totalitarian version which has gained the ascendancy, one whose lineage can be traced to the Committee of Public Safety (ibid., 251). Gottfried considers the central feature of the Revolution to be the fact that people were killed in the name of democracy, a

[30] Cf. "Rethinking Churchill," in Denson (2003, 360).

[31] Cf. Sowell (2002).

tradition which he now finds exemplified in the great leviathan latter-day American democracy has become, prescribing remedies for all ills. This present incarnation, which owes more to the French Revolution than the Founding Fathers, offers neither freedom nor self rule, serving only the interests of its ruling class, supported by its vast bureaucracy, and favoured industries.[32]

### 4.3.2 Democracy and Property

If recent liberalism and democracy have not shrunk from war, nor have they been averse to commandeering the resources necessary for the various wars and crusades undertaken by the state against both internal and external threats. Thus, we should perhaps not be surprised to see a diminishing respect for property rights, which Gottfried also recorded, and of which the Canadian Charter provides a good example, where protection of the life, liberty and security of the individual does not extend to the individual's rightfully acquired property. Even if it did, it would doubtless be subject to the notable proviso that it be limited by what is justifiable in a democratic society even though, as Jasay noted, questions of justice are not a matter of majority vote (1998).[33] In fact, Jasay writes that private property used to be seen as reinforcing the bulwarks of civil society against the state and therefore an important institution for both owners and non-owners (ibid., 144).[34] Or as the historian, Pipes, puts it, property has been the single most effective device for ensuring both civil rights and liberties, marking out a sphere in which the individual is sovereign (1999, 281). Thus, according to DeSoto, property was essential to the production of capital in the West for which the development of property title at law was essential (2000, 51).

---

32 In Denson (2003, 426–427, 429).

33 If it is a matter of deciding whether a proposed abridgement of Charter rights is reasonable in a liberal democratic society it will be up to a majority, not of the people, but of the unelected Supreme Court Justices, which, as Starkey tries to reassure us, is as Sir Edward Coke would have wished (2015, 154).

34 Among the non-owners having interests are bankers, governments of one sort or another and other suppliers of goods and services: cf. DeSoto (2000, 51).

Despite the clear benefits to all of a propertarian regime, sovereign democracy can override title in any way it sees as reasonably justified.[35] As observed earlier, Rex has not departed the political scene but has simply appeared in new finery, and as Jasay points out, about all the *legum leges* or constitutional charter guarantees, is that we and our property are no safer under the sovereign people than we were under the monarch, for the threat derives from sovereignty per se (ibid., 208–209). One of the chief sovereign prerogatives is what has latterly become known as redistribution, and which appears to be derived from earlier granting of land and privilege based on meritorious service to the monarch. According to the medieval constitution, as mainly revealed in its land law, all land is held of the king, though he may grant tenure to his subjects, for example, for military service, or perhaps knight service, which meant limited war service as a fully armed horseman. There was considerable disagreement between king and barons as to the scope of the latter, the upshot of which was that, contrary to modern conscription, it did not imply overseas service. Unlike modern democracy, medieval sovereignty was subject to increasing limitations beginning notably with Magna Carta.[36]

However, as Jasay reminded us, sovereign democracy knows no such bounds, supported as it is by the fiction that majority rule in its various manifestations is a direct pipeline to yet another fiction, namely the common good. Or as Salin has put it, democratic procedures are self justifying, assuming as they do that there is a way of ascertaining a demand for collective goods or that there is a common good which has priority over individual rights (2000, 112). The redistributive state possesses a vast array of goods to hand out as it sees fit to all and sundry, the most notable feature of such transfers being that they benefit some at the expense of others, or as Jasay writes, the state robs Peter to pay Paul, being apparently unable to contemplate a Pareto improvement where Paul's lot would be made better, but not at Peter's expense (1998, 255, 149). On the contrary, democratic competition necessarily makes some winners and others losers; benefits to one group are at the expense of

[35] Cf. Jasay (ibid., 144).

[36] Cf. Maitland (1965, 23–26).

some other group. Indeed, as Jasay further points out, democracy can be seen as an instance of a three-player distribution game where two of the players get to decide the size of the winnings to be distributed to their benefit and to the disadvantage of the third player left out of the ruling coalition (2002, 110).

Of course, we might ask why Pareto improvements where some gain and none lose are preferable to non-Pareto solutions where some gain while others lose. Jasay replies that, provided we can ignore envy, the former is by definition good, since some have ended up better off and no one worse off, while the latter would require an argument as to what was good about them, since some have been harmed as a result. As for the prospects of ruling out envy, as we have already had occasion to remark, Lucas thought that, at least for the egalitarian, they were rather slim (1971, 150). With respect to the frequent assimilation of inequality to injustice, Schumpeter, in a noteworthy obiter, believes we have democratic rhetoric to thank for equating inequality with injustice, which not only provides comfort to the less fortunate but a useful opportunity for political intervention (ibid., 254, n.3).

In addition to the general Pareto objection against redistribution, Jasay mentions a couple of others. First is the fact that the government's duty to protect rightly held property conflicts with its supposed democratic mandate to redistribute that property to others. Further, those such as Schumpeter's unsuccessful who press their eleemosynary petitions upon the emperor, may not always find sovereign power so beneficent since recipients of the sovereign's favour today may fall from grace tomorrow (2002, 84–85). Or as Friedman pointed out, once you invite the state to legislate against discrimination, the same power accorded to the state can also be used to discriminate, as in the Nuremberg or Jim Crow laws (1962, 113).[37] Thus when it claims to offer protection, the only hazard the state does not protect against are those inflicted by itself, which, contrary to what Walzer thought, are not confined to banana republics or populist democracies (1983, 83).

[37] Thus, the Jeffersonian principle that a government big enough to give you everything you want is strong enough to take everything you have.

### 4.3.3 Hayek and the State

If war is one of those crises which Higgs has suggested give rise to an expansion of the state (1987, 17), democratic or otherwise, such increased powers will also affect the life and liberty of its citizens. In fact, the past millennium from the Norman Conquest to the present day has proved singularly fatal to millions, with the twentieth century being the bloodiest of all. Indeed, Denson has estimated that some 170 million were killed by governments, of whom 60 million died in the two World Wars (2003, 17). With respect to one of the more recent enthusiasms of the war and welfare state, the so-called war on terror, Robin has also observed that when the war on terrorism comes to an end, we shall still be living in fear of our own governments who will have managed to dispose of any threat except that posed by themselves (2004, 25). Both war and welfare require the coercive redistribution which has come to be the hallmark of the contemporary state, despite the arguments that have been levelled against it.

Although as we mentioned at the outset, Hayek was on record as wishing to keep coercion to a minimum, he does not think that maximizing liberty will rule out all government activity, since there are supposedly non-coercive activities, which it would be reasonable to support by taxation (1978, 257). Hayek seems to think that there is some way to determine which actions of government are coercive, and which are not, other than by asking whether a proposed action would infringe upon someone's liberty, which we are not entitled to do unless that person threatens to harm someone else. Government coercion could be justified on similar law and order grounds, namely, to neutralize threats from those proposing to harm others, a justification which Sumner has, for example, reaffirmed as a reasonable approach to regulating freedom of speech (2004, 185). Sidgwick calls such a criterion for government intervention by its then fashionable name of individualism, according to which others are owed only duties of non-interference, and compensation in the case of harm (2005, 43).

However, Hayek reminds us that modern governments have never just confined themselves to the minimum required by individualism (ibid.,

257), influenced perhaps by Sidgwick's view that individualism or libertarianism cannot be counted on to deliver the requisite amount of social utility (ibid., 44). Hayek argues that all modern governments charged themselves with the welfare of the unfortunate, as well as with health and education (ibid.). To which we would respond that indeed they have, though generally with little to show for the enormous expenditure. The political crowding out of private charity, as Seldon observes, is no exception since charity supplied by taxation has not only led to a decline in private charity but also in the ability of people to look after themselves (2002a, 86).[38]

In our view, of course, nothing whatever follows from what recent governments have found themselves inclined to do. Similarly, we reject Hayek's claim that it is possible to supply needs collectively without affecting liberty (ibid., 257). Since collective action is mostly synonymous with government action, it restricts individual liberty, even though Hayek holds that some degree of state paternalism is not necessarily harmful. The criterion Hayek proposes for separating the non-harmful or non-coercive functions of government from the coercive and undesirable ones is that of freedom within the rule of law which is tantamount to the rule of the state. Thus we can distinguish the coercive measures of government from services such as health and sanitation, which do not involve coercion, or do so only to the extent that taxes are required to support them. In Hayek's view the provision of such services only becomes coercive if the government acts as monopoly provider (ibid., 220–223).

Working back from the last point, we argued in the previous chapter that once government decides there is a need for it to supply a service, before long it assumes it has an exclusive right to do so, just as it assumes it has an exclusive right to coerce compliance. The supposed importance of the need in no way mitigates the coerciveness of the taxation, for as Jasay writes, taking money and giving it to others is redistribution, regardless of the motive (2002, 90). As for the benefits of the rule of law

[38] Cf. Whelan's suggestion that if we could rediscover the motivations driving the private production of welfare before state takeover, we might be able to solve the problems of the bloated and inefficient welfare state (1996, 98).

adduced by Hayek, where the state's power to coerce is clearly circumscribed by law (ibid., 222), as Jasay has pointed out recently, it is not clear if the legal framework really acts the way many theorists claim. According to this received view, the state ensures that we do the right thing by providing monopoly enforcement, which we pay for, not only because we must, but because this is supposedly the most efficient way to stave off social breakdown. However, this monopoly is subject to all sorts of political hazards, with the result that it rarely delivers what it promises. Further, because enforcement is financed by taxes it invites free riding by individuals who download responsibilities onto the state that in a well functioning society, they would bear on behalf of themselves or their family and friends (2007, 1).

It should also be noted that Hayek is aware that the main concern of public finance is to raise as much money as possible with the least fuss. This has gone hand in hand with an attempt to hoodwink the taxpayer into paying more than he thinks by convincing him that others will really pay for it. As opposed to the Murphy/Nagel approach discussed above, the one way to counteract the law of growing public expenditure is not to have needs determine taxes, but the other way round. Hayek believed government should be reformed so that we could know what we were paying for, and get what we paid for, rather than paying for all government services regardless of whether we use them. Majoritarian democracy is not a recipe for rational public finance, but rather encourages people to resort to state coercion to have others pay for what they think they need (1979, 51–52).

Hayek also makes it clear that, while he favours a larger public sector than we have been advocating throughout this discussion, the concern for social justice which drives the Murphy/Nagel enterprise has no place in his, emphasizing as it does the spontaneous ordering of the market. Hayek argues that while it might be tempting to consider the misfortunes of life, including the unequal distribution of worldly goods, as unjust, no one has in fact acted unjustly towards another (1976, 69). The belief that in a socially just system wealth would be equally distributed is largely responsible for the contemporary so-called mixed economy, where government acts as though it could and should level the playing field.

Again, Hayek emphasizes, as we have done in discussing the Murphy/Nagel proposals, that morality consists of rules for individual conduct. In Hayek's Great or Open market society there would be no room for governments to chase the will-of-the-wisp of social justice, rather than performing their sole function of providing for law and order and any collective needs which might not be met by the market (1976, 82, 83). In his view social justice simply consists in supporting demands that have no basis in morality, whereas human society cannot function in the absence of morality (ibid., 97). In fact, Hayek even thinks it possible, as we have been intimating in this essay, that government may not be essential to the spontaneously ordered society, though moral rules may require some enforcement mechanism (1973, 47). Indeed, they might, though one suspects that a private court system could prove much more efficient than the hopelessly inefficient and corrupt government counterparts we are familiar with.

It is also worth noting that in the Great Society, where we simply enforce the rules of just conduct or laws prohibiting *malum in se*, much of the enterprise of law as we presently know it would disappear, consisting of *malum prohibitum* or statute law. The latter would include the host of regulations by which politicians have sought to control economic activity, for which in fact nothing more is needed than that people avoid force and fraud, and honour contracts. As an important step in providing capitalism with the tools required to do its job, Hayek recommends removing government monopoly on money, which was never intended to be a source of good money but rather of providing government with a licence to print it. Private monetary systems, on the other hand, will prove more stable in purchasing power. He believes that democracy where government is at the beck and call of endless pressure groups will never be able to give us reliable money, but rather will resort to inflation, followed by totalitarian price controls.[39] Indeed, as Hayek wrote more than 30 years ago, economic downturns are largely the fault

[39] The 2008 recession provided another excuse for government to shower money on all and sundry. But as Woods observes, it is difficult to cure overspending and debt by more of the same. The government borrowing necessary to fund bailouts will require the printing of more money which erodes the value of the dollar (2009, 150–151). There is no reason to believe that Covid bailouts will perform any differently.

of government monopoly, which has produced such resource misallocation that even the introduction of sound money might take a long time to correct (2008, 23–25, 27–28).

While Hayek appears to be ready at least in principle to overlook the coerciveness of taxes to provide some basic goods, he also thinks it important to distinguish laudable objectives from the actual policies used to put them into practice. Having desirable goals is one thing, but if many state welfare activities are seen as a threat to freedom, it is because they rely on coercion to maintain the state's monopoly (1978, 258). The paternalistic state then doles out portions of the income it has taken from its subjects as it sees fit (ibid., 260–261). Nor should we think that democracy will safeguard our liberty by somehow reigning in the bureaucrats, including the highly bureaucratized professions, who consider it their job to give us what they think we need (ibid.). Indeed, as we have already pointed out in this chapter, democratic control is as much a myth as the public good the *nomenklatura* are supposedly charged with safeguarding; for Hayek it is not surprising that in the name of welfare, an administrative monster is created as a law unto itself and not as the agent of the principal citizens (ibid., 262).

### 4.3.4 Democracy and Redistribution

The redistribution which is central to the doctrine of state sovereignty depends, as Jasay explains, on the further notion of a great amount of orphan wealth waiting for politicians to disperse at will (2002, 100). Such bounties typically spill over from two party contracts, where both parties consider themselves to have secured a good deal. The fact that a third party who is external to the contract happens to profit in some way puts him under no obligation to the contracting parties who undertook their contract solely to benefit one another. Nor do these inheritors of a supposed surplus owe anything to society in general or earlier generations since the original parties were satisfied with the terms of the contract (ibid., 103).

Even if there was something to be recaptured from the products of past contractors, as Jasay observes, society has no more claim on this supposed pool than the individuals who contributed them do (ibid., 104), nor is the state entitled to them, and as we have argued, democracy is in no position to underwrite any such claim. On the contrary, Chodorov points out that the periodic changing of the political guard tends to obscure the true nature of the state, allowing the rulers to convince themselves that they have been exalted above their fellows to serve a higher calling (1959, 99).

Further, as Jasay explains, the supposed unowned pool of wealth which is available for redistribution to the needy multitude appears upon closer inspection to be two rather different pools. The first consists of the sum of unintended consequences of various forms of social cooperation, while the second consists of those additional goods which we have at least metaphorically contracted with a government to supply, such as defence, law and contract enforcement. Indeed, some enthusiasts for redistribution, such as Judge Posner, have gone so far as to claim that the government's enforcement of property meant that one was in effect a trustee of government property. Thus, when eating something as humble as a potato chip, one does so by the government's grace, since it is thanks to its beneficence that one can assert rightful ownership of the chip.[40] However, what His Lordship needs to explain is in what sense one could still coherently be said under such a regime to have a property right in the chip.

If we have, as it were, contracted with government suppliers for certain goods, there may well be positive externalities available to non-contractors, as there were in the case of private contracts. Moreover, if the principle of *ne bis in idem* continues to hold, according to which someone who happens to benefit from a positive externality, as we all do when people refrain from attacking us, or plant nice gardens, is under no obligation to pay for the benefit, contracting taxpayers are not entitled to seek redistributive compensation from the non-taxpayers. For, as Jasay observes, it is not at all clear those who provide the externality owe anything by way of redistribution to those who don't (ibid., 103). Indeed, he concludes that just as we owe nothing to particular people

---

[40] cited by Jasay (ibid., 102 n.13).

whose actions contribute positive externalities, nor do we owe society for benefits of unknown provenance (ibid., 106).

We noted earlier that democracy was a distribution game where commonly Peter was robbed to pay Paul, but according to Jasay, redistribution often takes the form of churning, where both will be robbed at different times with Paul maybe netting a slight gain in the end (1998, 261). This is not to say that either Peter or Paul will be aware of what their net positions are, and as Tocqueville points out, this was as true in eighteenth-century France as it is now. Although the nobility supposedly benefited from tax exemptions, which caused great resentment on the part of the populace, because of tax liabilities relating to his tenants, the net difference was much less than it first appeared (1955, 87).

Rather, to divide and conquer, the state seems intent upon keeping both Peter and Paul, and their heirs and successors, in the dark, and according to Jasay, it is in the state's interest to have more people thinking they have come out on top and few who think they have lost out, so as to retain the loyalty of the former (ibid., 261–262).[41] Despite possible political benefits, there is always the chance that Peter and Paul will tire of playing the distribution game, as their French ancestors apparently did at the Revolution, because the state is in the end the only beneficiary of churning (ibid., 264).

## 4.4 Dworkin on Democracy

In the last chapter of his discussion of democracy, Dworkin asks whether indeed democracy is possible, concluding much as we did earlier that the prognosis for majoritarian democracy is in fact rather bleak. He cites the pitiful standards of public discourse and the abysmal ignorance of the average citizen about any matter of significance. Politicians have become so accustomed to dumbing-down their message that truth has been sacrificed to scoring quick soundbites against one's opponents (2006, 128). Worse still, politics is a matter of money, with politicians spending a

[41] Thus, the Shavian wisdom that a government which robs Peter to pay Paul can always depend on the support of Paul.

great deal of their time bagging as much of it as possible by peddling their influence to large donors.

In response to the pedestrian realities of everyday politics, rather than taking the sanguine view that things were ever thus, Dworkin offers the more serious assessment that the political process and its legitimacy are now very much in question (ibid., 130). Curiously enough, however, it doesn't occur to Dworkin that democracy itself might be the problem, as we have been suggesting. On the contrary, according to Dworkin, all of us accept the general superiority of democracy to other forms of government, believing that we could not in good conscience support any alternative (ibid.).[42]

But of course, that is exactly what we have been questioning here. The fact that a government is democratic, in some sense or other, and Dworkin admits that the US is far from being a pure example, in our view, adds nothing whatever to its legitimacy which it doesn't already possess *qua* government. The only legitimacy it could possess *qua* government is that we have contracted with it to perform certain functions on our behalf, which overall it appears we have not done, or if we thought we did, this supposed agent all too often acts like a super contractor/enforcer of some sort.

However, Dworkin claims that underneath a vaguely Churchillian cheer for democracy rests profound disagreement as to its nature. Views divide into two main camps—majoritarian versus partnership democracy. We have already had occasion to refer to the majoritarian view of democracy, but somewhat like Singer, Dworkin proposes his partnership view as a way of rescuing democracy from its majoritarian errors by meeting further criteria designed to guarantee full partnership of each voter in the democratic process (ibid., 131). This account of partnership democracy is somewhat vague, as Dworkin admits, but we have already questioned the notion that democracy amounts to people governing themselves, and no qualifications either of the Singer or Dworkin variety serve to render it any more intelligible. Attempting to solve collective action politically, it is hard to escape the absurdity noted so aptly by

[42] Kekes offers a similar view to the effect that democracy's imperfections are the least of all forms of government (2008, 213).

Rose Wilder Lane, that self government requires a government to govern oneself (1993, 208).

The essence of Dworkin's partnership view is acknowledgement of others which, however, appears to be little more than lofty goal since contemporary politics favours the simple majoritarian position. On the latter view the majority carries the day, even if that means, according to Dworkin, having the legitimacy of our democracy threatened by our unwillingness to dig ever more deeply into our pockets to rescue others from misfortune. Of course, Dworkin still thinks that redistribution schemes run by the government are actually capable of delivering much besides rents to the politicians and the various functionaries who administer such programmes. Indeed, redistribution seems to have it in common with any form of socialist calculation, that in the end it is impossible to make. Rather, as Salerno has pointed out, the state can only produce welfare for some by destroying the support for others.[43] Nor is it any surprise that Dworkin should be mistaken about the virtues of redistribution, since as Jasay has observed, the haphazard intricacies of the redistribution scheme make it difficult to obtain any clear picture of its consequences, both from the point of view of the government as well as its supposed beneficiaries (1998, 262).

Of course, Dworkin argues that the virtues he does see in redistribution in turn rest upon his analysis of liberty, of what we are free to do or not do, and to be sure, we are not simply free to do as we please (ibid., 69). Well, indeed we aren't, for as Narveson has noted our own freedom of action is constrained by what others have a right to do (1988, 7). Thus, one is subject to longstanding prohibitions against force and theft since such actions violate the right of others to live their lives free of such predations. Dworkin agrees with a similar limitation on one's liberty, but at the same time believes that government redistribution schemes do not constitute any such infringement (ibid., 69–70). What Dworkin seems to have overlooked is that restrictions upon my liberty imply restrictions upon my ability to compel or coerce others. If I am not at liberty to seize your property because I believe I need it more than you do, as we have argued all along, there is no reason to believe that a government is at

[43] Postscript to Mises (1990, 70).

liberty to do so either. As Nozick held, it is not as if there is a distributor in chief who is checking that we have all got equal slices of the mythical government pie. To the extent we get anything, it will be because we engaged in a mutual exchange with someone else (1974, 149).

Dworkin, however, subscribes to a doctrine of reasons of state or the view that the state may possess plausible justifications for its actions not morally available to individuals, such as how it is that a large-scale distribution of social goods may be adjudged as fair (ibid., 170). We have already addressed the question as to how a theory of distributive justice depends upon a questionable notion of an unowned pool of wealth which is supposedly not fully captured by commutative justice, but, according to Jasay defaults to political distribution (ibid., 101). Further, with respect to Dworkin's view that the state may rightfully seize some proportion of our assets to accomplish its ends, Nagel claims that taxation shows clearly that there is no way of deriving the state's morality from the widely accepted rules that constitute private morality. Those that apply to the state and its institutions are inevitably consequentialist, such as the collection of taxes for redistribution, which is not susceptible of justification by the moral criteria we would apply to individual acts (1978, 88).

Again, if there really is such a disconnect between the morality of the state and its institutions, and that of the private individual, as Machiavelli famously thought, it is not clear why the individual should feel morally compelled to take any notice of the state's predilection for redistribution. Although Dworkin thinks most of us don't in fact consider taxes an infringement of our rightful freedom, there is no moral reason why we shouldn't (ibid., 69). In fact, Dworkin appears to recognize as much when he suggests, in favour of his own view, that the mere fact that a majority supports a proposal is not a good reason to adopt it as policy (ibid., 134), and offers further criticisms of majoritarianism reminiscent of those made above. He claims, for example, that it is wrong to think that a majority vote is necessarily the right way to solve disagreements about a course of action (ibid., 139). Accordingly, it would probably be a mistake to use a majority vote to decide who in an overcrowded lifeboat had to take his chances with the sharks, who was to be drafted for military service, or whether some questions of sexual behaviour might be subject to collective oversight.

In reply to the view that there might be times when a majority vote is the only fair way to decide a collective political matter, Dworkin rightly reminds us that in a democratic regime where all appear to have equal political power the rulers in the three branches of government have much more power than any private individual. Being neither capable of delivering the truth, nor of equal political power, Dworkin concludes, again happily, that the majority principle tells us nothing important about the value of any policy (ibid., 141–143).

Other than thanking Dworkin for supporting many of the criticisms we had already made about majoritarian democracy, that should be an end of the matter, except that Dworkin thinks he has a cure for what ails democracy, namely that we take seriously the rights of others to fair treatment, something he has been advocating for the past 30 years. One plank in such a platform is equality of concern, to which we might give effect by electing officials by wide suffrage, and not from within their unaccountable bureaucracies. Given that their number is reminiscent of the ten thousand times ten thousand, and thousands of thousands gathered about the throne in heaven, the cure for unsatisfactory elections sounds like an everlasting dose of them. Of course, about the notion of equal concern in general, Jasay has aptly remarked that its meaning is so unclear as for it to be impossible to tell whether it was instantiated in any particular instance or not (1991, 40, n.1).

Another way to give effect to equal concern we are told is by including special individual rights in a constitution subject only to judicial interpretation, and by raising the bar for constitutional amendment (ibid., 144). However, recent writers have shown that the US had such a constitution, whose provisions for individual rights have apparently been whittled away by unelected judges. Thus, according to Barnett, what liberties existed have been eroded by the judicial branch of the state (2004, 1), and for Epstein, the Progressives used interpretation as a vehicle to make the Constitution a mere shadow of the founding document (2006, 135–136).

Both Barnett and Epstein mention the particularly egregious instance of rewriting in favour of more expansive government powers, which we raised in the previous chapter under the heading of eminent domain. With respect to the much-discussed Kelo case, Epstein comments that it represents a major setback for the security of possession of one's home in the face of the ever-growing Progressive state (ibid., 134). If constitutions have not proved the bulwark against the erosion of rights, which some had hoped they might, it was Dworkin who reminded us years ago that rights would be trumps unless some overriding collective purpose dictated otherwise (1977, xi).[44] Jasay rightly responds that about all this seems to mean is that rights are trumps except where they are not, which is a rather odd definition of a trump and about the best you can expect under the Progressive version of liberalism (1991, 39–40).

Dworkin does attempt to clarify when a majority will have the right to impose its will on a minority, by appealing to the notion of self government. While it would compromise my dignity for others to automatically assume coercive authority over me, equal participation on my part does not involve loss of dignity. While this is apparently an important condition for democratic legitimacy, it is by no means clear, as we noted above, what would count as fulfilling it. Thus, such a notion can be of no help in explaining in what sense democracy implies self government. It would appear to mean self government, except when it doesn't, just as rights are trumps, except when they aren't, which is much of the time. Instead of self-government in any literal sense, what you get are rights less likely to be abridged than some, such as sharing in a political decision, voting, or running for office. Similarly, it seems, while some restrictions are understandable, such as those relating to the use of seatbelts or pharmaceuticals (ibid., 73), one has a right to decide the role of religion or morals in one's life (ibid., 146) provided, I imagine, that one's religion is not, for example, a front for terrorism or female genital mutilation, or that one's morality includes Progressivism.

[44] Barnett considers allowing the defence of public *purpose* rather than *use*, as in the case of a road or park, to be an example of gutting a crucial limitation on the takings power (2004, 354). In Kelo et al. *v.* City of New London, Conn. the Supreme Court upheld the city's taking private houses under eminent domain so that Pfizer Inc. could redevelop the land on which they stood and bring increased revenues to the cash-strapped city.

Dworkin's schedule, as it turns out, parallels that of the Canadian Charter of Rights and Freedoms, which after acknowledging the supremacy of God in the preamble,[45] lists freedom of conscience and religion as the first right, including freedom of expression and assembly, to be protected from legislative encroachment, followed by the right to vote. The Charter acknowledges a rather vague criterion for abridging rights, namely what is legally reasonable in a free and democratic society, which has apparently permitted seatbelt and pharmaceutical legislation, no doubt as part and parcel of the nanny state. Should that condition prove insufficient, parliaments can enact overrides to any of the earlier provisions including the schedule of legal rights, the first of which is the right to life, liberty and security of the person. About this ordering of rights, Narveson correctly notes that this latter right should have been at the top since all other rights flow from it (2002a, 236). Lately all manner of restrictions, such as shutting businesses, preventing public gatherings, quarantines, distancing, masks and fines have been tolerated supposedly to mitigate the threat of Covid 19, all of which, including many others, were thought compatible with a supposedly free and democratic society. However, Bishop suggests that such measures are a reminder of the fact that democracy is no longer liberal in any sense that matters, and that forced vaccination is not off the Covidocracy's table (2021). In fact, Singer, writing from Melbourne, which has become synonymous with lockdowns, claims that "On Liberty" notwithstanding, vaccination nowadays must be imposed on people for their own good like seat belt laws (2021).

Again, with respect to the right which Narveson would have included in the preamble, the European Convention on Human Rights lists protection of the right to life as the first of its 66 articles, a protection which might be diminished by the circumstances of a given case, such as one's having engaged in unlawful violence, rather than by contrary legislation. The Convention also provides a right to private property [Protocol, Article 1], used, for example, to roll back union dues in

[45] No doubt lest we think that the doctrine of divine right was a relic of absolute monarchy.

Sweden,[46] a right which Dworkin does not mention, and which is notably absent from the Canadian Charter.[47]

If Dworkin was hoping to escape the curse of majority rule, schedules of rights are not handed down on tablets on the mount but are established by committees who very much rely on majority rule. Dworkin thought that one way to guarantee equal concern was by listing individual rights in a constitution interpreted by judges rather than politicians, since courts are independent from the other branches of government and the most suitable tribunal for adjudicating rights (1985, 27, 32). However, there is no escape from majority rule either in the appointment of judges in the first place, or in the decisions rendered *en banc*. Moreover, although Dworkin admits that while Americans have often considered lawyers to be one of the least honourable professions, they abound in government where they wield considerable power and influence (ibid., 31–32).

According to Martin, the government of Canada is also a paradise for lawyers despite a similar poor public image (2003, 180). No doubt there is the illusion that donning the mantle of legislator, or the robes of a judge, enables one to overcome the frailties all too evident in more humble pursuits. While politicians do not typically fare any better in the public estimation than perhaps they did as lawyers, *pace* Dworkin, judges are not always held in great esteem either. For example, Martin considers a one-time member of the Supreme Court of Canada, Justice L'Heureux-Dube, to have entirely lacked both the personal and legal stature required for the job (ibid., 195).

Of course, Dworkin admits that we are a long way from a democracy of equal partnership, a fact which undermines any claim to democratic legitimacy. In fact, we share Dworkin's criticism of the present state of democracy, where most notably our electoral procedures are not genuinely democratic and political disagreements are not conducted in a respectful manner (ibid., 147). While most of Dworkin's criticisms have

---

[46] Cf. Södergren (2007, 23–25).

[47] However, in the absence of such a provision, on the question of union membership, while the Supreme Court of Canada has, for example, read into freedom of association under Article 2. that one cannot be compelled to join an association, under Article 1. it has at the same time found such compulsion justified in a free and democratic society; cf. Södergren (ibid., 13).

already been anticipated earlier in this discussion, we fail to share his belief that there is a genuine democracy which would be revealed if we were to strip away the practices that have been carried on in its name over the past couple of centuries. In our view what you see is what you get, and as with other proposals for democratic rehabilitation, the solution is not to be found in yet more democracy. Even if political debate could rise to the level of a mutually respectful disagreement, we may well continue to disagree, and do so profoundly, and may well have to resort to a vote, if there appears to be no alternative to collective action of some sort.

Part of the problem is getting to some agreement in the first place as to what matters, if any, will unavoidably be the subject of collective action and what won't. Perhaps this requires settling upon a constitution which attempts to coordinate, as Hardin suggests, on some of the broader structures and functions of the state (2003, 84). Assuming we can agree on the matters which call out for some sort of collective resolution, a relatively short list, on my view, we will presumably have to agree on how those resolutions are to be taken. With respect to the US Constitution, for example, Dworkin claims that majoritarianism was never intended to carry the day (ibid., 146). Elsewhere, however, he considers the New Deal as the last liberal settlement, or benchmark for the latter-day liberalism which he espouses. A principal feature of this view is redistribution to reduce inequality, while not abandoning free enterprise, plus a general assortment of latter-day liberal causes such as affirmative action and the protection of civil liberties (1980, 122).

Following the example of the New Deal, the aim is for such positions to issue in firm government policy by the usual majoritarian routes of electing a party and president who support such causes. However, the end result may stray considerably from such objectives, as did Roosevelt's first New Deal which appeared to have more in common with Mussolini's fascist state than the customary liberal nostrums.[48] As for

[48] Cf. Flynn claimed that Roosevelt's plan had much in common with Italian corporativism which he simply rebranded as liberal progressivism (1940, 83). While Goldberg admits the influence of fascist Italy and Germany on the New Deal, he thinks that FDR did not need to go much further afield than Wilsonian socialism. If liberal fascism, a term coined by H.G.

the claim that Roosevelt rescued the US from the Depression by government spending, DiLorenzo comments that such strategies simply divert resources from the private to the government sector, depressing genuine economic growth, with the result that unemployment was higher in 1938 than in 1931. Rather than the New Deal being of any benefit to the needy, it was mostly designed to ensure FDR's re-election (2004, 199–200).

Thus it seems rather difficult to reconcile the New Deal with Dworkin's claim that it embodied a political morality whose constitutive element was supposedly treating its citizens with respect, a view reflected in his partnership conception of democracy, which is just a more recent elaboration of the liberal package inherited from FDR (1980, 120–121). Indeed, it is hard to see what is particularly liberal about the first liberal settlement, for as Holcombe observes, the growth of democracy in government came at the expense of liberty (2002, 231). Although Dworkin claims to have avoided the errors of majoritarian democracy, his political morality, such as it is, is clearly descended from that tradition, and despite much posturing to the contrary, never really departs from it.

Moreover, as Spencer asked well over a century ago, what is it that qualifies one or more to assume sovereignty over others? (1981, 128). The answer, as we have been suggesting, is that there is no such warrant, and according to Spencer it is superstitious to think otherwise, since we have just transferred the myth of divine right of the monarchy to legislatures. The oil which anointed kings now drops upon the chosen of the people sanctifying their pronouncements (ibid., 123). Further, Chodorov reminds us that in a republic the transfer of power to representatives is a done deal since our supposed agents can usually work around any constitutional restraints. Even if we vote the incumbents out at the next election, another crowd of hopefuls steps up to the plate, with the result that once more we hand over control of our lives to those who may be no more capable than the last lot. One way to end the eternal cycle

Wells, stopped short of its European counterparts, Goldberg believes it had to do with American exceptionalism (2007, 11, 21, 161).

of sovereignty is to take ever diminishing voter turnout to its conclusion and stay away from the polling booth, in the hope of conveying the message that we no longer need politics to manage our lives. No doubt, we may expect a reaction from those who have most to lose by any reduction of the state (1980, 199–202). Statists par excellence, such as Hitler, Mussolini and Stalin still liked to see a ballot, even if there was only one party to vote for, but politicians of every stripe are unlikely to view with equanimity losing the stamp of legitimacy conferred by the people, and could be expected to respond by enforcing voting, as has happened for years in Australia.

Among those who could be expected to support the status quo ante any reduction of the state are the legions who live full-time off the avails of government, from welfare recipients to deputy ministers. With respect to those on welfare, Mill famously held that anyone receiving such support should be automatically disqualified from voting, since if he cannot provide for himself, he has no claim on others to support him (1958, 134). As for the bureaucracy, Tullock thought that state employees or anyone who was in other ways on the state payroll should be denied the vote (2002, 55, 58). Thus, we agree with Spencer that if government is simply seen as a management committee, its authority will be limited to carrying out the fiduciary duties its principals assign to it (ibid., 161, 165–166).

Brennan has claimed that the main problem besetting democracy is that it leaves us at the mercy of the great unwashed who mostly have little clue what they are voting for and have even less incentive to do much about it because their vote counts for little, not that they are necessarily aware of that. Instead of universal suffrage democracy, Brennan suggests we consider limiting the vote to those who know what is needed for good government, likely by passing qualifying exams. Another possibly more palatable version would have experts elected to an epistocratic council, which would be able to veto political decisions by the electorate at large or its representatives if it considered them ill-advised. But as desirable as it might seem to have political decisions based on more reliable knowledge, Brennan considers various difficulties related to the qualifications and election of the epistocratic council. One is that the sort of well-educated voters likely to be elected to the epistocracy might not look much like a representative sample of the populace. Rather than that being an objection to epistocracy per se, Brennan suggests that we attempt to address the social issues underlying the apparently biased representation (2017, 228). Another is that the ability of such a body to override rather than simply advise other bodies may strike some as undemocratic. Brennan replies that if we find the fact of courts sitting in judgement on the decisions of other bodies tolerable in a democratic society, we should have no qualms about the epistocracy's rulings either (ibid., 219).

The question we need to ask in conclusion is whether this more recent proposal answers some of the questions we have raised, and I suspect not. The main problem is that we are still left with a top-down political order, a-*cracy* of some sort, in this case an aristocratic house of the knowledgeable with power to veto the decisions of other bodies. If majoritarianism is a worry as Dworkin claimed it was, then the various stages of getting such a body up and running as well will be subject to majority decisions and the gaming and political jobbery that goes along with them. With reference to the various forms of participatory democracy fashionable in some quarters, Brennan reminds us that such enthusiasm is generally bad for us and tends to make us enemies of one another (ibid. 73, 235ff), so it is not at all clear why the politics of an epistocracy would be much different.

While Brennan is probably right that plural voting such as Mill had in mind would not resurrect Plato's philosopher kings (ibid. 213), we might still wonder whether the proposal for an epistocracy would do so. Whether or not we agree with Kant that combining the two roles in one person is undesirable because of the tendency of power to corrupt reason (2007, 46), a lesson Frederick II may or may not have impressed upon him,[49] or with Popper that the philosopher king was simply Plato himself revealing his love of power (1971, 155), the fact that the philosophers of the epistocracy wield power, even if it is less than that of a king, is not obviously something we see much reason to welcome. Hayek pointed out that while a body of experts might be the best way to tap into the

[49] While Kant did not favour philosopher kings, nor did he think that kings should silence philosophers, since their unbiased and apolitical views would be beneficial to the state (2007, 46).

current state of knowledge, the real problem would be picking them in the first place. Moreover, to the extent that an epistocracy suggests that in virtue of its powers all the most relevant knowledge is possessed by its members, it ignores the widely dispersed knowledge held by every actor in the marketplace (1948, 80–81). Or as Mises observes, even if chosen by the competent and possessing the wisdom of Plato's philosophers, sitting atop a socialist state, they will lack a merchant's insight, even if that was something they originally possessed (1990, 39).

## 4.5 Summary

To determine how democracy might be called upon to underwrite the authority of the state, we began with Peter Singer's discussion (1974), where he considers three possible modes of government for his model common room association, ranging from the autocratic to the democratic. He expects that only the latter will generate the sort of obligations on the part of its members to support the decision favoured by the majority. No doubt influenced by Hart's argument from fairness, Singer thinks the dissenter will feel constrained to go along with the majority because he has as it were by his participation consented to the outcomes of the democratic machine. Even if this is true of a small-scale association, there is still a question of its relevance to the republic, and as we have argued elsewhere, we suspect the answer is very little. Indeed, if there are any reasons to obey, it would be because they are independently morally right reasons, and not because they were arrived at democratically.

To the extent that democracy continues to have any appeal, it is because it is often seen to be connected in some way with liberal rights, which themselves derive from a basic right of all to liberty. In fact, democracy is inimical to individual liberty, interfering with the latter on behalf of the special interests which constitute Dahl's polyarchy. Democracy is no guarantee of peace, nor of a quick end to war, any more than it has proved a defender of that central individual right, namely private property. Its main *raison d'etre* is redistribution, and it serves as a reminder that the sovereign people represent no less of a threat to individual liberty than the *ancien regime*, for example. Dworkin claims to see much wrong with majoritarian democracy, as we have done, but approves of its central tenet of redistribution; while he touts self government, we seem to end up with participation, which sounds like more of the same, rather than any cure for what ails democracy. As to whether some version of an epistocracy might repair democracy's failings, presumably the permanent bureaucracy or deep state already consists of an army of experts and to the extent that it is they who are really running the show, maybe we already have more epistocracy than we need.

## Works Cited

Ackerman, Kenneth D. *Boss Tweed.* New York: Carroll & Graf, 2006.

Arrow, Kenneth J. "Values and Collective Decision Making." In *Philosophy, Politics and Society*, 3rd Series, ed. Laslett and Runciman, 215–232. Oxford: Blackwell, 1967.

Ball, Molly. "The Secret History of the Shadow Campaign That Saved the 2020 Election." *Time Magazine*, February 4, 2021.

Barnett, Randy E. *Restoring the Lost Constitution.* Princeton, NJ: Princeton, 2004.

Bastiat, Frederic. *Selected Essays on Political Economy.* New York: Foundation for Economic Education, 1995.

Binmore, Ken. *Game Theory and the Social Contract: Playing Fair.* Boston: MIT Press, 1995.

Bishop, Tho. *Covid Tyranny Destroys the Myth of Liberal Democracy.* Auburn: Mises Institute, 2021.

Bovard, James. *Attention Deficit Democracy.* New York: Palgrave, 2005.

Brennan, Jason. *Against Democracy.* Princeton: Princeton University Press, 2017.

Buchanan, James M., and Wagner, Richard E. *Democracy in Deficit: The Political Legacy of Lord Keynes.* Indianapolis: Liberty Fund, 2000.

Cavallar, Georg. "Kant's Judgement on Frederick's Enlightened Absolutism." In *History of Political Thought* 14 No.1 [Spring 1993]. Imprint Academic Ltd.

Chodorov, Frank. *Fugitive Essays.* Indianapolis: Liberty Press, 1980.

———. *The Rise and Fall of Society.* New York: Devin-Adair, 1959.

Creveld, Martin van. *The Changing Face of War.* New York: Ballantine, 2006.

Dahl, Robert A. *A Preface to Democratic Theory.* Chicago: Chicago U. Press, 1956.
———. *Pluralist Democracy in the United States.* New York: Rand McNally, 1967.
———. *Polyarchy.* New Haven: Yale U. Press, 1971.
———. *A Preface to Economic Democracy*. Berkeley: California U. Press, 1985.
———. *Democracy and Its Critics.* New Haven: Yale U. Press, 1989.
———. *On Democracy.* New Haven: Yale U. Press, 1998.
———. *How Democratic Is the American Constitution.* New Haven: Yale U. Press, 2003.
———. *On Political Equality*. New Haven, Yale U. Press, 2006.
Denson, John V. *The Costs of War: America's Pyrrhic Victories.* New Brunswick: Transaction, 2003.
———. *A Century of War: Lincoln, Wilson, and Roosevelt.* Auburn: Mises Institute, 2006.
Dershowitz, Alan M. *Preemption: A Knife that Cuts Both Ways.* New York: Norton, 2006.
DeSoto, Hernando. *The Mystery of Capital.* New York: Basic Books, 2000.
DiLorenzo, Thomas J. *How Capitalism Saved America.* New York: Three Rivers Press, 2004.
Dworkin, Ronald. *Taking Rights Seriously.* London: Duckworth, 1977.
———. "Liberalism." In *Public & Private Morality*, ed. Stuart Hampshire, 113–143. Cambridge: Cambridge U. Press, 1978 [Reprint,1980].
———. *A Matter of Principle.* Cambridge: Harvard U. Press, 1985.
———. *Law's Empire.* Harvard U. Press, 1986.
———. *Is Democracy Possible Here?* Princeton: Princeton U. Press, 2006.
The Economist Intelligence Unit. *Democracy Index 2020, In Sickness and in Health?* London: The Economist, 2021.
Eland, Ivan. *The Empire Has No Clothes: US Foreign Policy Exposed*. Oakland: Independent Institute, 2004.
———. *How Progressives Rewrote the Constitution.* Washington: Cato Inst., 2006.
Evatt, Herbert Vere. *The King and His Dominion Governors.* London: Frank Cass, 1967.
Flynn, John T. *Country Squire in the White House.* New York: Doubleday, 1940.
Forcese, Craig, and Aaron Freeman. *The Laws of Government*. Toronto: Irwin Law, 2005.
Friedman, Milton. *Capitalism and Freedom.* Chicago. U. of Chicago Press, 1962.

Gelpern, Anna et al. *How China Lends: A Rare Look into 100 Debt Contracts with Foreign Governments.* AIDDATA: A research hub at William and Mary, March 2021.
Gibson, Gordon, ed. *Fixing Canadian Democracy.* Vancouver: Fraser Institute, 2003.
Gilbert, Martin. *The Will of the People.* Toronto: Vintage Canada, 2006.
Goerlitz, Walter. *The German General Staff 1657-1945.* New York: Praeger Inc., 1965.
Goldberg, Jonah. *Liberal Fascism: The Secret History of the American Left from Mussolini to the Politics of Meaning.* New York: Doubleday, 2007.
Goodin, Robert E. *Reflective Democracy.* Oxford: Oxford U. Press, 2003.
Green, Leslie. *The Authority of the State.* Oxford U. Press, 1988.
Hardin, Russell. "Public Choice Versus Democracy". In *The Idea of Democracy*, ed. David Copp et al. Cambridge: Cambridge U. Press, 1993.
———. *Liberalism, Constitutionalism and Democracy.* Oxford: Oxford U. Press, 2003a.
Hare, R.M. "The Lawful Government." In *Philosophy Politics and Society*, 3rd Series, ed. Peter Laslett and W.G. Runciman, 157–172. Oxford: Blackwell, 1967.
Harper, F.A. *Liberty: A Path to Its Recovery.* Irvington-on-Hudson: The Foundation for Economic Education, 1949.
Hayek, F.A. *Individualism and Economic Order.* Chicago: Chicago U. Press, 1948.
———. *Law, Legislation and Liberty*, Vol. I. Chicago: Chicago U. Press, 1973.
———. *Law, Legislation and Liberty*, Vol. 2. Chicago: Chicago U. Press, 1976.
———. *The Constitution of Liberty.* Chicago: Chicago U. Press, 1978.
———. *Law, Legislation and Liberty*, Vol. 3. Chicago: Chicago U. Press, 1979.
———. *A Free Market Monetary System.* Auburn: Mises Institute, 2008.
Hazlitt, Henry. *Man vs The Welfare State.* New Rochelle: Arlington House, 1969.
———. *The Conquest of Poverty*. New Rochelle: Arlington House, 1973.
Henderson, David. *Joy of Freedom.* Upper Saddle River: Prentice-Hall, 2002a.
———. "Myths about US Health Care." In *Better Medicine*, ed. David Gratzer, 175–195, Toronto: ECW Press, 2002b.
Higgs, Robert. *Crisis and Leviathan.* New York: Oxford U. Press, 1987.
Hobbes, Thomas. *Leviathan.* Oxford: Oxford U. Press, 1909.
Hoffman, Robert, ed. *Anarchism.* New York: Atherton, 1970.
Holcombe, Randall G. *From Liberty to Democracy.* Ann Arbor: Michigan U. Press, 2002.

Hoppe, Hans-Hermann. *Democracy: The God That Failed.* New Brunswick: Transaction, 2002.

Howard, Michael. *The Invention of Peace and the Reinvention of War*. London: Profile, 2002.

Hume, David. *A Treatise of Human Nature*, ed. Selby-Bigge. Oxford: Oxford U. Press, 1960.

Ibbitson, John. *The Polite Revolution.* Toronto: McClelland & Stewart, 2005.

Jarrett, Gregg. *The Russia Hoax: The Illicit Scheme to Clear Hillary Clinton and Frame Donald Trump.* New York: HarperCollins, 2018.

Jasay, Anthony De. *Choice Contract and Consent*. London: Institute of Economic Affairs, 1991.

———. *The State.* Indianapolis: Liberty Fund, 1998.

———. *Justice and Its Surroundings.* Indianapolis: Liberty Fund, 2002.

———. "Misbehavior, Punishment, Prosperity. Part I The Statist Legacy." *The Library of Economics and Liberty* [August 6, 2007]. http://www.econlib.org/library/Columns/y2007/Jasaypunishment.html

Kant, Immanuel. *Perpetual Peace.* Minneapolis: Filiquarian Publishing LLC, 2007.

Kekes, John. *The Art of Politics.* New York: Encounter, 2008.

Kheiriddin, Tasha and Adam Daifallah. *Rescuing Canada's Right.* Mississauga: Wiley, 2005.

Lane, Rose Wilder. *The Discovery of Freedom.* San Franscisco: Fox & Wilkes, 1993.

Laski, Harold. *Democracy in Crisis.* London: Allen & Unwin, 1933.

Locke, John. *Two Treatises of Government*, ed. Peter Laslett. Cambridge: Cambridge U. Press, 1960.

Lott, John Jr. *A Simple Test for the Extent of Vote Fraud with Absentee Ballots in the 2020 Presidential Election: Georgia and Pennsylvania Data.* Washington: US Dept of Justice, December 21, 2020.

Lucas, John. "Against Equality." In *Justice and Equality*, ed. Bedau, 138–151. Englewood Cliffs: Prentice-Hall, 1971.

McWhinney, Edward. *The Governor General and the Prime Ministers.* Vancouver: Ronsdale, 2005.

Maitland, F.W. *The Constitutional History of England.* Cambridge: Cambridge U. Press, 1965.

Martin, Robert Ivan. *The Most Dangerous Branch.* Montreal: McGill-Queen's, 2003.

Michels, R. *Political Parties.* New York: Dover, 1959.

Mill, J.S. *On Liberty.* London: Penguin Classics, 1974 [1988].

———. *Considerations on Representative Government.* Indianapolis: Bobbs-Merrill, 1958.

———. *Omnipotent Government*. Grove City: Libertarian Press, 1985 [1944].

———. *Economic Calculation in the Socialist Commonwealth.* Auburn: Mises Institute, 1990.

———. *Liberalism: The Classical Tradition.* Irvington-on-Hudson, Foundation for Economic Education, 1996.

———. *Economic Policy.* Irvington-on Hudson: Free Market Books, 2000.

Mueller, John. *Capitalism Democracy & Ralph's Pretty Good Grocery*. Princeton: Princeton U. Press, 1999.

Nagel, Thomas. "Ruthlessness in Public Life." In *Public and Private Morality*, ed. Stuart Hampshire, 75–91. Cambridge: Cambridge University Press (1978) 1980.

Narveson, Jan. *The Libertarian Idea.* Philadelphia: Temple U. Press, 1988.

———. *Classics of Political and Social Philosophy.* Waterloo: U. Waterloo, 2000a.

———. *Respecting Persons in Theory and Practice*. Lanham: Rowman & Littlefield, 2002a.

———. *A Fairly Short Introduction to Political Philosophy*. Lanham: Rowman & Littlefield, 2008a.

Navarro, Peter. *The Immaculate Deception: 6 Key Dimensions of Election Irregularities.* Independent Report: December 2020.

Nelson, William, N. *On Justifying Democracy.* London: Routledge, 1980.

Nisbet, Robert. *The Present Age.* New York: Harper, 1989.

Norberg, Johan. *Financial Fiasco: How America's Infatuation with Homeownership and Easy Money Created the Economic Crisis.* Washington, DC: Cato Institute, 2009.

Nozick, Robert. *Anarchy, State and Utopia.* New York: Basic Books, 1974.

O'Rourke, P. J. *Don't Vote: It Just Encourages the Bastards.* New York: Atlantic Monthly Press, 2010.

Pateman, Carol. *The Problem of Political Obligation.* Berkeley: California U. Press, 1979.

Pena, Charles. *Winning the Un-War: A New Strategy for Winning the War on Terrorism.* Dulles: Potomac Books, 2006.

Pipes, Richard. *Property and Freedom.* New York: Random House, 1999.

Plamenatz, J.P. *Consent, Freedom and Political Obligation.* Oxford: Oxford U. Press, 1968.

———. *Democracy and Illusion.* London: Longman, 1973.

Popper, Karl R. *The Open Society and Its Enemies, Vol. I, Plato.* Princeton: Princeton University Press, 1971.
Power, Samantha. "Beyond Elections: Foreign Interference with American Democracy." In *Can It Happen Here: Authoritarianism in America?* ed. Cass Sunstein. New York: HarperCollins, 2018.
Plato. "The Crito." In *The Dialogues of Plato,* ed. Jowett, Vol. I, 4th ed. Oxford: Oxford U. Press, 1953.
Radnitzky, Gerald. "Is Democracy More Peaceful Than Other Forms of Government?" In *The Myth of National Defense,* ed. Hans-Hermann Hoppe, 145–212. Auburn: Mises Institute, 2003.
Raico, Ralph. "Why Historical Revisionism Matters". article@mises.org, October 23, 2020.
Rectenwald, Michael. *Google Archipelago: The Digital Gulag and the Simulation of Freedom.* Nashville: New English Review Press, 2019.
Robin, Corey. *Fear: The History of a Political Idea.* New York: Oxford U. Press, 2004.
Rothbard, Murray. *For a New Liberty.* New York: Collier, 1978.
———. *What Has Government Done to Our Money.* Auburn: Mises Institute, 1990.
———. "The November Memorandum." 1994, www.lewrockwell.com/rothbard/rothbard155.html.
———. "Revisionism for Our Time." article@mises.org [June 29, 2007b].
Salin, Pascal. *Libéralisme.* Paris : Odile Jacob, 2000.
Schumpeter, J.A. *Capitalism Socialism and Democracy,* 4th ed. London: Unwin, 1954.
Schwab, Klaus, and Malleret, Thierry. *Covid 19-The Great Reset,* Geneva: World Economic Forum, 2020.
Schweizer, Peter, *Throw Them All Out.* New York: Houghton Mifflin Harcourt, 2011.
Seldon, Arthur. *Capitalism.* Oxford: Blackwell, 1990.
———. *The Dilemma of Democracy.* London: Institute of Economic Affairs, 2002a.
———. "Public Choice in Britain." In *Government Failure,* ed. Gordon Tullock, 129–176. Washington: Cato Institute, 2002b.
Shapiro, Ian, *Democratic Justice.* New Haven: Yale U. Press, 1999.
———. *The Moral Foundations of Politics.* New Haven: Yale U. Press, 2003.
Sidgwick, Henry. *The Elements of Politics.* London. Macmillan, 1897 [Elibron Classics reprint 2005].

Simmons, A. John. *Moral Principles and Political Obligations*. Princeton: Princeton U. Press, 1979.
———. *On the Edge of Anarchy*. Princeton: Princeton U. Press, 1993.
Simpson, Jeffrey. *The Friendly Dictatorship*. Toronto: McClelland & Stewart, 2001.
Singer, Peter. *Democracy and Disobedience*. Oxford: Oxford U. Press, 1974.
———. "Remember Seat Belts? Why Vaccination Should Be Compulsory." *The Globe and Mail*, August 7, 2021.
Södergren, Jan. No Forced Union Membership or Dues for Politics: It's a Human Right. Toronto: Canadian Association of Counsel to Employers, 2007.
———. *The Quest for Cosmic Justice*. New York: Simon & Schuster, 2002.
Spencer, Herbert. *The Man Versus the State*. Indianapolis: Liberty Classics, 1981.
Starkey, David. *Magna Carta: The True Story behind the Charter*. London: Hodder and Stoughton Ltd, 2015.
Sumner, L.W. *The Hateful and the Obscene*. Toronto: U. Toronto Press, 2004.
Talmon, J.L. *The Origins of Totalitarian Democracy*. London: Sphere Books, 1970.
Taylor, A.J.P. *The Origins of the Second World War*. London: Penguin, 1964.
Tocqueville, Alexis de. *The Old Regime and the French Revolution*. New York: Doubleday, 1955.
———. *Democracy in America*. London: Penguin, 2003.
Tullock, Gordon. *Government Failure: A Primer in Public Choice*. Washington, DC: Cato Institute, 2002.
———. *The Vote Motive*. London: Institute of Economic Affairs, 2006.
Walzer, Michael. *Spheres of Justice*. New York: Basic Books, 1983.
Whelan, Robert. *The Corrosion of Charity*. London: Institute of Economic Affairs, 1996.
Wollheim, R. "A Paradox in the Theory of Democracy." In *Philosophy Politics & Society*, 2nd Series, ed. Peter Laslett and Walter Garrison Runciman. Oxford: Blackwell, 1962.
———. *Meltdown: A Free-Market Look at Why the Stock Market Collapsed, the Economy Tanked, and Government Bailouts Will Make Things Worse*. Washington, DC: Regnery, 2009.

# 5

# The Non-fallacy of Anarchism

Edmundson concludes his *Three Anarchical Fallacies* by reviewing arguments he has made in favour of the legitimacy of the state and against the sceptical view I have been advancing, for example, that we have a duty of non-interference with respect to the orders of a legitimate state (1998, 79). However, while legitimacy might conceivably entail such a duty, it simply begs the question as to whether there are any such states to begin with, something we cannot tell simply by inspection of its prerogatives. Indeed, it seems more likely that there are no such states, or as Jasay, has put it, binding contracts are not dependent on the myth of a legitimate state (1997, 36).

The second sceptical fallacy which Edmundson claims to have exposed is that of the coerciveness of law, which would make it harder to believe that we have a duty not to stand in its way (ibid.). We have argued that the law is indeed coercive, but whether that makes compliance more difficult seems to depend less on the presence or absence of coercion, but rather on whether coercion, by individuals or their agents, is justified in any particular case. In his attack on the third anarchical fallacy, Edmundson thought it important to show that whatever morality can

© The Author(s), under exclusive license to Springer Nature Switzerland AG 2022

G. Booker, *Coercion, Authority and Democracy*, Palgrave Studies in Classical Liberalism, https://doi.org/10.1007/978-3-031-16883-3_5

enforce the state may do likewise, which will have the benefit of showing law at its least coercive (ibid.).

Again, I suggested earlier that Edmundson has things the wrong way round, since the anarchist is generally more interested in legal requirements that appear to have little basis in morality. However, Edmundson thinks it an important question, whether morality can extend beyond law, such that there is conduct which is open to moral but not legal appraisal (1998, 127). Mill thought there was such a space reserved from the prying eye of the state, with the only question being where the boundary was to be drawn (1985, 306). Latterly this question reappeared when the Wolfenden Committee held that crime is the business of the law whereas sexual behaviours considered sinful by some remain beyond the law's reach.[1] According to Hart, such a view is not unlike Mill's in "On Liberty" where state coercion can only be justified by the need to avoid harm to others (1963, 15, 20). Lord Devlin, on the other hand, found fault with the Committee's approach since the law may rightly be called upon to defend the moral norms of society (ibid., 11) and in his opinion morality is not a private matter, since as such it could leave the vulnerable open to exploitation. Moreover, even when behaviour involves consenting adults, the need to maintain moral norms could override privacy rights (ibid., 19).

Hart denies that there is any such public interest which may rightfully be offended by private acts, for which it may demand relief at law; unless there are stronger grounds than disapproval, individual liberty should carry the day (ibid., 47). While Hart thinks it important to avoid Devlin's error of legal moralism, where the law, rather than being an instrument to protect one man from another, is deployed in a crusade against moral wickedness, he finds no inconsistency between his enthusiasm for individual liberty and his claim that protecting people against themselves is entirely justifiable. If indeed paternalism has become more fashionable since the days of Mill and laissez faire it is apparently merely a fact of social history, of which we should duly take note, just as we should find it equally unremarkable that as a result, for example, supplying non-pharmaceutical drugs is a crime (ibid., 31–32).

---

[1] Cited in Devlin (1975, 2).

No doubt it is similarly a matter of social history that a generation later Hamowy found himself declaring just the opposite, namely that in a liberal society we are no more entitled to prevent others from using certain drugs we disapprove of than we are the books they choose to read. We may attempt to persuade them, but the bully pulpit of the state has no business trying to rid us of sin (1987, 34). Some years later Healy hoped that the trend of drug liberalization would continue (2008, 129), and given that pot shops are now springing up like mushrooms, no doubt fuelled by the Covid crisis, it seems that far from being preoccupied with the cure of souls, the state has found a new industry to mismanage, which was probably not the sort of liberalism Healy was looking for.

In support of his claim that criminal law has historically never been separate from morals, Devlin noted that the law had never allowed victim consent as a defence (1963, 6), implying of course that it would be inconsistent to permit such a defence in the case of homosexual relations. The fact that we don't permit the defence of consent in a murder case, however, Hart thinks is still better explained by paternalism than by appeal to widely held moral rules, as Devlin would have it. However, Devlin is also right to wonder what the distinction between legal moralism and paternalism amounts to, something which Hart does not bother to explain (ibid., 133). While conceding that paternalism is one explanation, Hart appears to sidestep any question about its moral status by simply characterizing it as a fact of social history.

But of course, paternalism is not only a fashionable policy, but it is also a moral principle telling us that on at least some occasions we may be entitled to go further than Mill's non-maleficence principle and act as our brother's keeper, as Hart himself recommends. With respect to the rule which does not permit consent as a defence to murder, it seems a little odd to describe this as a case of paternalism since it is already too late to speak of protecting the victim; Devlin is right to see it as a case of punishing the wrongdoer for his immoral act. Moreover, it isn't obvious that Mill's principle needs to give way—it clearly provides for coercion to be used against murderers, and, *pace* Hart, is right to question paternalist legislation against drugs. As for Hart's claim that euthanasia or killing someone with their consent is still murder (ibid., 30), in some countries the criminal law has been amended to permit euthanasia by physicians,[2] following changes recommended by the Wolfenden Committee in the case of homosexuality and prostitution.

As for Edmundson's believing that he has uncovered another of the errors of anarchism, it seems that he has mostly been misled by rhetoric reminiscent of Wolfenden to the effect that there are acts, which some consider still to raise moral questions, but which ought no longer to fall under the purview of the criminal law and are best left up to the individual. If others participate in such acts, provided they have done so freely, there is no harm which the law need to protect them from, which is to say they raise no genuine moral questions. Curiously enough, Edmundson admits that legal change inspired by Mill's principle does not necessarily commit one to hold that delegalized moral requirements exist. Rather, following Feinberg, the harm principle leads moral and legal rules to overlap (1998, 128). Indeed, the sort of liberalism to which I am inclined, does suggest that the harm principle determines both the content of morality and that of law, which is to say, it is in Hart's words a general moral principle against which to measure both moral rules and social practice (1963, 20), though talk of law should not be taken to mean the whole edifice of the law and state as Edmundson seems to understand it. Moreover, as we have already had occasion to point out, the more interesting question is the one which Edmundson doesn't ask, namely whether there are any strongly demoralized legal requirements of the *malum prohibitum* variety, as opposed to those picked out by the harm principle as *malum in se*, to which we have offered a clearly affirmative answer.

As for the view that the harm principle determines the content of both morality and law, according to Edmundson, many liberals worried about making such a claim since it may get them involved in controversies about value or religion (ibid., 129). Well, it seems that liberalism, at least in the form of it latterly called libertarianism, as both a moral and political theory, quite clearly circumscribes both morality and law.

[2] For recent information about euthanasia in Canada see "Medical Assistance in Dying" Government of Canada, March 17, 2021, one of the more notable provisions of which was that it will be another two years before mental health or lack thereof will qualify as a criterion for medically assisted dispatch from this vale of tears.

Indeed, it is the view that individual liberty is paramount and that the only grounds for preventing someone from doing what she wants is that, as Narveson notes, her doing so would infringe upon the rightful liberty of someone else (1988, 7).

With respect to Edmundson's concern that, for many people, value may be connected to religion, we would simply point out that while that may be true as a matter of historical fact, it is of no great philosophical importance. The libertarian view is not itself dependent upon any religious view, but rather, as Narveson again has remarked, adding a divine stamp of approval to a supposedly right action contributes nothing to the explanation of what it is for it to be right (1999, 23). Edmundson agrees that liberals are generally agnostic and following Nagel that prudential considerations might militate against any overt hostility to religion.

Moreover, in Nagel's account of liberalism there is of necessity a discontinuity between political or public morality and private morality, at least to the extent that the latter may involve religious or other views of the good not shared by all (1991, 158). Such a view can probably be traced to Rawls who thought it important to distinguish between an account of political justice and a more fundamental moral or religious view (1993, 174). While Rawls admitted to some similarity between his liberalism and that of Kant and Mill, there are significant differences between the latters' interest in the basis for the autonomous moral life of the individual and Rawls's narrower focus on political justice (ibid., 200, 175).

According to the more modest goals of Rawls's non-comprehensive liberalism, rather than attempting to convince the young of the virtues of autonomy and individuality, their civic education should mainly consist in their being apprised of their rights at positive law. However, it seems that not even Rawlsian civics will entirely eschew the sorts of principles derived from Kant and Mill, since we are told that children's education should prepare them to participate as fully autonomous members of society (ibid., 199–200), for which purpose they will be indoctrinated in the values essential to fair cooperation. Such political values and their concomitant virtues will take precedence over the basic rights familiar to earlier liberalisms to ensure that all have equal access to them (ibid., 157).

Indeed, although Rawls assures us that political justice in a democracy will in general be liberal (ibid., 156) one cannot help wondering at what point such a latitudinarian view ceases to be liberalism at all. The usual way to ensure that those who the *nomenklatura* believe lack resources commensurate with their rights is to give them a right via redistribution to the resources of others, who supposedly have more than they need, a right we have already suggested is both non-liberal and non-existent. Rawls also claims that his variety of pluralist liberalism takes off the political table items of disagreement which might stand in the way of cooperative solutions (ibid., 157). Again, it is not clear how much, or why pluralism will count as a good thing, though no doubt those who claim to set the political agenda will think they have answers, just as they can determine which items are on the table and which, in the interests of something called reasonable social cooperation, must be left off. Of course, one suspects that those things which it is supposedly reasonable to do are just those things which Rawls's so-called liberalism holds dear, which is to say that he has been no more successful than either Kant or Mill before him in avoiding what he considers the besetting sin of comprehensiveness.

## 5.1 Abortion and Liberalism

Abortion is apparently one of those questions, about which there is such fundamental disagreement that, according to Nagel it should be left off any political agenda (1991, 164, 169). From a survey showing that while there is no great enthusiasm for abortion, nor is there any for regulating it, Edmundson concludes that such results imply that there are moral norms beyond the reach of the law and further, that liberals such as Nagel typically hold that politics respect such a view. As we have seen, what some might now call *woke* liberals deny that the demands of morality coincide with those of the state (ibid., 130). However, although Edmundson claims to understand the attraction of such liberals to this view, since in the case of abortion it allows one to hold both that it is wrong and that it is not amenable to legal prohibition, he does not find the language of Wolfenden congenial, namely that there is an inner sphere of morality which is not the state's business. On the contrary, it is Edmundson's view that whatever we can sanction morally is subject to legal coercion (ibid., 157). We agree of course that moral requirements, which attempt to curtail the class of *malum in se* actions, can be enforced by coercion, wielded either by the individual affected or his allies. Customs of enforcement may well have long since distilled into rules backed up by tribunals of one sort or another, resulting in legal sanctions. However, we are still a long way from Edmundson's state with a monopoly of enforcement.

As discussed earlier, Edmundson thinks that there are reasons for such a monopoly to prevent the undesirable consequences of us taking the law into our own hands, as the saying goes (ibid.). We might well ask whether it is a case of eliminating one set of hazards, or simply replacing one set with another, perhaps even greater, for the king's justice through the ages has hardly proved to be an unqualified boon to its petitioners. Monopoly guarantees overwhelming threat, and there is little the individual can do to counter such disproportionate and possibly unjustified use of the enforcement prerogative, as the much-discussed case of a would-be immigrant in Vancouver demonstrated.[3] Nor does Edmundson think we should attempt to do so, holding that at a minimum there is a *prima facie* duty incumbent upon all subjects not to interfere with the administration of enforcement.

Edmundson also claimed that the state may enforce requirements above and beyond those available to the individual, which is yet another implication of the doctrine of sovereign prerogative, such as enforcing taxes, or keeping the peace (ibid.). Of course, it is not surprising that the state should insist on presiding over its personal fiefdoms, since both taxes and public spaces are paradigmatic creatures of the state. The view that the state may create duties and enforcements not available to individuals leads one to question Edmundson's support for the perfect coincidence view, according to which the harm principle serves as both a moral and legal criterion. While noting that recent liberal opinion was

[3] In 2009 an inquest was held into the death of Robert Dziekanski who had exhibited symptoms of psychological distress after arrival in Vancouver airport, which led to his being tasered 5 times by police. Brennan has suggested that if such officials are acting unjustly, as many thought they were in this case, we may even have a duty to intervene (2019, 235).

divided on the question, Edmundson opted for the coincidence view, no doubt as a way of blocking the existence of a moral domain not amenable to the reach of the law. The fact that there are laws beyond the reach of the moral principles available to individuals apparently doesn't trouble him nearly so much.

That is, as noted earlier, according to Edmundson, the law does not confine its purview to the class of *malum in se* actions, as a coincidence view might suggest, but can declare other actions to be illegal which do not meet a test of harm to others, though the government may attempt to claim that it or society is harmed by non-compliance. These are the *malum prohibitum* actions, those whose wrongfulness simply derives from the fact that they fall under a state prohibition. If indeed the state presides over an arsenal of rules and enforcement not available to ordinary mortals, as Edmundson argues, and is able to prohibit by fiat, then it is not clear why we have any obligation not to interfere in the administration of its prohibitions, since according to Junius, a loyal subject will not advise or consent to arbitrary measures. Reminiscent of *Euthyphro*, the other alternative, which I favour, is for morality to be independent of the state, in which case, if it is a liberal state, like any individual, it will be constrained at the very least by a principle of non-maleficence. Should it have any inclination to beneficence, following Pareto, it may improve a lot of some, and worsen the lot of none.

Not only are there supposedly moral requirements that only the state may enforce, Edmundson claims in support of this asymmetrical enforcement that there are moral obligations which the individual has no power to enforce (ibid., 157). By way of illustration, he offers the case of a passer-by who fails to render assistance to a blind man who has dropped his cane. While a third party might well upbraid the passer-by for his want of charity, the observer may not force the passer-by to retrieve the blind man's cane, for as Epstein reminds us, the customary prohibitions against force and fraud do not compel us help to those in danger. Duties of charity are not subject to enforcement by individuals or the state, a view with which the law has historically agreed (2003, 100–101).

According to Edmundson, to recognize a moral duty is to agree to its being socially enforced in some way (ibid., 176). Perhaps we need to clarify what it is for X to be morally required and for that matter to be enforced. With respect to the first, Narveson recommends that we distinguish between strong moral requirements such as non-aggression, and moral virtues, such as charity, which go beyond what we must do. While the pursuit of virtue is much to be commended, including the virtue of pursuing one's own health and well-being, we are not required to benefit others in the same way that we are required to refrain from harming them.[4] As for enforcement, Narveson suggests we distinguish that from less direct attempts to reinforce behaviour by persuasion and exhortation (2000b, 316, 318).

However, it is not at all clear how Edmundson's case of the blind man supports the view that the state can go one better than any of us when it comes to enforcing or reinforcing a moral principle. States have generally avoided the sort of Good Samaritan law which might compel direct assistance to those in distress, such as Edmundson perhaps has in mind, though, of course they have had no hesitation in compelling various forms of indirect assistance via taxation, something which on our view they are not justified in doing. Thus, to the extent that states have arrogated powers to themselves unavailable to individuals, this is not something we should commend, as Edmundson does, but rather declare their actions to be morally *ultra vires*, or unjustified.

While a genuine moral requirement may well be backed up by social sanctions ranging from reinforcement to enforcement, Edmundson has a distinct preference for the latter, because it reflects the majestic authority of the state. In an age when social networks are not as strong as they once were, leaving correction to individuals can be an uncertain affair (ibid., 170, 175–176). On the other hand, according to Morgan, state intervention is a source of moral hazard which encourages people to take less responsibility for themselves and their offspring, leading some to argue that the state is at least partly to blame for weakening family supports (2007, 13). In agreeing with Devlin's view that the state is not to be excluded from the enforcement of morals, Edmundson holds that we may on balance benefit from its oversight, though that question cannot be settled a priori. However, he does seem to have forgotten that morals

[4] Brennan notes that while many think we have a duty to obey the law, it isn't as fundamental as the duty to avoid harming others for no good reason (2019, 72).

are the paradigm instance of a privately supplied public good and are mostly reinforced by upbringing. Where further enforcement is required, there is no reason to think that cannot be adequately supplied privately as well.

## 5.2 Private Enforcement

With respect to the alleged deficiencies of private correction, we have offered various arguments suggesting that state intervention would suffer from similar shortcomings, if not more. By way of some sort of non a priori backing for his claims about the greater reliability of government enforcement, Edmundson asks us to imagine a case where a citizen who is concerned about someone's driving pulls him over to complain about it. Were we confronted by such a highway vigilante, he claims we would find it much more annoying than being pulled over by police (1998, 171) If indeed that were our reaction, it hardly qualifies as an empirical account of the deficiencies of private enforcement. For many, reactions to police intervention are not much different. Such a scenario might constitute a citizen's arrest, the effect of which is humiliating and intrusive, as the use of coercion tends to be, leading to police involvement. If private intervention is any more galling than that by public officials, it may just be that this is not what we are accustomed to, at least on the highway.

In addition to its perhaps unusual and erratic features, Edmundson thinks that public and private correction also differ with respect to the state having the exclusive right to punish and to delegate it to its officials. Thus, a private citizen is not backed up by a right of non-interference, whereas, according to Edmundson, those operating at the behest of the state do possess such immunity. While we are quite aware that the state claims such monopoly rights, which entail a duty of non-interference, we contend that Edmundson never quite managed to produce any satisfactory grounds for such a claim. As for the protection against interference which piggybacks on such a claim right, the private citizen who attempts an arrest may have to be prepared to defend himself if challenged. If so, his situation is probably no different from that of many police officers, though his weaponry may fall short of standard police issue, at least in

Commonwealth countries. Brennan has also denied that state officials possess any immunity when it comes to their acting unjustly. They do not possess a special moral status by dint of working for a state which claims to possess one. Officials are liable to the same countermeasures we would use to defend ourselves or others against unjust actions which are to say the state's officers are morally on a par with us. The fact that policing can be riskier than some occupations does not entitle them to act as they see fit; they have a responsibility to respect the rights of their moral equals (2019, 10–11, 237).

Edmundson, again, sums up what he takes to be the defining characteristics of state, as opposed to other forms of social enforcement as, first, the right to award an official sticker of social disapproval and to possess a monopoly on doing so (ibid., 175). To which we reply that we know what it is they claim but have no idea what it is to justify such a claim. Presumably morality itself expresses the disapproval of society, and it is unclear what officialdom can contribute to that process, other than the social cost of having yet another special producer group, as Friedman noted, be granted a favour at our expense (1962, 148). However, the anointing of authorities, if not of kings, appears to have continued unabated, and the ancient myth of the divine right of kings has simply been replaced with that of states. Or according to Burke, each state constitution is a part of the everlasting constitution of human society, a notion inspired by Cicero in *De Republica* who thought that nothing was more pleasing to the Supreme Ruler of the Universe than lawful societies or states (1955, 110–111).

Edmundson seems to be of a similar mind, since he has trouble imagining a society where correction of wrongs is handled privately. Besides the fact that the gods smile kindly upon those entities called states, the right to punish for Edmundson is clearly a social one, which is to say in the power of the state alone (ibid., 175). He is also pleased to note that Nozick was reluctantly forced to a similar conclusion given the problems faced by a doctrine of punishment under an anarchic order (1974, 139). Not that it is surprising that Nozick should be found under the same tent as Edmundson, since the aim of both their endeavours was to subject anarchism to serious scrutiny to reassert the legitimacy of the state. If the latter has commonly been characterized by a monopoly on the use of force, including punishment, then Nozick famously set himself the task of showing how we might get there without abridging anyone's rights in the process.

Of course, there would be holdouts, who refused to get on the dominant protection agency bandwagon and preferred dealing with offenders on their own terms, enlisting the aid of allies when needed. Nozick thought that rights-preserving compensation could be offered to the non-joiners, to secure their participation in the great public protection racket, commonly known as the state. But to preserve the state's monopoly on enforcement (ibid.,14), Nozick needs to circumscribe Locke's right of every person to punish judiciously according to the law of nature (1960, II, 272).

## 5.3 Locke on Punishment

Although he admits that such a doctrine may seem odd to some, including apparently Nozick and Edmundson, Locke contends that the power of the magistrates to punish aliens flows from such a right held by each person (ibid., 273). Nozick for his part thinks the doctrine strange, preferring to see punishment as a liberty rather than a right. Moreover, the difference between punishment and compensation serves to underscore the fact that punishment is a right of all in common since it is not owed to the victim in particular (ibid., 138).

Locke also speaks of two separate rights to punishment, that of protection and deterrence belonging to everybody, and reparation, which belongs only to the victim (ibid., 273). While Locke agrees with Nozick that restitution is owed to the victim or third parties who sustain collateral damage, Locke also holds that every individual has the natural power to punish, including killing a murderer as an example to others and to prevent a repeat offence. Thus, it is not clear why Nozick thinks some permission from on high is required over and above the power which everyone has to respond with lethal force where necessary against someone who according to Locke has become an enemy of society preying on his fellows like a wild animal (ibid., 274).

As for lesser crimes than murder, Locke allows that the severity of the punishment will be enough to make a perpetrator realize his mistake and deter others from repeating it (ibid., 274). Nozick, however, thinks the devil is in the details, and that a system of open punishment is likely to become a shambles, and thus prove an entirely unreliable method of correction. If Nozick is concerned that leaving punishment up to anyone who feels disposed to dish it out is problematic, we could insist that the victim, if willing and able, should have the first crack, assisted by anyone inclined to help. Nozick would again object that while a victim is owed compensation, he is not owed punishment, so he has no right to return the favour, though it would seem he may well have the liberty of doing so (ibid., 138), assuming that this is a distinction with a difference, something Narveson rightly doubts (2002a, 227).

## 5.4 Nozick on Punishment

Because it is supposedly difficult to determine who has a right to punish, Nozick considers punishment necessarily a collective operation which would in turn require an institutionalized decision mechanism (ibid., 139). Such a suggestion would reinforce Nozick's view that what Rothbard called the immaculate conception of the state is not prejudiced by preventing the last holdouts against monopoly provision of protection services from resorting to self-help, provided that the non-joiners are compensated for being thus disadvantaged. Requiring that all together have a right to punish, rather than just the victim or his surrogates, virtually guarantees that it will be difficult to provide a coherent account of punishment in the state of nature. Of course, it also leaves Nozick with the task of defending collective rights, something which may well prove less than straightforward.[5]

However, in his enthusiasm for the minimal state, Nozick has overlooked at least one famous chapter in legal history, namely outlawry as

[5] cf. Narveson, "Collective Rights" (2002a, 225ff). Nozick apparently thinks that the greater the number of people who authorize an agency to act for them, the greater is its entitlement, the whole being necessarily greater than the sum of its parts and the apotheosis of the state at hand (ibid., 139).

a way of allowing the participation of anyone in punishment. Nozick thought it important that the offender not owe a duty of punishment to the victim. Maybe so, but under the outlaw doctrine the offender is placed beyond the protection of the law, which is to say he is subject to the same open season as he declared upon his victims, which *pace* Nozick, appears well suited to the state of nature. As Pollock and Maitland explain, outlawry is an ancient weapon for communities lacking professional enforcement, where any law-abiding person has the right to treat the outlaw as a wild animal, or in the parlance of the Middle Ages, as one who bears the wolf's head (1978, 476).

With reference to Nozick's interest in having some institutional oversight of punishment, Rothbard reminds us again that since law can develop quite independently of any state, the appropriate institutions for adjudication and dispute resolution would also be produced as needed (2002, 236). Nozick thinks that the dominant protection agency is right to prevent holdouts from using such less reliable methods of enforcement, a prohibition which in turn transforms the agency into a de facto state. However, as Rothbard again points out, the ugly history of the state is unlikely to inspire much confidence in its reliability. As for the right to prevent holdouts from engaging in the risky activity of not getting on the bandwagon, Rothbard considers such coercion as an unwarranted attack on their rights (ibid., 238–239), a criticism which could also apply to the various mechanisms being employed by states to coerce people into taking experimental medical treatments.

However, Nozick insists that there is nothing wrong with coercing the holdouts, which is to say, contrary to what I have suggested, that the protective association is not a racket, because the former provides beneficial protection, whereas the latter does not (ibid., 86). Such a distinction supposedly allows Nozick to rule out blackmail, since it produces no benefit, which is to say that victims of blackmail would be better off in the absence of such threats. Productive exchanges, on the other hand benefit both buyer and seller (ibid., 85, 83). An example of the latter is neighbour A, who agrees for a fee not to go ahead with plans to put up a structure that B would find offensive. If A did not have bona fide plans to build anything but attempted to cash in on the threat of doing so, this would not be a productive exchange.

## 5.5 Blackmail Revisited

Blackmail is a similarly unproductive activity for Nozick though it apparently has nothing to do with the blackmailer's threat not being genuine. It is simply a matter of the entirely gratuitous presence of the blackmailer, such that his victims would be better off if he had never appeared. Of course, the same could be said of the real or imaginary neighbourhood developer, which is to say that the distinction between productive and unproductive exchanges sounds more and more like the proverbial distinction without a difference. If so, it will prove quite unable to do the work Nozick had planned for it, namely, to justify compensation for the coercion of holdouts against a protective monopoly/proto state. Indeed, Rothbard and Gordon have suggested turning Nozick's notion of unproductive exchange back on his own derivation of the state, since in the absence of the dominant agency, clients of independent agencies would prefer to continue being served by them. In that case they are not better off by being dragooned into the monopoly association, which is to say it is non-productive and should be prohibited.[6]

Since Nozick's valiant effort to distinguish the genuine protective services of the nascent state from those of a protection racket (ibid., 86) has amounted to nought, we should take stock as to where this leaves us. As Narveson has recently pointed out, there are those who want to be governed, that is, hand over their right to protect themselves to an agency they believe can do a better job of it, and those who don't. While it is true that a democracy can ride roughshod over the wishes of the minority, when it comes to contracting with a protective agency, as we have seen, unmade contracts are nullities and give rise to no rights of enforcement, or anything else, for that matter. Rather, as Narveson suggests, a would-be state can only get the right to decide all matters in heaven or earth if those who want it to do so have agreed (2008, 107).

[6] cf. Rothbard (2002, n.35, 245).

## 5.6 Anscombe on Authority

If, as we have suggested, individuals have not conferred any such right on a central agency, then there is much to be said for the view considered by Anscombe that government is a glorified Mafia parading in the robes of authority. While Anscombe is to be commended for such a characterization of the libertarian position, like Nozick, she herself holds on the contrary that the civil authority does have a right based in human need to coerce and use violence in a way that the Mafia does not. The task of government could not be accomplished without the obedience of its citizens and the right of the governors to use force. Thus, they have the authority we need them to have to do what they need to do (1981, 136–137).

While Anscombe's attempt to derive the right to govern from human need appears at least *prima facie* to avoid the question of consent, we should press her further on her first premise, where the need for government was thought to follow from the fact that some are not content to let others go about their lives peacefully (ibid., 135–136). However, as we have observed, while the use of force against those who do not let others live and work in peace is justifiable, Anscombe has not shown why something called government should have a monopoly on such force, or why such decisions need to come from the top (ibid., 153).

While not addressing the question of a monopoly, as such, Anscombe implies that such decision-making is of necessity in the hands of the anointed few charged with coordinating the activities of large masses of humanity (ibid., 137). We would respond, of course, that if we can manage, for example, to feed, house and clothe most people without the aid of government, there is some question as to whether we really need it for any of the activities which have historically fallen under its mandate. Anscombe, however, believes that private coordination, or Hayek's spontaneous order (1973, 41), cannot supply the requisite machinery in large societies, with the customary practice being only a feature of primitive ones.

Thus, on Anscombe's account we cannot hope to explain the right of the civil authority to forcefully impose solutions as one derived from ways in which communities had historically developed their own procedures. Authoritative acts of the civil governors are not acts of self-help writ large. Contrary to the Lockean tradition which assumes a private right of punishment, Anscombe holds that coercive rights held by government are not comparable with those in the state of nature (ibid., 146–147). In supposedly rejecting the view that civil authority arises by surrendering prior rights in the state of nature, Anscombe is no closer to explaining how it is that the state can acquire rights sharply discontinuous with those of ordinary mortals. Indeed, she acknowledges that to the extent that state authority can defend its rule by coercion, it is a case of bootstrapping par excellence (ibid., 153). In this respect the source of the authority of the state turns out to be on a par with transubstantiation, about which Anscombe thought that *qua* mystery it would likely remain forever beyond our understanding (ibid., 109).

*Pace* Anscombe, we hold with Jasay that authority must indeed be generated in anarchy, which is to say, as Green claimed, it could be produced without top-down enforcement (1988, 147). If it can't be generated in the absence of higher-level enforcement, as Anscombe suggests, then we have a situation where according to Jasay the principals cannot contract with an agent without yet another to enforce the agreement, and we could well be stuck with an endless procession of meta-agents (1997, 21). Moreover, in addition to Juvenal's ancient question: *Quis custodiet ipsos custodes?* coming back with a vengeance, there is also Green's question that if authority can be generated in the absence of higher-level enforcement, why we would need to provide political authority in the first place. With respect to taxes, it is not obviously easier to convince people to comply with tax laws than it is to convince them of the benefits of doing so, assuming of course there are any. Green thinks we could do so, given that authority is likely to prove a tougher sell than the goods it is thought necessary to produce (ibid., 147, 149). Thus, Jasay concludes that lacking a higher enforcer we won't be able to contract to leave the state of nature in the first place, nor for similar reasons can we contract into a state (ibid., 22).

## 5.7 The Appeal of Anarchy

During this discussion, we have responded to Edmundson's attack on anarchy, undertaken in the name of state legitimacy, though as he points out one needs to go further than simply demonstrating where one's opponents have gone wrong (1998, 180). In this respect, we have not simply exposed Edmundson's errors but have considered other attempts to stave off the anarchic day of reckoning, finding them similarly wanting. So where then does this leave the question of an apolitical or stateless order, one which Nozick considered the starting point of political philosophy (1974, 4). At the very least, as Boettke has observed, it continues to be a lively research programme having both theoretical as well as practical value (2005, 215–216). Further, as Leeson noted, it is everywhere, if we care to look (2014, 225); Hasnas agrees, though sometimes we fail to see it, even when it is staring us in the face (2008, 111).

Perhaps we should emphasize that in questioning the authority of the state, we are not questioning the need for order. Or according to Hasnas, to consider managing without the endless layers of what currently goes by the name of government, is not to welcome a society without structure. With respect to coercion, with which we began this discussion, to make a case for anarchy Hasnas is not proposing a non-coercive society, but only one where people can live in harmony without central control (2008, 112). To those who think that government is necessary to produce the laws which will enable us to live together in peace and harmony, he reminds us of the long tradition of common law which preceded anything like government as we now know it. Common law has the advantage of not being derived from political sources, but of having grown up in the context of settling actual disputes between individuals, creating rules essential to maximizing peace and personal freedom (ibid., 116). Such rules are part of the communal heritage, and unlike much contemporary legislation, do not run counter to the ordinary moral understandings of the proverbial man in the Clapham omnibus.

As for the courts, which Hasnas sees recovering their powers of independent adjudication, he reminds us that publicly supported courts came late in legal history (ibid., 121). We noted earlier that the commercial courts continue to this day to mediate mercantile disputes, quite independent of any government oversight, to say nothing of the myriad tribunals and systems of private arbitration, which have burgeoned as their public counterparts have become mired in inefficiency. Thus, we would have no trouble envisaging how other bodies might fill the spaces left by the eventual departure of much of the machinery of the public administration of justice.

While many have little trouble in imagining a largely private and independent system of arbitration, which assesses fees directly on litigants, some may contend that policing must remain a government monopoly. Hasnas reminds us again that government supported police are also a relatively recent development, beginning with the Runners of the Bow Street Magistrates' Court in London in the late eighteenth century (ibid., 122). However, as Benson shows, the establishment of the metropolitan police did not happen overnight, since many Britons were not anxious to emulate the aggressive style of French policing developed under the *ancien regime* (1990, 74–75). Similar suspicions were confirmed by the arrival of police departments in American cities around the middle of the nineteenth century, where as Benson notes, they were mostly creatures of their political bosses. In many ways not much has changed in the intervening century or so, since corruption still exists, and much crime goes unreported, suggesting we may have something to gain from a return to the privately managed justice once crowded out by powerful monarchs (1998, 224–226).

Of course, in another sense the private provision of security has never quite died out, no doubt because many have always realized that sovereign monopoly had little to do with individual security. Benson reminds us, for example, that the period when public police were in the ascendant also saw the establishment of many prominent private protection agencies which have continued to prosper, apparently because of their ability to provide better service than their tax-supported counterparts (ibid.). Indeed, Hasnas argues that a private system could hardly do worse than a publicly funded one, which requires everyone to contribute through taxes, with no control over the quality or level of service (ibid., 125). While Morris seems to agree that a private security system may perform the same functions at least as well as a public one, he reminds us that in doing so, a private system inevitably provides goods to noncontributors so that it may not be possible to efficiently provide law and order in the absence of a state. This is the standard public goods defence of the state, to the effect that free riding would cause privately produced order to be underproduced, which Morris admits has been much criticized (1998, 61), including in this discussion.

However, as Hasnas notes, the fact that private policing would generate uncompensated positive externalities in the form of deterrence is no reason to think that such services would be underproduced. On the contrary policing and courts have it in common with more recent developments such as light houses and the internet that they have historically been supplied apolitically. Moreover, just about any productive activity will spill over onto others not party to the contract (ibid., 128). In addition to paying attention to such matters as personal hygiene and dress, most of us perform duties of non-maleficence, as well as the occasional duty of beneficence. Indeed, as Hasnas reminds us, if we want examples of the anarchic production of public goods, they are all around us. Or as we saw earlier, schemes for providing such goods are not dependent on an entrepreneurial political class, but according to Jasay, there are private suppliers happy to risk being played for a sucker because they themselves want some good badly enough. Under non-political provision people make their own choices about being sucker or free rider, rather than having those roles assigned via the political process (2002, 29).

Although many would have little trouble seeing how we might increase the share of the private market in protection services within a country, they may have more trouble doing so when it comes to the defence of the whole country. Hasnas admits that if we are talking about the sort of massive defence spending that now goes on, it is hard for that to be provided without a government. What isn't clear of course is how much of the massive defence arsenal of a country such as the US is necessary for the defence of its citizens. Indeed, in view of the colossal security failure of 9/11, it seems about as effective as the Maginot Line. If the purpose of spending the following twenty years in Afghanistan was to move the country from 139 on the Economist Democracy scale to something closer to the US rank of 25 then that hasn't happened any more than Kabul came to resemble Westminster after the three British

Afghan wars. Crawford has estimated the costs of this venture to the US alone to be over 2 trillion dollars with a similar amount needed for the care of veterans and compensation for families of those who didn't return (2021, 1).

Of course, to decide if the US is in the business of protection, and not of latter-day Caesarism, then, as Hasnas suggests, we need some reliable assessment both of the external threat, and of the defence spending proportional to that threat (ibid., 33). If Hasnas is right that it is not reasonable to expect the state to wither away overnight, the provision of national defence may well be one of the last bastions of government to fall. While the best solution would be for all states to disarm, leading by example may not be the wisest move, though as Huemer suggests, it might be a start since national protection paradoxically begets hostility (2013, 301). For Jasay it is also paradoxically the case that unless the nation state is much attenuated, a credible threat of war may also reduce the chance of conflict (2002, 70). But the nation offers its nostrums by collective choice which prevents any attempt to weigh costs against benefits. While collective choice suppresses some free riding it gives rise to others, such as that some improve their lots while others go to war to defend king and country.

## 5.7.1 The Private Production of Defence

As Hoppe points out, the sovereign is no exception, in that he obtains his security at the expense of others. The way in which he is different is that he has arrogated to himself the monopoly of protection within his domain and the power to collect taxes to pay for it (2003, 336). The fact that the sovereign claims to both defend property while at the same time seizing it should make one wonder how it is that he is able to provide protection for his subjects that they could not provide for themselves. On the contrary, as Hoppe argues, it is not a matter of collectively provided security being superior to what citizens could purchase for themselves, but rather that the security of the state is purchased by confiscating wealth from its citizens (ibid., 337). Indeed, pious pronouncements about the protection of life notwithstanding, as Jasay observes, such expropriation including loss of life or limb is only good for flattering the ego of the rulers (ibid.), often obscured by what Owen called the old lie, *Dulce et decorum est pro patria mori* (1987, 188–189).

However, Hoppe offers us an interesting way out of the contradictions of collective choice in the service of the nation/state by reminding us that defence is a form of insurance. Companies which agreed to underwrite such risks would possess the resources necessary to deal with real or imagined threats, being part of the vast insurance and reinsurance industry, whose networking and wealth exceed that of many sovereign nations. Just as regular insurance excludes certain misadventures initiated by the client, so defence insurance would rule out hostilities initiated by its clients (ibid., 346–348). Under the present arrangement of states there is not the same disincentive to aggressive behaviour as under an international insurance market since a state can externalize the costs of its aggression onto its taxpayers. Indeed, Hoppe argues that there is a tendency for hostilities to escalate into total war, for example, of all Israelis against all Palestinians, since all subjects are implicated in the wars waged by their respective states which monopolize protection and taxation. However, in a possible post-state world, aggressors would have an incentive to confine hostilities to their uninsured foreign counterparts, lest they provoke response from very powerful international insurers with strong incentives to protect their clients. Such insurers would no doubt contract out protective services in the way states have done in recent years to the private military industry, whose ability to wage war, as P. W. Singer notes, extends worldwide like that of a great variety of international players (2003, 242).

Moreover, Hoppe further contends that a free territory consisting only of private property owners and their insurers could exist with a state nearby, which is more aggressive, and therefore a threat to such owners and their insurers. The latter of course have a strong incentive to neutralize threats coming both from within and from without; thus, they would expel criminals from their neighbourhood, as well as control any influx of government agents from outside. Hoppe also argues that a nearby state might have some difficulty in convincing its agents to attack a non-aggressive free territory, since as Hume observed, governments of all types depend on opinion rather than on force (2003, 16).[7]

Even if we think that the favourable opinion of his subjects and the possible loss of legitimacy might not be a strong enough bulwark against unilateral aggression, Hoppe reminds us that in a free territory its citizens would not have been disarmed like their state counterparts, and therefore able to defend their property, with defence contractors supplying more sophisticated weaponry if needed. However, unlike a state, an insurance company cannot afford to allow a counterattack to degenerate into total war and will therefore confine itself to surgical strikes against particular aggressors, thus minimizing collateral damage. In delivering such a precise response, they could sway public opinion against the state aggressors, perhaps leading to the latter's downfall, and the eventual replacement of state protection by private profit–loss underwriters (ibid., 368).

### 5.7.2 Responses to Holcombe

After canvassing most of the common arguments in support of the state, many of which have been discussed in one form or another above, Holcombe concludes that all encounter major difficulties (2007, 159). For example, with respect to the claim that government is necessary to produce public goods, often government has simply decided to offer unrestrained access to certain goods, not that it was impossible to restrict access. Typically, state production of such goods results in inefficiencies of overproduction near empty transit buses or underproduction—20% of the population without a primary care physician. As an example of a public good which the market supplies very effectively, Holcombe cites computer software, which has in practice turned out to be non-excludable because it can be easily copied, not that Microsoft has failed to turn a profit as a result (1996, 111).

On the other hand, if the rationale for government is to control externalities, Holcombe holds that most of those are generated by poorly

---

[7] For further discussion of the limits public opinion might set on military adventurism see Huemer (2013, 309).

defined property rights, but rather than expedite the latter, states often place all sorts of stumbling blocks in the way.[8] Indeed as he argues, there are law and contract traditions antedating the state which have proved much better at internalizing externalities, whereas government often passes laws allowing them. As for the view that it is reasonable for us to contract into a government to solve problems which would arise in the absence of one, he argues that such a view does not tell us why we have government in the first place, or why we should (2007, 155–156).

As we have argued above, various writers have shown that government coercion is not necessary for establishing a cooperative order. Indeed, without cooperation we could not establish a government in the first place. As Holcombe concludes, instead of universal agreement to a state which improves a lot of some while worsening none, we have redistributive democracy which robs Peter to pay Paul (ibid., 157). Although Holcombe agrees with our contention that the standard arguments for the state do not withstand critical scrutiny, he does not think it is time to abandon the ship of state altogether. When we ask why governments exist, it is because some people have forcibly imposed them on others. If anarchy is not an appealing option, in the absence of government, albeit forcibly imposed, there will be nothing to prevent other predatory gangs from plundering the peaceful citizenry. Were such a Mafia to establish a monopoly in a given area, it would become the de facto government, exchanging protection for tribute, as has been the habit of governments throughout history, and as could well be the case with the Taliban in Afghanistan.

Not only does the establishment of a monopoly enforcer bring an end to the cycle of predation, but according to Holcombe, citizens will find it in their interest to constrain the maximizing tendencies of their inevitable rulers by pre-emptively setting up limited government. However, if governments come about because some manage to impose them by force, then jumping the gun by seizing the reins of government would seem to be the exception rather than the rule. Holcombe thinks something like this happened in the case of the US, though he agrees, that if the purpose was to create limited government, the exercise has

[8] cf. DeSoto (2000, 20).

long since failed (ibid., 163) with democracy having supplanted liberty as the driving principle of American government (2002, 250).

By arguing that we are better to govern ourselves than have someone even more predatory do it for us, assuming we can reliably separate the more from the less predatory, Holcombe implies that the redistributive game called democracy is a case of governing ourselves, a view we earlier questioned. Even if we thought that one of the good features of democracy as we know it was that it enabled us to ride with the hunt, rather than run with the hounds, or something offering even less opportunity for predation, as we noted above, the churning associated with redistribution does not guarantee that it is invariably Peter who is robbed to pay Paul.

Nevertheless, Holcombe is convinced that if anarchy is not on the table, limiting the reach of government might be one way to restore liberty. Although he admits on the one hand that the US appears to have been much more interested in preserving democracy rather than liberty, it remains among the freest of all countries (2007, 163), something we have also had occasion to question. We would of course suggest to an advocate of the minimal state, such as Holcombe, that he not only heed Thoreau's support for minimal government, but also that for him it implied a one which didn't govern at all (1993, 1, 27). Indeed, as Narveson concludes, if it is realism we are after, then minimal government doesn't seem any more realistic than anarchism (2008b, 110). Hasnas reminds us that although most of us no longer subscribe to the divine right of kings, we think that order is not possible without government operating under another fiction called the rule of law (2008, 130–131). If we do believe that, it is likely because we sat at the feet of some naïve civics teacher who was schooled in the same errors.

## 5.8 Summary

While Edmundson appears to have taken the role of democracy as a source of authority largely for granted, in our concluding discussion we pick up the thread of his argument again, paying particular attention to the third of the fallacies which anarchism allegedly ran afoul of, namely, by declaring an area of private morality off limits to the state. While we have contended that the privately produced good of morality can render most state activity redundant, our concern has been rather that in the dominant *malum prohibitum* variety of law, the state claims authority to legislate in an area which is off limits to morality. According to Edmundson the state also rightly asserts a duty of non-interference in the administration of its laws, the failure to recognize which is another of anarchism's supposed fallacies. But the duty to obey laws which are moral nullities, consisting as they do of prohibitions having no other rationale than that the state has prohibited them, cannot be a moral one.

To respond to this difficulty, some writers such as Nagel proclaim a discontinuity between the morality of individuals and that of the state. In our view, however, the state does not possess moral rationales unavailable to individuals, which is to say we reject any doctrine of *raison d'état*. While Edmundson claims to deny Nagel's discontinuity thesis, to ensure that the law may reach wherever morality does, he also holds that there are moral requirements only the state may enforce, such as rendering aid to those in distress. Indeed, the state claims an exclusive right to enforcement, which we also reject, since it appears to have no other foundation than the myth of the Supreme Ruler of the Universe who smiles kindly upon his earthly vice-regents. Anscombe also favours sharply discontinuous state rights, which she insists are not simply rights of self-help writ large. As to how the state pulls itself up by its bootstraps appears to be as much of a mystery as she thought transubstantiation was.

For those of us who hold that individual morality clearly underwrites self-help, without which, moreover, there is no exit from the state of nature, non-coercive solutions are available to questions of both internal and external security, for both of which the state has typically been thought essential. Hoppe proposes an insurance model for defence which is more likely to prevent hostilities from escalating than the present statist regime. As to the possible threat posed by a state to an adjacent non-state jurisdiction, defence insurance contracts held by members of the latter, coupled with the fact that they would not have been disarmed by a monopoly protection agency masquerading as a state, should mean that they could neutralize any such threat. Indeed, if anyone is guilty of fallacies, it is statists, like Edmundson, rather than the anarchists he attempts to call to account.

## Works Cited

Anscombe, G.E.M. Collected Philosophical Papers, Vol. 3. Oxford: Blackwell, 1981.

Benson, Bruce L. *The Enterprise of Law*. San Francisco: Pacific Research Institute, 1990.

———. *To Serve and Protect*. New York: New York U. Press, 1998.

Boettke, Peter, ed. *Anarchy State and Public Choice*. Cheltenham: Edward Elgar, 2005.

Brennan, Jason. *When All Else Fails: The Ethics of Resistance to State Injustice*. Princeton: Princeton U. Press, 2019.

Burke, Edmund. *Reflections on the Revolution in France*. New York: Bobbs-Merrill, 1955.

Crawford, Neta C. "Calculating the Costs of the Afghanistan War in Lives, Dollars and Years." In *The Conversation*. Boston: Boston University, 2021.

DeSoto, Hernando. *The Mystery of Capital*. New York: Basic Books, 2000.

Devlin, Patrick. *The Enforcement of Morals*, 6. Oxford: Oxford U. Press, 1965 [1975].

Edmundson, William A. *Three Anarchical Fallacies*. Cambridge: Cambridge U. Press, 1998.

Epstein, Richard. *Scepticism and Freedom*. Chicago: Chicago U. Press, 2003.

Friedman, Milton. *Capitalism and Freedom*. Chicago U. of Chicago Press, 1962.

Green, Leslie. *The Authority of the State*. Oxford: Oxford U. Press, 1988.

Hamowy, Ronald. *Dealing with Drugs: Consequences of Government Control*. San Francisco: Pacific Research Institute for Public Policy, 1990 [1987].

Hart, H.L.A. *Law, Liberty and Morality*. Oxford: Oxford U. Press, 1963.

Hasnas, John. "The Obviousness of Anarchy." In *Anarchism/Minarchism*, ed. T. Long and Tibor R. Machan, 111–131. Aldershot: Ashgate, 2008.

Hayek, Friedrich A. *Law Legislation and Liberty*, Vol. I, 41. Chicago: Chicago U. Press, 1973 [1983].

Healy, Gene. “Drug Prohibition.” In *The Encyclopedia of Libertarianism*, ed. Ronald Hamowy, 128–129. Thousand Oaks: Sage, 2008.
Holcombe, Randall G. *Public Finance*. St Paul: West, 1996.
———. *From Liberty to Democracy*. Ann Arbor: Michigan U. Press, 2002.
———. “Why Government?” In *Ordered Anarchy: Jasay and His Surroundings*, ed. Hardy Bouillon and Hartmut Kliemt, 147–166. Aldershot: Ashgate, 2007.
Hoppe, Hans-Hermann, ed. *The Myth of National Defense*. Auburn: Mises Institute, 2003.
Huemer, Michael. *The Problem of Political Authority*. Basingstoke: Palgrave Macmillan, 2013.
Hume, David. *Political Essays*. Ed. Haakonssen. Cambridge U. Press, 2003.
Jasay, Anthony De. *Choice Contract and Consent*. London: Institute for Economic Affairs, 1991.
———. *Against Politics*. London: Routledge, 1997.
———. *Justice and Its Surroundings*. Indianapolis: Liberty Fund, 2002.
Leeson, Peter T. *Anarchy Unbound*. New York: Cambridge University Press, 2014.
Locke, John. *Two Treatises of Government*. Ed. Peter Laslett. Cambridge: Cambridge U. Press, 1960.
Mill, J.S. *Principles of Political Economy, Books IV, and V*. London: Penguin Classics, 1985.
Morgan, Patricia. *The War Between the State and the Family: How Government Divides and Impoverishes*. London: Institute for Economic Affairs, 2007.
Morris, Christopher W. *An Essay on the Modern State*. Cambridge: Cambridge U. Press, 2002 [1998].
Nagel, Thomas. *Equality and Partiality*. New York: Oxford U. Press, 1991.
Narveson, Jan. *The Libertarian Idea*. Philadelphia, Temple U. Press, 1988.
———. *Moral Matters*, 2nd ed. Peterborough: Broadview, 1999.
———. “Libertarianism.” In *The Blackwell Guide to Ethical Theory*, ed. Hugh LaFollette. Oxford: Blackwell, 2000b.
———. *Lectures on Political Philosophy*. Waterloo: U. Waterloo Dept of Philosophy, 2000c.
———. *Respecting Persons in Theory and Practice*. Lanham: Rowman &, Littlefield, 2002a.
———. “The State: From Minarchy to Anarchy.” In *Anarchism/Minarchism: Is Government Part of a Free Country?* ed. Roderick Long and Tibor Machan, 103–110. Aldershot: Ashgate, 2008b.
Nozick, Robert. *Anarchy, State and Utopia*. New York: Basic Books, 1974.

Owen, Wilfred. "Dulce et Decorum est." In *Oxford Book of War Poetry*, ed. Jon Stallworthy, 188–189. Oxford: Oxford U. Press, 1987.

Pollock, Sir Frederick, and Frederic William Maitland. *The History of English Law*, Vol I. Cambridge: Cambridge U. Press 2nd ed. 1898 [Reissued with new intro. 1978].

Rawls, J. *Political Liberalism.* New York: Columbia U. Press, 1993.

Rothbard, Murray. *The Ethics of Liberty*. New York: New York U. Press, 2002.

Singer, P.W. *Corporate Warriors: The Rise of the Privatized Military Industry*. Ithaca: Cornell U. Press, 2003.

Thoreau, Henry David. *Civil Disobedience and Other Essays*. New York: Dover, 1993.

# Works Cited


Ackerman, Kenneth D. *Boss Tweed*. New York: Carroll & Graf, 2006.

Aerztekammer Berlin. *The Value of the Human Being: Medicine in Germany 1918-1945*. Berlin: Aerztekammer Berlin, 1991.

Alden, Markus et.al. "Intracellular Reverse Transcription of BioNTech Covid-19 mRNA Vaccine BNT162b2 in Vitro in Human Liver Cell Line." *Current Issues in Molecular Biology* 44 (2022): 1115–1126.

Ambati, Balamurali K. et.al. "MSH3 Homology and Potential Recombination Link to Sars-Cov-2 Furin Cleavage Site." *Frontiers in Virology* 2 (February 2022): 834808.

Anderson, Terry L., and Peter J. Hill. *The Not so Wild, Wild West*. Stanford, CA: Stanford, 2004.

Anscombe, G.E.M. *Collected Philosophical Papers*, vol. 3. Oxford: Blackwell, 1981.

Aquinas, Thomas. *The Political Ideas*. New York: Hafner, 1953.

Arrow, Kenneth J. "Values and Collective Decision Making." In *Philosophy, Politics and Society*, 3rd Series, ed. Peter Laslett and W.G. Runciman, 215–232. Oxford: Blackwell, 1967.

Arthur, Terry. *Crap: A Guide to Politics*. London: Continuum, 2007.



© The Editor(s) (if applicable) and The Author(s), under exclusive license to Springer Nature Switzerland AG 2022



G. Booker, *Coercion, Authority and Democracy*, Palgrave Studies in Classical Liberalism,
https://doi.org/10.1007/978-3-031-16883-3

Axfors, Cathrine, and John P.A. Ioannidis. "Infection Fatality Rate of COVID-19 in Community-dwelling Populations with Emphasis on the Elderly: An Overview." medRXiv, BMJ Yale preprint. August 2021.
Ball, Molly. "The Secret History of the Shadow Campaign That Saved the 2020 Election." *Time Magazine*, February 4, 2021.
Barclay, Harold. *The State*. London: Freedom Press, 2003.
Barnett, Randy E. *The Structure of Liberty.* New York: Oxford, 1998.
———. *Restoring the Lost Constitution.* Princeton, NJ: Princeton, 2004.
Barua, Bacchus et al. *Waiting Your Turn: Wait Times for Healthcare in Canada, 2018 Report.* Vancouver: Fraser Institute, 2018.
Bastiat, Frederic. *Selected Essays on Political Economy*. New York: Foundation for Economic Education, 1995.
———. *The Law*. London: IEA, 2001.
Bennett, James T., and Thomas J. DiLorenzo. *Underground Government: The off-Budget Public Sector*. Washington: Cato Institute, 1983.
Benson, Bruce L. *The Enterprise of Law*. San Francisco: Pacific Research Institute, 1990.
———. *To Serve and Protect*. New York: New York U. Press, 1998.
Bentham, Jeremy. *A Fragment on Government*. Cambridge: Cambridge U. Press, 1994.
Bergland, David. *Libertarianism in One Lesson*. Cartersville: The Advocates for Self Government, 2005.
Binmore, Ken. *Game Theory and the Social Contract: Playing Fair*. Boston: MIT Press, 1995.
———. *Just Playing*. Boston: MIT Press, 2002.
Bishop, Tho. *Covid Tyranny Destroys the Myth of Liberal Democracy.* Auburn: Mises Institute, 2021.
Black, D. *Theory of Committees and Elections*. Cambridge: Cambridge U. Press, 1958.
Blainey, Geoffrey. *The Tyranny of Distance*. Melbourne: Sun Books, 1966.
Block, Walter. "Cut the Murder Rate in New Orleans." http://www.lewrockwell.com/2007/01/walter-e-block/cut-the-murder-rate-in-new-orleans/.
Blundell, John, and Colin Robinson. *Regulation Without the State*. London: IEA, 2000.
Boetie, Etienne De La. *The Politics of Obedience: The Discourse of Voluntary Servitude.* Whitefish: Kessinger Reprint, n.d.
Boettke, Peter, ed. *Anarchy State and Public Choice*. Cheltenham: Edward Elgar, 2005.

Bolick, Clint. *Leviathan: The Growth of Local Government and the Erosion of Liberty*. Stanford: Hoover Institution, 2004.

Bouillon, Hardy, and Hartmut Kliemt, eds. *Ordered Anarchy: Jasay and His Surroundings*. Aldershot: Ashgate, 2007.

Bovard, James. *Freedom in Chains: The Rise of the State and the Demise of the Citizen*. New York: St Martin's Press, 1999.

———. *Attention Deficit Democracy*. New York: Palgrave, 2005.

Brennan, Geoffrey. 2005. "'The Myth of Ownership' Liam Murphy and Thomas Nagel: A Review Essay." *Constitutional Political Economy* 16: 207–219.

Brennan, Jason. *Against Democracy*. Princeton: Princeton U. Press, 2017.

———. *When All Else Fails: The Ethics of Resistance to State Injustice*. Princeton: Princeton U. Press, 2019.

Browne, Harry. *Why Government Doesn't Work*. New York: St Martin's Press, 1995.

———. *The Great Libertarian Offer*. Great Falls: Liam Works, 2000.

Brubaker, Elizabeth. *Property Rights in the Defence of Nature*. London: Earthscan, 1995.

Buchanan, James M., and Richard E. Wagner. *Democracy in Deficit: The Political Legacy of Lord Keynes*. Indianapolis: Liberty Fund, 2000.

Burke, Edmund. *Reflections on the Revolution in France*. New York: Bobbs-Merrill, 1955.

Canada, Government of. "Medical Assistance in Dying." Ottawa, March 17, 2021.

Canadian Covid Care Alliance. "The Pfizer Inoculations for Covid-19: More Harm than Good." Report, December 16, 2021. www.CanadianCovidCareAlliance.org.

Canadian Institute for Health Information. *Waiting for Health Care in Canada*. Ottawa: CIHI, 2006.

Canadian Taxpayers Federation. *On the Dole: Businesses, Lobbyists, and Industry Canada's Subsidy Programs*. Toronto: CTF, 2007.

Carter, April. *Authority and Democracy*. London: Routledge, 1979.

Cavallar, Georg. "Kant's Judgement on Frederick's Enlightened Absolutism." In *History of Political Thought* 14, no.1 (Spring 1993). Imprint Academic Ltd.

Centers for Disease Control and Prevention. "Immunization: The Basics; Understanding mRNA COVID-19 Vaccines." September 1, 2021.

Chodorov, Frank. *The Rise and Fall of Society*. New York: Devin-Adair, 1959.

———. *Fugitive Essays*. Indianapolis: Liberty Press, 1980.

Coase, R.H. *The Firm, the Market, and the Law*. Chicago: Chicago U. Press, 1988.
Cohen, G.A. *Self-Ownership, Freedom and Equality*. Cambridge: Cambridge U. Press, 1995.
College of Physicians and Surgeons of Ontario. "Covid-19 FAQs for Physicians." www.cpso.on.ca. 2022.
Crawford, Neta C. "Calculating the Costs of the Afghanistan War in Lives, Dollars and Years." In *The Conversation*. Boston: Boston University, 2021.
Creveld, Martin van. *The Rise and Decline of the State*. Cambridge: Cambridge U. Press, 1999.
———. *The Changing Face of War*. New York: Ballantine, 2006.
Cutler, A. Claire. *Private Power and Global Authority*. Cambridge: Cambridge U. Press, 2003.
Cusan, Alfred G. "Do We Ever Really Get Out of Anarchy." *Journal of Libertarian Studies* 3, no. 2 (1979): 151–158.
Dahl, Robert A. *A Preface to Democratic Theory*. Chicago: Chicago U. Press, 1956.
———. *Pluralist Democracy in the United States*. New York: Rand McNally, 1967.
———. *Polyarchy*. New Haven: Yale U. Press, 1971.
———. *A Preface to Economic Democracy*. Berkeley: California U. Press, 1985.
———. *Democracy and Its Critics*. New Haven: Yale U. Press, 1989.
———. *On Democracy*. New Haven: Yale U. Press, 1998.
———. *How Democratic Is the American Constitution*. New Haven: Yale U. Press, 2003.
———. *On Political Equality*. New Haven: Yale U. Press, 2006.
Davis, Iain. *Pseudo Pandemic: New Normal Technocracy*. London: Independently Published, 2021.
Denning, Lord. *The Discipline of Law*. London: Butterworths, 1979.
Denson, John V. *The Costs of War: America's Pyrrhic Victories*. New Brunswick: Transaction, 2003.
———. *A Century of War: Lincoln, Wilson, and Roosevelt*. Auburn: Mises Institute, 2006.
Dershowitz, Alan M. *Preemption: A Knife That Cuts Both Ways*. New York: Norton, 2006.
DeSoto, Hernando. *The Mystery of Capital*. New York: Basic Books, 2000.
Devlin, Patrick. *The Enforcement of Morals*, 6. Oxford: Oxford U. Press, 1965 [1975].

DiLorenzo, Thomas J. *How Capitalism Saved America.* New York: Three Rivers Press, 2004.
———. The Rise of Economic Fascism in America. mises.org., August 27, 2021.
Dunn, John. *The Cunning of Unreason.* New York: Basic Books, 2000.
———. *Democracy: A History*. Toronto: Penguin, 2005.
Dworkin, Ronald. *Taking Rights Seriously*. London: Duckworth, 1977.
———. "Liberalism." In *Public & Private Morality*, ed. Stuart Hampshire, 113–143. Cambridge: Cambridge U. Press, 1978 [Reprint,1980].
———. *A Matter of Principle.* Cambridge: Harvard U. Press, 1985.
———. *Law's Empire.* Harvard U. Press, 1986.
———. *Sovereign Virtue.* Cambridge: Harvard U. Press, 2002.
———. *Is Democracy Possible Here?* Princeton: Princeton U. Press, 2006.
Edmundson, William A. *Three Anarchical Fallacies.* Cambridge: Cambridge U. Press, 1998.
Eland, Ivan. *The Empire Has No Clothes: US Foreign Policy Exposed*. Oakland: Independent Institute, 2004.
Ellickson, Robert C. *Order Without Law: How Neighbors Settle Disputes.* Cambridge: Harvard U. Press, 1991.
Elshtain, Jean Bethke. *Sovereignty: God, State and Self.* New York: Basic Books, 2008.
Emsley, Clive. *The Great British Bobby: A History of British Policing from the 18th Century to the Present*. London: Quercus, 2010.
Engdahl, F. William. "There Is More to Blackrock Than You Might Imagine." WilliameEngdahl.com, June 18, 2021.
Engelbrecht, Torsten, Claus Koehnlein, Samantha Bailey, and Stephano Scoglio. *Virus Mania* (Books on Demand). Bloomington: Trafford, 2021.
Epstein, Richard. *Bargaining with the State*. Princeton: Princeton U. Press, 1993.
———. *Forbidden Grounds*. Cambridge: Harvard U. Press, 1995.
———. *Simple Rules for a Complex World*. Cambridge: Harvard U. Press, 1997.
———. *Principles for a Free Society.* Reading: Perseus, 1998.
———. *Scepticism and Freedom.* Chicago: Chicago U. Press, 2003.
———. *Free Markets Under Siege.* Stanford: Hoover Institution, 2005.
———. *How Progressives Rewrote the Constitution.* Washington: Cato Institute, 2006.
Essex, Christopher, and Ross McKittrick. *Taken by Storm: The Troubled Science, Policy and Politics of Global Warming.* Toronto: Key Porter, 2002.

Evatt, Herbert Vere. *The King and His Dominion Governors*. London: Frank Cass, 1967.
Faust, Drew Gilpin. *This Republic of Suffering: Death and the American Civil War*. New York: Vintage, 2008.
Feinberg, Joel. *Social Philosophy*. New York: Prentice-Hall, 1973.
———. *Harm to Others*. New York: Oxford U. Press, 1984.
———. *Harm to Self*. New York: Oxford U. Press, 1986.
Fitzgerald, Randall. *Mugged by the State*. Washington: Regnery, 2003.
Fleming, Richard M. *Is Covid-19 a Bioweapon? A Scientific and Forensic Investigation*. New York: Skyhorse, 2021.
Flynn, John T. *Country Squire in the White House*. New York: Doubleday, 1940.
Foot, Philippa. *Natural Goodness*. Oxford: Oxford U. Press, 2001.
Forcese, Craig, and Aaron Freeman. *The Laws of Government*. Toronto: Irwin Law, 2005.
Foster, Peter. *Self Serve*. Toronto: Macfarlane Walter & Ross, 1992.
Freeman, Samuel. "Illiberal Libertarians: Why Libertarianism Is Not a Liberal View." *Philosophy & Public Affairs* 30, no. 2 (Spring 2001): 105–151.
Fried, Charles. *Right and Wrong*. Cambridge: Harvard U. Press, 1980.
Friedman, David. *The Machinery of Freedom*. La Salle: Open Court, 1989.
Friedman, Milton. *Capitalism and Freedom*. Chicago: Chicago U. Press, 1962.
———. *Capitalism and Freedom*. Chicago: Chicago U. Press, 1982.
Friedman, Milton, and Rose Friedman. *Freedom to Choose*. New York: Avon, 1981.
Frijters, Paul, Gigi Foster, and Michael Baker. *The Great Covid Panic. What Happened, Why and What to do Next*. Austin: The Brownstone Institute, 2021.
Gauthier, David. *Morals by Agreement*. Oxford: Oxford U. Press, 1987.
Gelpern, Anna et al. *How China Lends: A Rare Look into 100 Debt Contracts with Foreign Governments*. AIDDATA: A Research Hub at William and Mary, March 2021.
Gibson, Gordon, ed. *Fixing Canadian Democracy*. Vancouver: Fraser Institute, 2003.
Gilbert, Martin. *The Will of the People*. Toronto: Vintage Canada, 2006.
Godwin, William. *Enquiry Concerning Political Justice*. London: Penguin, 1976.
Goerlitz, Walter. *The German General Staff 1657–1945*. New York: Praeger Inc, 1965.
Goldberg, Jonah. *Liberal Fascism: The Secret History of the American Left from Mussolini to the Politics of Meaning*. New York: Doubleday, 2007.
Goodin, Robert E. *Reflective Democracy*. Oxford: Oxford U. Press, 2003.

Gould, Carol. *Globalizing Democracy and Human Rights.* Cambridge: Cambridge U. Press, 2004.
Graetz, Michael J., and Ian Shapiro. *Death by a Thousand Cuts: The Fight Over Taxing Inherited Wealth.* Princeton: Princeton U. Press, 2005.
Gratzer, David. *Code Blue.* Toronto: ECW Press, 1999.
———, ed. *Better Medicine.* Toronto: ECW Press, 2002.
Grazia, Alfred De. *Political Organization.* New York: Free Press, 1952.
Green, Leslie. *The Authority of the State.* Oxford: Oxford U. Press, 1988.
———. "Associative Obligations and the State." In *Dworkin and His Critics,* ed. J. Burley, 267–284. Oxford: Blackwell, 2004.
Greenhut, Steven. *Abuse of Power: How the Government Misuses Eminent Domain.* Santa Ana: Seven Locks Press, 2004.
Gwartney, J.D., and R.L. Stroup. *What Everyone Should Know About Economics and Prosperity.* Vancouver: Fraser Institute, 1993.
Hamowy, Ronald. *Canadian Medicine: A Study in Restricted Entry.* Vancouver: Fraser Institute, 1984.
———, ed. *Dealing with Drugs: Consequences of Government Control.* San Francisco: Pacific Research Institute for Public Policy, 1990 [1987].
———, ed. *The Encyclopedia of Libertarianism.* Thousand Oaks, CA: Sage 2008.
Hampshire, Stuart, ed. *Public and Private Morality.* Cambridge: Cambridge U. Press, 1980.
Hardin, Russell. "Public Choice Versus Democracy". In *The Idea of Democracy,* ed. David Copp et al. Cambridge: Cambridge U. Press, 1993.
———. *One for All: The Logic of Group Conflict.* Princeton: Princeton U. Press, 1995.
———. *Indeterminacy and Society.* Princeton: Princeton U. Press, 2003a.
———. *Liberalism, Constitutionalism and Democracy.* Oxford: Oxford U. Press, 2003b.
Hare, R.M. "The Lawful Government." In *Philosophy Politics and Society,* 3rd Series, ed. Peter Laslett and W.G. Runciman, 157–172. Oxford: Blackwell, 1967.
———. *Essays on Political Morality.* Oxford: Oxford U. Press, 1998.
Harper, F.A. *Liberty: A Path to Its Recovery.* Irvington-on-Hudson: The Foundation for Economic Education, 1949.
Harris, Mike, and Preston Manning. *Building Prosperity in a Canada Strong and Free.* Vancouver: Fraser Institute, 2006.
Hart, H.L.A. *The Concept of Law.* Oxford: Oxford U. Press, 1961.
———. *Law, Liberty and Morality.* Oxford: Oxford U. Press, 1963.

———. "Are There Any Natural Rights?" In *Theories of Rights*, ed. J. Waldron, 77–90. Oxford: Oxford U. Press, 1984.
———. *Essays in Jurisprudence and Philosophy*. Oxford: Oxford U. Press, 1985.
Hasnas, John. "Toward a Theory of Empirical Natural Rights." *Social Philosophy & Policy* 22, no. 1 (Winter 2005): 111–147.
———. "Some Reflections on the Argument for the State." [unpubl.].
———. "Unethical Compliance and the Non-sequitur of Academic Business Ethics." *Journal of Private Enterprise* 22, no. 20 (Spring 2006a): 87–105.
———. *Trapped: When Acting Ethically Is Against the Law.* Washington, DC: Cato Institute, 2006b.
———. "The Myth of the Rule of Law." In *Anarchy and the Law*, ed. Edward P. Stringham, 163–192. New Brunswick: Transaction Publishers, 2007.
———. "The Obviousness of Anarchy." In *Anarchism/Minarchism*, ed. Roderick T. Long and Tibor R. Machan, 111–131. Aldershot: Ashgate, 2008.
Hayek, F.A. *Individualism and Economic Order*. Chicago: Chicago U. Press, 1948.
———. *Law, Legislation and Liberty*, Vol. I, 41. Chicago: Chicago U. Press, 1973 [1983].
———. *Law, Legislation and Liberty*, Vol. 2. Chicago: Chicago U. Press, 1976.
———. *The Constitution of Liberty*. Chicago: Chicago U. Press, 1978.
———. *Law, Legislation and Liberty*, vol. 3. Chicago: Chicago U. Press, 1979.
———. *A Free Market Monetary System*. Auburn: Mises Institute, 2008.
Hazlitt, Henry. *Man vs The Welfare State*. New Rochelle: Arlington House, 1969.
———. *The Conquest of Poverty*. New Rochelle: Arlington House, 1973.
———. *Is Politics Insoluble?* Irvington-on-Hudson: Foundation for Economic Education, 1997.
Healy, Gene. "Drug Prohibition." In *The Encyclopedia of Libertarianism*, ed. R. Hamowy, 128–129. Thousand Oaks: Sage, 2008.
Heath, Joseph. *The Efficient Society*. Toronto: Penguin, 2001.
Hebert, Philip C. *Doing Right*. Toronto: Oxford U. Press, 1996.
Henderson, David. *Misguided Virtue: False Notions of Corporate Social Responsibility*. London: IEA, 2001.
———. *Joy of Freedom*. Upper Saddle River: Prentice-Hall, 2002a.
———. "Myths About US Health Care." In *David Gratzer*, ed. Better Medicine, 175–195. Toronto: ECW Press, 2002b.
Higgs, Robert. *Crisis and Leviathan*. New York: Oxford U. Press, 1987.
———. *Against Leviathan*. Oakland: The Independent Institute, 2004.

———. *Resurgence of the Warfare State*. Oakland: The Independent Institute, 2005.

Hobbes, Thomas. *Leviathan.* Oxford: Oxford U. Press, 1909.

Hoffman, Robert, ed. *Anarchism.* New York: Atherton, 1970.

Hogue, Arthur R. *Origins of the Common Law*. Bloomington: Indiana U. Press, 1966.

Holcombe, Randall G. *Public Finance*. St Paul: West, 1996.

———. *Writing off Ideas.* Oakland: Independent Institute, 2000.

———. *From Liberty to Democracy*. Ann Arbor: Michigan U. Press, 2002.

———. "Why Government?" In *Ordered Anarchy: Jasay and His Surroundings*, ed. Hardy Bouillon and Hartmut Kliemt, 147–166. Aldershot: Ashgate, 2007.

Holmes, Stephen, and Cass R. Sunstein. *The Cost of Rights*. New York: Norton, 1999.

Hoppe, Hans-Hermann. *Democracy: The God That Failed*. New Brunswick: Transaction, 2002.

———, ed. *The Myth of National Defense.* Auburn: Mises Institute, 2003.

Hospers, John. *Libertarianism.* Santa Barbara: Reason Press, 1971.

Howard, Michael. *The Invention of Peace and the Reinvention of War*. London: Profile, 2002.

Huemer, Michael. *The Problem of Political Authority*. Basingstoke: Palgrave Macmillan, 2013.

Hume, David. *A Treatise of Human Nature*. Ed. L.A. Selby-Bigge. Oxford: Oxford U. Press, 1960.

———. *Enquiries Concerning Human Understanding and Concerning the Principles of Morals*, 3rd ed., ed. Peter H. Nidditch. Oxford: Oxford U. Press, 1975.

———. *Political Essays*. Ed. Knud Haakonssen. Cambridge: Cambridge U. Press, 2003.

Hurd, Heidi. *Moral Combat*. Cambridge: Cambridge U. Press, 1999.

Ibbitson, John. *The Polite Revolution.* Toronto: McClelland & Stewart, 2005.

Ignatieff, Michael. *The Lesser Evil*. Toronto: Penguin Canada, 2004.

International Criminal Court. *Brief Alleging Crimes Against Humanity in Violation of the Nuremberg Code.* The Hague: December 6, 2021.

Ioannidis, John P.A. "A Fiasco in the Making? As the Coronavirus Pandemic Takes Hold, We Are Making Decisions Without Reliable Data." *Stat-Journal for the Rapid Dissemination of Statistical Research.* Wiley: March 17, 2020.

———. "Global Perspective of COVID-19 Epidemiology for a Full-Cycle Pandemic." *European Journal of Clinical Investigation* 50 (2020): e13423. Wiley online: October 6, 2020.

Jacobs, Jane. *The Death and Life of Great American Cities*. New York: Vintage, 1992.

Jarrett, Gregg. *The Russia Hoax: The Illicit Scheme to Clear Hillary Clinton and Frame Donald Trump*. New York: HarperCollins, 2018.

Jasay, Anthony De. *Choice Contract and Consent*. London: Institute of Economic Affairs, 1991.

———. *Against Politics*. London: Routledge, 1997.

———. *The State*. Indianapolis: Liberty Fund, 1998.

———. *Justice and Its Surroundings*. Indianapolis: Liberty Fund, 2002.

———. "Justice, Luck, Liberty." In *Liberty and Justice*, ed. Tibor Machan. Stanford: Hoover Institution, 2006.

———. "Misbehavior, Punishment, Prosperity. Part I The Statist Legacy." *The Library of Economics and Liberty*. http://www.econlib.org/library/Columns/y2007/Jasaypunishment.html, August 6, 2007.

Kant, Immanuel. *Perpetual Peace*. Minneapolis: Filiquarian Publishing LLC, 2007.

Kater, Michael H. *Doctors Under Hitler*. Chapel Hill and London: The U. of North Carolina Press, 1989.

Kekes, John. *The Art of Politics*. New York: Encounter, 2008.

Kendrick, Malcolm. "A Few Thoughts on Covid 19 Vaccination." http://drmalcolmkendrick.org/2022/02/23/a-few-thoughts-on-covid-19-vaccination/.

———. "Vaccination-silencing Doctors in the UK." http://drmalcolmkendrick.org/2022/02/27/vaccination-silencing-doctors-in-the-uk/.

Kennedy, Robert F. Jr. *The Real Anthony Fauci: Bill Gates, Big Pharms, and the Global War on Democracy and Public Health*. New York: Skyhorse, 2021.

Kheiriddin, Tasha, and Adam Daifallah. *Rescuing Canada's Right*. Mississauga: Wiley, 2005.

Kibbe, Matt. *Don't Hurt People and Don't Take Their Stuff: A Libertarian Manifesto*. New York: Harper Collins, 2014.

King, Anthony and Ivor Crewe. *The Blunders of Our Governments*. London: One World, 2014.

Laband, D. and D. Zhang. "Softwood Lumber: Americans Have Been Bush-whacked." *Globe & Mail*, August 16, 2001.

Lane, Rose Wilder. *The Discovery of Freedom*. San Franscisco: Fox & Wilkes, 1993.

Laski, Harold. *Democracy in Crisis*. London: Allen & Unwin, 1933.

———. *The State in Theory and Practice*. New York: Viking, 1935.

Laslett, Peter, and W.G. Runciman. *Philosophy, Politics and Society*, 2nd Series, Oxford: Blackwell, 1962.

———. *Philosophy, Politics and Society*, 3rd Series. Oxford: Blackwell, 1967.

Leeson, Peter T. *Anarchy Unbound*. New York: Cambridge U. Press, 2014.

Lemieux, Pierre. *In Defense of Bribery*. Auburn: Mises Institute, August 8, 2005.

Leoni, Bruno. *Freedom and the Law*. Indianapolis: Liberty Fund, 1991.

Leroy, Sylvia. "How Giving Are Canadians? The 2004 Generosity Index." *Fraser Forum*, December 2004–January 2005, 9–13.

Lester, Jan. *Escape from Leviathan*. London: St Martin's Press, 2000.

Lieberman, Myron. *The Teacher Unions*. New York: Encounter, 2000.

Locke, John. *Two Treatises of Government*. Ed. Peter Laslett. Cambridge: Cambridge U. Press, 1960.

Lomasky, Loren E. "Libertarianism at Twin Harvard." *Social Philosophy and Policy* 22, no. 1 (Winter 2005): 178–199.

Long, Roderick, and Tibor Machan. *Anarchism/Minarchism: Is Government Part of a Free Country?* Aldershot: Ashgate, 2008.

Lowey, Mark. *Business Edge* 1, no. 15 (July 2004).

Lott, John Jr. *A Simple Test for the Extent of Vote Fraud with Absentee Ballots in the 2020 Presidential Election: Georgia and Pennsylvania Data*. Washington: US Dept of Justice, December 21, 2020.

Lucas, John. "Against Equality." In *Justice and Equality*, ed. H.A. Bedau, 138–151. Englewood Cliffs: Prentice-Hall, 1971.

———. *The Principles of Politics*. Oxford: Oxford U. Press, 1985.

MacCormick, Neil. *Legal Right and Social Democracy*. Oxford: Oxford U. Press, 1982.

Macey, Jonathan. "On the Failure of Libertarianism to Capture the Popular Imagination." In *Problems of Market Liberalism*, ed. Ellen Frankel Paul. Cambridge: Cambridge U. Press, 1998.

Machan, Tibor, ed. *Liberty and Equality*. Stanford: Hoover Institution Press, 2002a.

———. *Liberty and Hard Cases*. Stanford: Hoover Institution Press, 2002b.

Machan, Tibor R., and James E. Chesher. *A Primer on Business Ethics*. Lanham: Rowman and Littlefield, 2002.

Machiavelli, Nicolo. *The Prince*. New York: Norton, 1992.

Maitland, F.W. *The Constitutional History of England*. Cambridge: Cambridge U. Press, 1965.

Martin, J.C. *Martin's Annual Criminal Code*. Toronto: Canada Law Book, 1971.

Martin, Robert Ivan. *The Most Dangerous Branch.* Montreal: McGill-Queen's, 2003.

Martin, David E., *The Fauci/Covid 19 Dossier.* 205pp. Creative Commons License CC-BY-NC-SA, 2021.

Mavor, James. *Niagara in Politics*. New York: Dutton, 1925.

McChesney, Fred S. "Government Prohibitions on Volunteer Firefighting in 19th Century America: A Property Rights Perspective." *The Journal of Legal Studies* 15, no. 1 (January 1986): 69–92.

———. *Money for Nothing: Politicians, Rent Extraction and Political Extortion.* Boston: Harvard U. Press, 1997.

McCullough, Peter et al. "Multifaceted Highly Targeted Sequential Multidrug Treatment of Early Ambulatory, High Risk SARS-CoV-2 infection (Covid-19)." *Reviews in Cardiovascular Medicine* 21, no. 4 (2020): 517–530.

———. "The State of Covid Treatment." Transcript of Talk Given at Andrews University Village Church in Berrien Springs, Michigan, August 20, 2021.

McWhinney, Edward. *The Governor General and the Prime Ministers.* Vancouver: Ronsdale, 2005.

Mencken, H.L. *Notes on Democracy*. New York: Knopf, 1926.

———. *Prejudices: A Selection.* Ed. James T. Farrell. New York: Vintage, 1958.

Mercola, Joseph. "The Truth Is Coming Out About Covid Deaths." *Epoch Times*, March 2, 2022.

Mercola, Joseph, and Ronnie Cummins. *The Truth About COVID-19, Exposing the Great Reset, Lockdowns, Vaccine Passports, and the New Normal*. White River Junction, VT: Chelsea Green Publishing, 2021.

Michels, R. *Political Parties*. New York: Dover, 1959.

Milke, Mark, *Tax Me I'm Canadian.* Calgary: Thomas & Black, 2002.

———. *A Nation of Serfs*. Mississauga: Wiley, 2006.

Mill, J.S. *Considerations on Representative Government.* Indianapolis: Bobbs-Merrill, 1958.

———. *On Liberty*. London: Penguin Classics, 1988 [1974].

———. *Principles of Political Economy. Books IV and V*. Harmondsworth: Penguin, 1970 [1985].

Miller, David, ed. *Liberty*. Oxford: Oxford U. Press, 1991.

Mises, Ludwig von. *The Anti-Capitalistic Mentality.* Spring Mills: Libertarian Press, 1972.

———. *Omnipotent Government*. Grove City: Libertarian Press, 1985 [1944].

———. *Economic Calculation in the Socialist Commonwealth.* Auburn: Mises Institute, 1990.

———. *Liberalism: The Classical Tradition.* Irvington-on-Hudson: Foundation for Economic Education, 1996.

———. *Economic Policy.* Irvington-on Hudson: Free Market Books, 2000.

Molinari, Gustave De. "The Production of Security." Translated by J. Huston McCulloch, *Occasional Papers*, Series 2, ed. R. Ebeling. New York: The Center for Libertarian Studies, 1977.

Montanini, Chris. "Stratford Surgeon Slams Hospital Group's Mandatory Vaccination Policy." *The Beacon Herald Marketplace.* Stratford, November 4, 2021.

Montreal Economic Institute. *Economic Note*, February 2007.

Morgan, Patricia. *The War Between the State and the Family: How Government Divides and Impoverishes*. London: Institute for Economic Affairs, 2007.

Morris, Christopher W. *An Essay on the Modern State.* Cambridge: Cambridge U. Press, 2002 [1998].

———. "Are States Necessarily Coercive?" [unpubl.], 2003.

Mueller, John. *Capitalism Democracy & Ralph's Pretty Good Grocery*. Princeton: Princeton U. Press, 1999.

Mueller, Antony, "Coronavirus Crisis Management—What Really Happened and Why It Failed." Medium: May 15, 2020.

Murphy, Liam, and Thomas Nagel. *The Myth of Ownership.* New York: Oxford U. Press, 2002.

Nagel, Thomas. "Ruthlessness in Public Life." In *Public and Private Morality*, ed. Stuart Hampshire, 75–91. Cambridge: Cambridge U. Press, 1980 [1978].

———. *Equality and Partiality*. New York: Oxford U. Press, 1991.

Narveson, Jan. *The Libertarian Idea.* Philadelphia: Temple U. Press, 1988.

———. *Ethics in the Business and Professional Life.* Waterloo: U. Waterloo, 1998.

———. *Moral Matters*, 2nd ed. Peterborough: Broadview, 1999.

———. "Liberalism v. Democracy." [unpubl.].

———. "Government by Soundbyte." [unpubl.].

———. "Democracy by Main Force." [unpubl.], ed.

———. *Classics of Political and Social Philosophy.* Waterloo: U. Waterloo, 2000a.

———. "Libertarianism." In *The Blackwell Guide to Ethical Theory*, ed. Hugh LaFollette. Oxford: Blackwell, 2000b.

———. *Lectures on Political Philosophy.* Waterloo: U. Waterloo Dept of Philosophy, 2000c.

———. "Coercion: A Few Obvious Things." [unpubl.], October 2001.

———. *Respecting Persons in Theory and Practice*. Lanham: Rowman & Littlefield, 2002a.

———. "Liberty and Equality: A Question of Balance." In *Liberty and Equality*, ed. Tibor Machan, 35–59. Stanford: Hoover Institution Press, 2002b.

———. "The Free Market: How to and How Not to Defend It." [unpubl. 2006].

———. *A Fairly Short Introduction to Political Philosophy*. Lanham: Rowman & Littlefield, 2008a.

———. "The State: From Minarchy to Anarchy." In *Anarchism/Minarchism: Is Government Part of a Free Country?* ed. Roderick Long and Tibor Machan, 103–110. Aldershot: Ashgate, 2008b.

National Commission on Terrorist Attacks on the US. *The 9/11 Report*. New York: St Martin's Press, 2004.

Navarro, Peter. *The Immaculate Deception: 6 Key Dimensions of Election Irregularities.* Independent Report, December 2020.

Nelson, William N. *On Justifying Democracy.* London: Routledge, 1980.

Newton, Chris. *Written Evidence Submitted* [CLL0112] Center for Immune-Metabolism, Microbiome and Bio-energetic Research. UK, June 2021.

Nicholas, Barry. *An Introduction to Roman Law*. Oxford: Oxford U. Press, 1984.

Nisbet, Robert. *The Present Age*. New York: Harper, 1989.

Nock, Albert Jay. *Our Enemy the State.* San Francisco: Fox & Wilkes, 1994.

Noel, Ted. "Why Do Doctors Go Along with COVID Panic Porn and CDC Prescriptions." *American Thinker*, September 22, 2021.

Norberg, Johan. *Financial Fiasco: How America's Infatuation with Homeownership and Easy Money Created the Economic Crisis.* Washington, DC: Cato Institute, 2009.

Nozick, Robert. *Anarchy, State and Utopia.* New York: Basic Books, 1974.

———. *Socratic Puzzles.* Cambridge: Harvard U. Press, 1997.

OECD. "Economic Survey of Canada, 2006." Policy Brief, June 2006.

Olson, M. *The Logic of Collective Action.* Cambridge: Harvard U. Press, 1965.

Ontario Ministry of Northern Development and Mines. Factsheet, January 2004.

O'Rourke, P.J. *Don't Vote: It Just Encourages the Bastards.* New York: Atlantic Monthly Press, 2010.

Otteson, James R. *Actual Ethics.* New York: Cambridge U. Press, 2006.

Owen, Wilfred. Dulce et Decorum est. In *Oxford Book of War Poetry*, ed. Jon Stallworthy, 188–189. Oxford: Oxford U. Press, 1987.

Oye, Kenneth A., ed. *Cooperation under Anarchy*. Princeton: Princeton U. Press, 1986.

Palmer, Michael. "Open Letter to UW Officials: Repeal the COVID Vaccination and Testing Mandates." August 26, 2021.

Palmer, Michael, Sucharit Bhakdi, and Stefan Hockertz. "Expert Statement Regarding Comirnaty-COVID-19-mRNA-Vaccine for Children." doctors4c ovidethics.org, 2021.

Pateman, Carol. *The Problem of Political Obligation*. Berkeley: California U. Press, 1979.

Pena, Charles. *Winning the un-War: A New Strategy for Winning the War on Terrorism*. Dulles: Potomac Books, 2006.

Phelps, Edmund. *Mass Flourishing: How Grassroots Innovation Created Jobs, Challenge and Change*. Princeton: Princeton U. Press, 2013.

Pipes, Richard. *Property and Freedom*. New York: Random House, 1999.

Pipes, Sally C. *Miracle Cure: How to Solve America's Health Care Crisis and Why Canada Isn't the Answer*. San Francisco: Pacific Research Institute/ Vancouver: Fraser Institute, 2004.

Plamenatz, J.P. *Readings from Liberal Writers*. New York: Barnes & Noble, 1965.

———. *Consent, Freedom and Political Obligation*. Oxford: Oxford U. Press, 1968.

———. *Democracy and Illusion*. London: Longman, 1973.

Plimer, Ian. *Not for Greens*. Ballarat: Connor Court, 2014.

Pollock, Sir Frederick, and Frederic William Maitland. *The History of English Law*, Vol I. Cambridge: Cambridge U. Press 2nd ed. 1898 [Reissued with new intro. 1978].

Ponesse, Julie. *My Choice: The Ethical Case Against Covid-19 Mandates*. Toronto: The Democracy Fund, 2021.

Popper, Karl R. *The Poverty of Historicism*. New York: Harper and Row, 1961.

———. *The Open Society and Its Enemies, Vol. I, Plato*. Princeton: Princeton U. Press, 1971.

Power, Samantha. "Beyond Elections: Foreign Interference with American Democracy." In *Can It Happen Here: Authoritarianism in America?* ed. Cass Sunstein. New York: HarperCollins, 2018.

Plato. *The Republic*. Ed. Cornford. Oxford: Oxford U. Press, 1970 [1941].

———. "The Crito." In *The Dialogues of Plato*, ed. Jowett, Vol. I, 4th ed. Oxford: Oxford U. Press, 1953.

Popper, Karl. *The Poverty of Historicism*. New York: Harper & Row, 1961.

Porter, Bruce. *War and the Rise of the State*. New York: Free Press, 1994.

Proudhon, J-P. "An Anarchist View of Democracy." In *Anarchism*, ed. R. Hoffmann. New York: Atherton, 1970.
Quinton, Anthony, ed. *Political Philosophy*. Oxford: Oxford U. Press, 1967.
Radnitzky, Gerald. "Is Democracy More Peaceful Than Other Forms of Government?" In *The Myth of National Defense*, ed. Hans-Hermann Hoppe, 145–212. Auburn: Mises Institute, 2003.
Raico, Ralph. "Rethinking Churchill." In *The Costs of War: America's Pyrrhic Victories*, ed. John V. Denson, 321–360. New Brunswick: Transaction Publisher, 2003.
———. "Why Historical Revisionism Matters". article@mises.org, October 23, 2020.
Rand, Ayn. *Capitalism: The Unknown Idea*. New York: New American Library, 1967.
Rawls, J. "Justice as Fairness." In *Philosophy Politics and Society*, 2nd Series., ed. Peter Laslett and W.G. Runciman, 132–157. Oxford: Blackwell, 1962.
———. *A Theory of Justice*. Cambridge: Harvard U. Press, 1971.
———. *Political Liberalism*. New York: Columbia U. Press, 1993.
Raz, J. *The Authority of Law*. Oxford: Oxford U. Press, 1979.
———. *Morality of Freedom*. Oxford: Oxford U. Press, 1988.
———. *Practical Reason and Norms*. Princeton: Princeton U. Press, 1990a.
———. *Authority*. New York: New York U. Press, 1990b.
Rectenwald, Michael. *Google Archipelago: The Digital Gulag and the Simulation of Freedom*. Nashville: New English Review Press, 2019.
Reiss, Karina, and Sucharit Bhakdi. *Corona False Alarm: Facts and Figures*. White River Junction, VT: Chelsea Green Publishing, 2020.
———. "The Vaccination Craze": Prepublication of Chapter from *Corona Unmasked*. Berlin and Vienna: Goldegg Verlag, 2021.
Rhodes, Michael. "The Nature of Coercion." *The Journal of Value Inquiry* 34 (2000): 369–381.
Robb, Graham. *The Discovery of France*. New York: Norton, 2007.
Robin, Corey. *Fear: The History of a Political Idea*. New York: Oxford U. Press, 2004.
Rockwell, Lew. "The Right to Bribe." *The Free Market* 15, no. 8 (August 1997).
Rothbard, Murray. "Robert Nozick and the Immaculate Conception of the State." *Journal of Libertarian Studies* 1, no. 1 (1977a): 45–57.
———. *Power and Market*, Kansas City: Sheed Andrews & McMeel, 1977b
———. *For a New Liberty*. New York: Collier, 1978.

———. *What Has Government Done to Our Money.* Auburn: Mises Institute, 1990.
———. "The November Memorandum." www.lewrockwell.com/rothbard/rothbard155.html, 1994.
———. *Making Economic Sense.* Auburn: Mises Institute, 1995.
———. *The Logic of Action Two.* London: Edward Elgar, 1997.
———. *Education: Free and Compulsory.* Auburn: Mises Institute, 1999.
———. *Man, Economy and State.* Auburn: Mises Institute, 2001.
———. *The Ethics of Liberty.* New York: New York U. Press, 2002.
———. "Libertarians of Will, Intellect and Action." article@mises.org, February 9, 2007.
———. "Revisionism for Our Time." article@mises.org, June 29, 2007.
Rummel, R.J. *The Blue Book of Freedom: Ending Famine, Poverty, Democide, and War.* Nashville: Cumberland House, 2007.
Salin, Pascal. *Libéralisme*. Paris: Odile Jacob, 2000.
Sandefur, Timothy. *Property Rights in 21st Century America.* Washington, DC: Cato Institute, 2006.
Sanders, John T. The Free Market Model Versus Government. *Journal of Libertarian Studies* 1, no.1 (1977): 35–44.
———. *The Ethical Argument Against Government*. Washington, DC: U. Press of America, 1980.
Sanders, John T., and Jan Narveson. *For and Against the State*. Lanham: Rowman & Littlefield, 1996.
Scahill, Jeremy. *Blackwater: The Rise of the World's Most Powerful Mercenary Army*. New York: Nation, 2007.
Schmidtz, David. *The Limits of Government*. Boulder: Westview, 1991.
———. "Justifying the State." In *For and Against the State*, ed. John T. Sanders and Jan Narveson, 81–97. Lanham: Rowman and Littlefield, 1996.
———. *Elements of Justice*. New York: Cambridge U. Press, 2006.
Schumpeter, J.A. *Capitalism Socialism and Democracy*, 4th ed. London: Unwin, 1954.
Schwab, Klaus, and Thierry Malleret. *Covid 19-the Great Reset*. Geneva: World Economic Forum, 2020.
Schweizer, Peter. *Throw Them All Out*. New York: Houghton Mifflin Harcourt, 2011.
———. *Secret Empires*. New York: Harper, 2019.
Seldon, Arthur. *Capitalism.* Oxford: Blackwell, 1990.
———. *The Dilemma of Democracy*. London: Institute of Economic Affairs, 2002a.

———. “Public Choice in Britain.” In *Gordon Tullock*, ed. Government Failure, 129–176. Washington: Cato Institute, 2002b.

Selgin, George. *Good Money*. Ann Arbor: U.Michigan Press for the Independent Institute, 2008.

Shapiro, Ian. *Democratic Justice*. New Haven: Yale U. Press, 1999.

———. *The Moral Foundations of Politics*. New Haven: Yale U. Press, 2003.

Sharansky, Natan. *The Case for Democracy*. New York: Public Affairs, 2004.

Sidgwick, Henry. *The Elements of Politics*. London: Macmillan, 1897 [Elibron Classics reprint, 2005].

Simmons, A. John. *Moral Principles and Political Obligations*. Princeton: Princeton U. Press, 1979.

———. *On the Edge of Anarchy.* Princeton: Princeton U. Press, 1993.

———. “Philosophical Anarchism.” In *For and Against the State*, ed. Sanders John T. and Jan Narveson, 19–39. Lanham: Rowman and Littlefield, 1996.

———. *Justification and Legitimacy.* Cambridge: Cambridge U. Press, 2001.

Simpson, Jeffrey. *The Friendly Dictatorship*. Toronto: McClelland & Stewart, 2001.

Singer, Peter. *Democracy and Disobedience*. Oxford: Oxford U. Press, 1974.

———. “Remember Seat Belts? Why Vaccination Should Be Compulsory.” *The Globe and Mail*, August 7, 2021.

Singer, P.W. *Corporate Warriors: The Rise of the Privatized Military Industry*. Ithaca: Cornell U. Press, 2003.

Skoble, Aeon. “Liberty, Policy and Natural Disasters.” In *Liberty and Hard Cases*, ed. Tibor Machan, 83–102. Stanford: Hoover Institution, 2002.

Skoble, Aeon J. *Deleting the State: An Argument about Government*. Chicago and La Salle: Open Court, 2008.

Smith, Adam. *The Wealth of Nations*, vol. 2. Oxford: Oxford U. Press, 1976.

Södergren, Jan. *No Forced Union Membership or Dues for Politics: It's a Human Right*. Toronto: Canadian Association of Counsel to Employers, 2007.

Sowell, Thomas. *The Vision of the Anointed*. New York: Harper-Collins, 1995.

———. *Basic Economics*. New York: Basic Books, 2000.

———. *The Quest for Cosmic Justice*. New York: Simon & Schuster, 2002.

———. *Affirmative Action Around the World: An Empirical Study*. New Haven: Yale U. Press, 2004.

———. *Black Rednecks and White Liberals*. New York: Encounter Books, 2005.

———. *Intellectuals and Society*. New York: Basic Books, 2011.

———. *Discrimination and Disparities*. New York: Basic Books, 2018.

———. *Charter Schools and Their Enemies*. New York: Basic Books, 2020.

Spencer, Herbert. *The Man Versus the State*. Indianapolis: Liberty Classics, 1981.
Spooner, Lysander. *The Lysander Spooner Reader*. San Francisco: Fox & Wilkes, 1992.
Stallworthy, Jon, ed. *The Oxford Book of War Poetry*. Oxford: Oxford U. Press, 1984.
Stanbury, W.T. *The Politics of Milk in Canada*. Vancouver: Fraser Institute, 2002.
Starkey, David. *Magna Carta: The True Story Behind the Charter*. London: Hodder and Stoughton Ltd, 2015.
Stone, Julius. "Justice in the Slough of Equality." *Hastings Law Journal* 29 (May 1978): 995.
Stossel, John. *Give Me a Break*. New York: Harper Collins, 2004.
Stringham, Edward P., ed. *Anarchy, State and Public Choice*. London: Edward Elgar, 2005.
———. *Anarchy and the Law: The Political Economy of Choice*. Oakland: Independent Institute, 2007.
Sumner, L.W. *The Hateful and the Obscene*. Toronto: U. Toronto Press, 2004.
Sunstein, Cass R. *The Cost Benefit State*. Chicago: American Bar Association, 2002.
Svorny, Shirley. "Medical Licensing: An Obstacle to Affordable Quality Care." *Policy Analysis* No. 621. Washington: Cato Institute, 2008.
Symonds, Richard. *Oxford and Empire*. Oxford: Clarendon Press, 1991.
Talmon, J.L. *The Origins of Totalitarian Democracy*. London: Sphere Books, 1970.
Tamanaha, Brian Z. *Law as a Means to an End*. Cambridge: Cambridge U. Press, 2006.
Taylor, A.J.P. *The Origins of the Second World War*. London: Penguin, 1964.
Taylor, Michael. *Community Anarchy & Liberty*. Cambridge: Cambridge U. Press, 1982.
———. *The Possibility of Cooperation*. Cambridge: Cambridge U. Press, 1987.
The Economist Intelligence Unit. *Democracy Index 2020, In Sickness and in Health?* London: The Economist, 2021.
Thoreau, Henry David. *Civil Disobedience and Other Essays*. New York: Dover, 1993.
Tocqueville, Alexis de. *The Old Regime and the French Revolution*. New York: Doubleday, 1955.
———. *Democracy in America*. London: Penguin, 2003.

Treitschke, Heinrich von. *Politics*. Ed. Hans Kohn. New York: Harcourt Brace and World, 1963.

Tullock, Gordon. *Government Failure: A Primer in Public Choice*. Washington, DC: Cato Institute, 2002.

———. *The Vote Motive*. London: Institute of Economic Affairs, 2006.

Tyson, Brian, and George Fareed. *Overcoming the Covid Darkness: How Two Doctors Successfully Treated 7000 Patients*. Brawley, CA: El Centro, 2021.

Vedder, Richard K., and Lowell E. Galloway. *Out of Work*. Oakland: The Independent Institute, 1997.

Veldhuis, Nick, and Milagros Palacios. "Canadians Celebrate Tax Freedom Day on June 19." Fraser Forum, July–August, 2006.

Viminitz, Paul. "Coercion." [unpubl.], July 2001.

Waldron, Jeremy. *Theories of Rights*. Oxford: Oxford U. Press, 1984.

———. *Liberal Rights*. Cambridge: Cambridge U. Press, 1993.

Walzer, Michael. *Spheres of Justice*. New York: Basic Books, 1983.

Wang, Joe. "Pandemic Lessons Learned: Omicron Versus Bill Gates." *Epoch Times*, February 26, 2002.

Wertheimer, Alan. *Coercion*. Princeton: Princeton U. Press, 1987.

West, E.G. "The Political Economy of American Public-School Legislation." *Journal of Law and Economics* 10: 101–128, 1967.

———. *Education and the State*. Indianapolis: Liberty Fund, 1994.

Westen, John Henry, "Physicians Pushing Experimental COVID Jabs Are 'Complicit' in People's Deaths: 'Cancelled' Doctor." *Lifesite News*, February 25, 2022.

Whelan, Robert. *The Corrosion of Charity*. London: Institute of Economic Affairs, 1996.

Wolff, R.P. *In Defense of Anarchism*. New York: Harper & Row, 1970.

Wollheim, R. "A Paradox in the Theory of Democracy." In *Philosophy Politics & Society*, 2nd Series, ed. Peter Laslett and Walter Garrison Runciman. Oxford: Blackwell, 1962.

Woods, Thomas. *The Politically Incorrect Guide to American History*. Washington, DC: Regnery, 2004.

———. *Meltdown: A Free-Market Look at Why the Stock Market Collapsed, the Economy Tanked, and Government Bailouts Will Make Things Worse*. Washington, DC: Regnery, 2009.

Zakaria, Fareed. *The Future of Freedom*. New York: Norton, 2003.

Zumwalt, Robert. "The Global Minimum Corporate Tax Exposes the G7's Hypocrisy." mises.org., July 1, 2021.

# Index


A

abortion 240
*Academie francaise* 110
accountability 107, 117
Ackerman,Kenneth D. 102, 188
affirmative action 104, 105, 223
aggression 16, 122, 256, 257
anarchism, philosophical 49, 71, 73
*ancien regime* 202, 203, 228, 253
Anderson, Terry L. 110, 111
anonymity 135, 136
Anscombe, G.E.M. 5, 250, 251
Aquinas, Thomas 77
aristocracy 171, 190, 201
Arrow, Kenneth J. 131, 194
Arthur, Terry 95
Athens 49, 119
Augustine 77
Austin, John 32, 33
Australia 101, 109, 225
  New South Wales 101
authority, political 49, 51, 54, 58, 80, 81, 88, 90, 124, 251

B

Balkans 87
Ball, Molly 196
Barclay, Harold 83
Barnett, Randy E. 40, 61, 65, 81, 219, 220
Bastiat, Frederic 61, 165
Bennett, James T. 107
Benson, Bruce L. 43, 72, 113–115, 122, 253
Bentham, Jeremy 76, 79
Bergland, David 103
Binmore, Ken 138, 139, 156
Birkenhead, Lord 159
Bishop, Tho 221


© The Editor(s) (if applicable) and The Author(s), under exclusive license to Springer Nature Switzerland AG 2022
G. Booker, *Coercion, Authority and Democracy*, Palgrave Studies in Classical Liberalism, https://doi.org/10.1007/978-3-031-16883-3

Bismarck, Otto von 94
blackmail 19, 20, 248, 249
Blainey, Geoffrey 59
Block, Walter 103
Blundell, John 106
Boetie, Etienne de la 83
Boettke, Peter 252
Bolick, Clint 78, 97
Bovard, James 90, 193
Brennan, Geoffrey 91
Brennan, Jason 225, 226, 241, 243, 245
bribes 48
Browne, Harry 103
Brubaker, Elizabeth 16
Buchanan, James 199, 200
Burke, Edmund 174, 245
Bush Doctrine 203

C

Caesar 89, 94
Canada 3, 58, 70, 78, 90, 94, 95, 100, 103, 107, 128, 129, 132, 178, 183, 185, 187, 191, 194, 222
  Charter of Rights and Freedoms 221
  Criminal Code 5
  euthanasia 237, 238
  health care 128, 132, 184
  Supreme Court 222
  Wheat Board 78
capital 25, 107, 198, 206
capitalism 9, 93, 117, 118, 157, 212
Carter, April 82
Cartright, Sir Richard 94, 95
caste systems 57
Cavallar, Georg 204
Chicago 101, 110
China, debt 198
Chodorov, Frank 183, 214, 224
Churchill, Winston 70, 71, 100, 154, 179, 195, 203, 205
Cicero 43, 245
citizen's arrest 244
Clapham omnibus, man in the 33, 42, 77, 117, 252
Clinton, Hillary 196
Clinton, William 202–204
Coase, R.H. 15, 16, 133
coercion 1, 2, 5, 9–12, 20–33, 35, 36, 38, 40, 44, 47, 48, 50, 52, 65, 70, 71, 84, 88, 97, 103, 104, 109, 125, 163, 166, 193, 197, 205, 209–211, 213, 235–237, 241, 244, 248, 249, 251, 252, 258
Cohen, G.A. 119
collective 2, 42, 49, 57, 58, 126, 127, 139, 173, 194, 195, 207, 210, 212, 216, 219, 220, 223, 247, 255, 256
  action 195, 210, 216, 223
  orderings 49
Collective Rights 247
common good 38, 175, 207
compromise 2, 60, 61, 81, 86, 153–156, 161, 162, 166, 171, 174, 175, 179–181, 186, 188, 191, 220
  fair 153–156, 162, 171, 174, 175, 179–181, 186, 188
consent 2, 3, 50–55, 65, 67, 72, 79, 81, 90, 118, 133, 135, 140, 151, 157–162, 200, 237, 242, 250
  express 50, 53, 158

hypothetical 50, 51
non-intentional 54
quasi 55, 158, 159
contract 5, 14, 27, 29, 40, 48–50, 54, 55, 59, 63, 64, 80, 87, 91, 102, 105, 118, 119, 121, 125, 126, 136, 139, 140, 159, 184, 201, 212–214, 235, 249, 251, 254, 256, 258
tacit 63
convention 51, 93, 109, 120, 121, 125, 221
cooperation 100, 109, 110, 114, 115, 133, 138, 161, 214, 239, 240, 258
social 67, 214, 240
coordination 2, 3, 83–85, 88, 108–111, 140, 250
decentralized 108
self-enforcing 109
cost–benefit 68, 105
courts, King's 114, 121
Crawford, Neta C. 254
Creveld, Martin van 94, 99, 100, 202, 203
Crewe, Ivor 122
Crito 49
CSR 117
CTF 90
Cusan, Alfred G. 6
Cutler, A. Claire 115–119, 122, 136

D

Dahl, Robert A. 156, 171–173, 175, 177–179, 181–185, 188–190, 192–197, 227
Daifallah, Adam 187
democracy 3, 43, 55, 83, 84, 117, 124, 130, 149–151, 154, 160, 162–179, 181–184, 186–194, 196–199, 201–208, 211–217, 219–228, 240, 249, 258, 259
Athenian 151, 171
partnership 216, 222, 224
polyarchal 178
representative 43, 171, 174, 175, 181
Denning, Lord 54, 55
Denson, John V. 99, 203, 205, 206, 209
Dershowitz, Alan M. 203
Devlin, Lord 236, 237, 243
DiLorenzo, Thomas J. 92, 107, 224
discrimination 57, 104, 156, 208
disobedience, civil 76, 77, 167
divine right 83, 123, 124, 192, 224, 245, 259
of kings 245, 259
Doctrine of Certainty 89
Dodgson, Charles–Lewis Carroll 150
drugs, non-pharmaceutical 236
due process 111
Dunn, John 47, 52
duty 2, 13, 19, 20, 28, 29, 33, 39, 41, 48–50, 53, 54, 56, 57, 61–66, 68–80, 84, 89, 90, 94, 106, 139, 158, 159, 164, 170, 208, 209, 225, 235, 241, 242, 244, 248, 254
of charity 242
of non-interference 2, 41, 53, 63, 73, 74, 209, 235, 244
positive 53, 63, 64
prima facie 50, 62, 69–71, 73, 76, 79, 241

Dworkin, Ronald 5, 31, 37, 50, 56–62, 64–66, 68–71, 112, 113, 149, 150, 177, 215–224, 226, 228

E

Easement 16
*Economist Democracy Index* 178
Edmundson, William A. 235, 236, 238–246, 252
education 3, 102, 128–130, 132, 140, 151, 152, 166, 186, 210, 239
Ellickson, Robert C. 110, 111
eminent domain 15, 78, 79, 97, 98, 104, 220
  seizure 97
Emsley, Clive 123
enforcement, of morals 242, 243
Engdahl, F. William 117
England, Bank of 200
epistocracy 225–228
Epstein, Richard 20, 23, 29, 48, 78, 87, 105, 219, 220, 242
equal 37, 41, 56, 57, 59–62, 152, 153, 155, 157, 170, 181, 182, 184, 186, 188, 218–220, 222, 239
  concern 57, 59–62, 219, 222
  treatment 57
equality 9, 37, 57, 93, 102, 130, 151, 181, 182, 184, 189, 190, 201, 219
ESG 117
Essex, Christopher 89
estoppel 54, 55, 140, 158–160, 162
  doctrine of 54, 55
  promissory 54
*etatism* 191
Europe, Convention on Human Rights 221
Evatt, H.V. 191
exclusion costs 132
externality 98, 106, 127, 214, 215, 254, 257, 258
  negative 127
  positive 127, 214, 215, 254

F

fair-go 55
fairness 2, 38, 39, 44, 61, 62, 66–70, 119, 120, 140, 152–154, 156, 157, 179, 227
fascist, dictatorships 70
Faust, Drew Gilpin 81, 82
Feinberg, Joel 18, 36, 238
firefighting 101, 102
Flynn, John T. 223
Folk Theorem 135, 139
Foot, Philippa 52, 136
Foster, Peter 100, 107
Franklin, Benjamin 94, 95
fraternity 59, 61
Frederick 204
  Frederick II 226
  the Great 204
Freeman, Samuel 63, 125, 191
free riding 67, 126, 127, 137, 160, 211, 254, 255
Friedman, David 43, 107
Friedman, Milton 108, 130–132
*Fuehrerprinzip* 150

G

Gates, Bill 92

Gauthier, David 134, 136
Gelpern, Anna 198
Gibson, Gordon 172, 178, 194
Gilbert, Martin 70, 71, 100, 154, 179, 205
Goerlitz, Walter 201
Goldberg, Jonah 223, 224
Goodin, Robert E. 172–174, 177
goods, public 3, 96, 104, 106, 108, 128, 132, 133, 140, 161, 254, 257
Gottfried, Paul 205, 206
government 4–6, 15, 34, 35, 43, 44, 48, 49, 51–53, 65, 67, 71, 72, 76–78, 80, 81, 83, 85–108, 110–116, 118, 120–127, 129–133, 149–154, 158, 163, 165, 166, 171, 172, 175–179, 181–187, 191–199, 201, 208–214, 216–220, 222–225, 227, 242, 244, 250–259
  by consent 53, 193
  responsible 53, 99, 132, 193
Graetz, Michael J. 92
Gratzer, David 128, 129
Grazia, Alfred de 83
Great Reset 117, 187
Greenhut, Steven 79, 97
Green, Leslie 1, 2, 6, 49, 51–56, 64, 65, 158–160, 162, 251
guild system 131

H

Hamowy, Ronald 129, 237
Hardin, Russell 85, 87, 109, 111, 189, 190, 194, 195, 223
Hare, R.M. 119, 152, 153
harm principle 122, 125, 137, 238, 241
harms, compensable 92
Harper, F.A. 173
Hart, H.L.A. 2, 22, 31–33, 37–39, 43, 62–68, 160, 161, 227, 236–238
Hasnas, John 6, 87, 88, 113, 116, 137, 252–255, 259
Hayek, F.A. 9–11, 14, 94, 97, 113, 114, 127, 197, 198, 209–213, 226, 250
Hazlitt, Henry 113, 165, 166
Healy, Gene 237
Heath, Joseph 133, 134, 136–139
Hebert, Philip C. 51, 52
Henderson, David 21, 166
Higgs, Robert 72, 82, 121, 209
Hill, Peter J. 110, 111
Hitler, Adolf 225
Hobbes, Thomas 25, 76, 77, 82, 83, 110, 137, 190, 193
Holcombe, Randall G. 34, 121, 224, 257–259
Holmes, Stephen 101, 103, 106
Homesteading 16
Hoppe, Hans-Hermann 198–202, 255–257
Horace 82
Hospers, John 21, 37, 95, 96
Huemer, Michael 30, 255, 257
Hume, David 93, 109, 111, 112, 114, 120–126, 137, 195, 257
Hurd, Heidi 83, 84, 88
Hurricane Katrina 60, 98, 100, 103, 126

I

Ibbitson, John 183
Ignatieff, Michael 91
independence 132, 134, 135, 174
Indians, North American 121
Individualism 209, 210
insurance, defence 256
integrity 58, 61, 112
irrelevance 134, 135

J

Jacobs, Jane 98
Jarrett, Gregg 196
Jasay, Anthony de 4, 25, 36, 40, 88, 89, 92, 96, 97, 102, 118–121, 126–128, 132–141, 158, 159, 195–197, 206–208, 210, 211, 213–215, 217–220, 235, 251, 254, 255
Jim Crow 87, 208
Junius 79, 242
justice 5, 37, 49, 61, 65, 70, 71, 73–76, 93, 94, 111, 112, 119–122, 124, 125, 130, 136, 156, 166, 170, 177, 206, 211, 218, 239–241, 253
  distributive 65, 218
  natural 112
  social 125, 211, 212
justification 1, 3, 19, 24, 25, 33, 35, 36, 38, 43, 48, 51, 54, 65, 82, 91, 127, 128, 157, 163, 185, 195, 199, 201, 209, 218
Juvenal, *Quis custodiet Ipsos custodes* 140, 251

K

Kant, Immanuel 200–202, 204, 226, 239, 240
Kekes, John 216
Kheiriddin, Tasha 187
Kibbe, Matt 122
King, Anthony 122
King, Mackenzie 70
King, Martin Luther 76, 77, 79, 80

L

laissez faire 118, 236
Lane, Rose Wilder 3, 4, 217
Laski, Harold 83, 194
Laurier, Sir Wilfred 95
law 1–5, 20, 24, 25, 27, 29–33, 35–38, 41, 43, 44, 47–50, 61, 62, 65, 69, 70, 73–77, 79, 80, 83–85, 87–89, 91, 103, 111–116, 120, 122, 125, 137, 140, 151, 153, 157, 165, 167, 170, 183, 184, 186, 192, 206–214, 221, 235–243, 246, 248, 251, 252, 254, 258, 259
  coerciveness of 2, 30–33, 35–38, 43, 44, 235
  common 111–113, 122, 125, 137, 252
  customary 113–115
  decentralized 112
  just 32, 50, 69
  *legum leges* 207
  *lex mercatoria*-Merchant 115
  natural 112
  positive 112, 239
  rule of 210, 259
Leeson, Peter 114, 120, 252
legal moralism 236, 237

legal system, decentralized 43
legitimacy 173
legitimacy, moral 58
Lemieux, Pierre 48
Leoni, Bruno 61, 81, 84
Leroy, Sylvia 101
Lester, Jan 36, 66
liberal 24, 33, 63, 95, 101, 103, 105, 106, 115–117, 174, 184, 189, 197, 205, 206, 221, 223, 224, 227, 237, 240–242
liberalism, classical 104, 118
libertarianism 63, 90, 91, 125, 210, 238
liberty, presumption of 36, 37, 43
Lieberman, Myron 129, 130
light house 254
Locke, John 40, 41, 158, 246, 247
logrolling 154–156
Lomasky, Loren E. 37
London 97
Lott, John 196
Louis XIV 185
Lucas, John 1, 93, 208

M

MacCormick, Neil 31, 32, 34, 35
Macey, Jonathan 91
Machan, Tibor 48
Magna Carta 207
Maitland, F.W. 207, 248
majoritarianism 218, 223, 226
majority rule 123, 162, 173, 177, 180, 182, 192, 195, 207, 222
*malum in se* 2, 38, 40, 44, 48, 212, 238, 241, 242
*malum prohibitum* 2, 5, 38–40, 44, 47, 48, 140, 212, 238, 242
Martin, J.C. 74, 75
Marx, Karl 93, 122, 184
mateship 55
Mavor, James 100
maximization 134
McChesney, Fred S. 101, 102, 104, 108, 112
McKittrick, Ross 89
Mencken, H.L. 4, 106, 107
*mens rea* 20, 87
*mercatocracy* 115, 116
Michels, R. 182, 183, 185, 188
Microsoft 92, 186, 257
Middle Ages 116, 248
Milke, Mark 33, 94, 95
Mill, J.S. 34, 122, 125, 133, 137, 152, 153, 156, 166, 167, 171, 184, 192, 193, 225, 226, 236–240
Mises, Ludwig von 115, 117, 118, 157, 165, 166, 191, 197–199, 227
Molinari, Gustave de 83, 123, 124
monopoly, producer 131
moral hazard 243
morality, of taxes 88, 90
Morgan, Patricia 243
Morris, Christopher W. 32–35, 253, 254
Mueller, Antony 121, 184
Murphy, Liam 65, 90–93, 211, 212
Mussolini, Benito 223, 225

N

Nagel, Thomas 65, 90–93, 211, 212, 218, 239, 240
Napoleon 181, 201

Narveson, Jan 9, 13–15, 21, 24, 29, 37, 50, 60, 63, 64, 66, 73, 86, 88, 93, 105, 106, 116, 117, 119, 120, 122, 124, 125, 154, 157, 160, 173, 175, 176, 182, 184, 189, 192, 197, 198, 217, 221, 239, 243, 247, 249, 259
Nash equilibrium 134, 138
National Commission report on 9/11 98
National Health Service 128
Navarro, Peter 196
Nazi 69, 70, 129, 180
  Germany 50, 69, 75, 169, 203
  laws 50, 70
  state 5, 69, 70, 75
Nelson, William N. 160, 162
New Deal 223, 224
Nicholas, Barry 43
Nisbet, Robert 204
*noblesse oblige* 73, 201
Nock, Albert Jay 123
non-excludability 96, 127
non-maleficence 237, 242, 254
*non-rivalry* 96
Norberg, Johan 199
Norman Conquest 209
Nozick, Robert 1, 3, 5, 11–31, 38, 39, 41–44, 49, 66–68, 91, 92, 118–120, 152, 161, 218, 245–250, 252
Nuisance 15, 16

O

obedience, prima facie 68
objector, conscientous 63, 167
obligation 2, 27, 33, 49–54, 56–60, 62–68, 70, 71, 73, 74, 77, 79, 80, 84, 85, 88, 90, 92, 140, 149–152, 158–161, 164, 170, 213, 214, 227, 242
  associative 56, 58–60, 64, 66, 140
  political 2, 53, 57–60, 62–66, 71, 73, 74, 77, 79, 80, 150, 159
  to obey the law 49, 50, 170
OECD 3, 90
Ontario 100, 128
Oregon 110
O'Rourke, P.J. 183, 185
Otteson, James R. 103
Owen, Wilfred 82, 256
Oxford 62, 82, 150, 152
Oye, Kenneth 6

P

*pacta sunt servanda* 54
Palacios, Milagros 90, 96
paradoxes, voter 156
Pareto 15, 85, 86, 126, 137, 138, 207, 208, 242
parties, political 182–185
Pateman, Carol 150
paternalism 90, 210, 236, 237
patronage 102
*pax democratica* 203, 204
Pearl Harbor 98, 99, 203
Petrocan 100, 107
Pipes, Richard 94, 104, 111
Pipes, Sally C. 129
Plamenatz, J.P. 51–53, 159, 162, 179–181, 192
Plato 49, 82, 151, 183, 192, 226, 227
Plimer, Ian 89
Pollock, Frederick 248

Popper, Karl 86, 226
Porter, Bruce 82, 99
prerogative, administrative 74–77, 79
pre-tax income 90–92
principal-agent 139
prisoners' dilemma 108, 109, 133, 134, 137–141
privatization 115, 122
property, rights 15, 16, 90, 97, 110, 132, 206, 214, 258
protection 10, 19, 42–44, 72, 76, 102, 104, 123, 125–127, 206, 208, 221, 223, 244, 246–249, 253–258
  agency 44, 102, 246, 248, 253
  racket 10, 19, 246, 249
protective services 249, 256
public goods, non-excludable 96
punishment, open 41, 247
punish, natural executive right to 40, 41

Q

*quanxi* 117

R

Radnitzky, Gerald 200, 202–204
Raico, Ralph 203–205
rail gauge 109, 110
  Iberian 109
  standard 109
Rawls, John 2, 24, 31, 33, 36–38, 60, 62–64, 66, 68, 120, 161, 239, 240
Raz, J. 1, 35, 51, 53–56, 71–74, 80–82, 108, 109, 140
*Realpolitik* 124
reasons of state, *raison d'etat* 218
reciprocity 56–59, 62
redistribution 90–93, 100, 140, 207–210, 213–215, 217, 218, 223, 227, 228, 240, 259
rents 110, 182, 198, 217
representation 174, 192, 226
Revolution, The French 202, 206
Rhodes, Michael 21–26, 28, 29
right 2, 13, 15, 16, 18, 20, 23, 26, 27, 29, 31, 33, 35, 37, 40–43, 48, 52–55, 61–63, 65–68, 72–74, 76, 78, 81–84, 86, 91, 101, 104, 106, 107, 109–114, 116, 124, 125, 154, 160–166, 168, 169, 171, 173, 181–183, 189–197, 206, 207, 210, 211, 217–222, 226, 227, 236, 237, 239, 240, 244–251, 255
  group 67
  natural 67, 116
  negative 63
  particular 63
  positive 63
  riparian 111, 112
  special 63, 67
  to punish 40–42, 244–247
  to tax 65
robber baron 92
Robb, Graham 93
Robespierre 61
Robinson, Colin 106
Rockwell, Lew 48
Roman Law, Twelve Tables of 43
Roosevelt, F.D. 70, 78, 82, 99, 223, 224
Roosevelt, Theodore 110, 111

Rothbard, Murray 3, 14–16, 19, 21, 39–42, 44, 48, 66, 90, 92, 95, 113, 116, 122, 123, 125–127, 129, 130, 132, 165, 166, 187, 199, 202, 247–249
rule 5, 6, 11, 12, 16, 19, 22, 30, 33, 39, 57, 58, 60, 62, 72, 73, 80, 82, 84, 88, 93, 109–114, 117, 119, 120, 122, 124, 126, 133, 134, 137, 138, 149, 150, 152, 155, 159, 160, 162, 170, 171, 173, 176, 177, 180, 184, 185, 191–194, 196, 197, 203, 206, 209, 210, 212, 218, 237, 238, 241, 242, 248, 251, 252, 256, 258
  arbitrary 80, 191
  non-hierarchical 112
Russell, Bertrand 163, 167, 169
Russia 65, 196

S

Salerno, Joseph T. 129, 217
Salin, Pascal 207
sanctions 24, 30, 31, 33, 35, 97, 110, 114, 125, 134, 136, 241, 243
Schmidtz, David 42, 51, 120
Schumpeter, Joseph 175–177, 179–181, 187, 188, 193, 194, 208
Schwab, Klaus 117, 118, 172, 187
Schweizer, Peter 73, 176
Seldon, Arthur 34, 66, 81, 86, 96, 98, 127–129, 132, 182, 186, 187, 195, 210
self government 184, 190, 192, 197, 217
Selgin 113
services, government 65, 66, 210, 211
Shapiro, Ian 92, 93, 177, 185–187
Sidgwick, Henry 133, 209, 210
Simmons, A. John 2, 48, 49, 53, 78, 150, 158–162
Simpson, Jeffrey 42, 183, 185
Singer, Peter 149–153, 155–175, 177, 179–181, 186, 188–190, 193, 216, 221, 227
Singer, P.W. 256
Skoble, Aeon 24, 99, 101
slavery 26, 66, 91, 119
Smith, Adam 97, 136
social contract 51, 138–140
*social transaction costs* 15
Socrates 49, 50, 151–153, 157
sovereign prerogative 44, 207, 241
sovereignty 43, 83, 91, 140, 151, 190, 191, 207, 213, 224, 225
Sowell, Thomas 14, 105, 125, 130, 205
Spencer, Herbert 224, 225
Spooner, Lysander 78, 95
spot exchange 136
*Stadtluft macht frei* 111
Stalin, Joseph 70, 205, 225
Starkey, David 206
state 1–6, 10, 15–17, 21, 24, 25, 30–35, 40–44, 47–56, 58, 61, 64, 65, 67, 70–76, 78–80, 82, 83, 85, 87, 89, 90, 92, 93, 97, 99–105, 108–110, 112–115, 117, 120–124, 126–141, 149, 151–153, 155, 159–162, 164, 165, 168, 171, 176–178, 180, 183, 184, 190, 191, 194, 196, 198, 201, 202, 205–211,

213–215, 217–223, 225, 227, 228, 235–238, 240–249, 251, 252, 254–259
fascist 223
immaculate conception of 247
welfare 34, 99, 100, 103, 165, 204, 209, 213
Stone, Julius 93
Sumner, L.W. 122, 209
Sunstein, Cass R. 101, 103, 105, 106
Svorny, Shirley 131, 132
Symonds, Richard 82

T

Talmon, J.L. 205
Tamanaha, Brian Z. 61
Tammany Hall 97, 102, 188
taxation, progressive 94, 100
taxes 3, 34, 44, 65, 66, 90–92, 94–97, 106, 111, 113, 118, 140, 195, 199, 210, 211, 213, 218, 241, 251, 253, 255
Taylor, A.J.P. 204
Taylor, Michael 100
Tertullian 89
the Revolution 61, 82, 190, 205, 215
Third Reich 64
Thoreau, Henry David 259
Thrasymachus 73, 192
Tocqueville, Alexis de 183, 189–194, 197, 200, 201, 204, 215
Toronto, City of 78
transubstantiation 251
treatment, preferential 105
Treitschke, Heinrich von 83
Trump, Donald 178, 196, 220
Tullock, Gordon 86, 154, 155, 186, 187, 225
Tweed, William 102

U

United States (U.S.) 21, 70, 101, 258

V

Veldhuis, Nick 90, 96
Viminitz, Paul 9, 10
Voltaire 123, 165, 204
voluntarism 58
voter, turnout 183, 225
voting, plural 226

W

Waldron, J. 51
Walzer, Michael 208
war 75, 97, 99, 100, 103, 110, 114, 118, 121, 167, 200–207, 209, 227, 254–257
Iraq 202, 203
of all against all 51, 138
World War I 99, 154, 183, 202–204
World War II 99, 100, 199
WEF 117, 118
Wells, H.G. 224
Wertheimer, Alan 18, 19, 25, 29
West, E.G. 102, 129, 206
Whelan, Robert 210
will 10, 175, 176, 179–181, 183
collective 175, 180
of the people 175, 176, 179, 181, 183

Wilson, Woodrow, President 202, 204
Wolfenden Report 5
Wolff, R.P. 49, 72
wolf's head 248
Wollheim, R. 167–171, 176, 177
Woods, Thomas 21, 199, 212

Z

Zakaria, Fareed 79

The manufacturer's authorised representative in the EU is Springer Nature Customer Service Centre GmbH, Europaplatz 3, 69115 Heidelberg, Germany. If you have any concerns regarding our products, please contact ProductSafety@springernature.com

Printed and bound by CPI Group (UK) Ltd, Croydon, CR0 4YY
30/09/2026
02225243-0007